DATE DUE

~~R 1 8 98~~			
~~AP 13 00~~			
~~MY 2 00~~			
~~MY 23 00~~			

DEMCO 38-296

POET AND HERO IN THE
PERSIAN BOOK OF KINGS

A volume in the series

MYTH AND POETICS

edited by GREGORY NAGY

A list of titles appears at the end of the book.

POET AND HERO
IN THE PERSIAN
BOOK OF KINGS

Olga M. Davidson

CORNELL UNIVERSITY PRESS

ITHACA AND LONDON

First published 1994 by Cornell University Press.

Library of Congress Cataloging-in-Publication Data
Davidson, Olga M.
    Poet and hero in the Persian Book of kings / Olga M. Davidson.
        p.   cm.
    Includes bibliographical references and index.
    ISBN 0-8014-2780-0
    1. Firdawsī. Shāhnāmah.   I. Title.   II. Series.
  PK6459
  891'.5511—dc20   93-26257

Printed in the United States of America

⊚ The paper in this book meets the minimum requirements
of the American National Standard for Information Sciences—
Permanence of Paper for Printed Library Materials, ANSI Z39.48–1984.

To my parents

Contents

Foreword

GREGORY NAGY

Poet and Hero in the Persian Book of Kings, by Olga M. Davidson, addresses a central concern of the Myth and Poetics Series: how can we explain a Classical literary form as the continuation of an earlier oral tradition? This book about the *Shāhnāma* of Ferdowsi, a medieval Persian epic that far surpasses in sheer length the Homeric *Iliad* and *Odyssey* combined, offers important answers. The story told by the *Shāhnāma* or "Book of Kings" is not only about the kings and heroes of Iran from the beginnings of time to the Arab conquest; it is also about the *Shāhnāma* itself. That is, the *Shahnāma* is meant to be a book about the ultimate Book. Davidson's own book about this book seizes on the self-reflexiveness of the *Shāhnāma,* linking it with the history and prehistory of the Iranian song culture and showing that the very idea of a book is not at all incompatible with oral tradition in this culture. More than that, the idea of the Book becomes a driving metaphor for oral tradition itself.

The most striking example Davidson adduces is Ferdowsi's vision of a lost archetype, described as the ultimate model for his own Book of Kings. The story is told in the *Shāhnāma* that this archetypal Book of Kings became lost in time and disintegrated, only to be recovered all at once and literally reintegrated through oral performance. The oral performers are *mōbad*s, wise men assembled by a wise vizier from every corner of the empire, each holding a "fragment" of the long-lost Book of Kings. The vizier lines up the *mōbad*s, and each recites his fragment in order. The Book is thus reassembled by this assembly, just as the disintegrating empire is implicitly reintegrated by the Book. By laying claim to this book as his model, Ferdowsi appropriates his own ultimate authority as author.

The *mōbad*s in this story are oral performers not only because they are pictured as performing the Book of Kings. More important, Ferdowsi throughout his *Shāhnāma* keeps naming as his sources the performances of individual *mōbad*s that he himself has heard. Whether or not these references to performances by *mōbad*s are to be interpreted as stylized gestures, much like the references to the archetypal Book, the point remains that Ferdowsi is treating the concepts of oral performance and book as interchangeable visualizations of the poet's authority.

The poet is authorized by the empire of the successive *shāh*s of Iran, or even by the very idea of kingship. Reciprocally, the poet authorizes that same idea, gives it authority, by becoming the author of his Book of Kings. But there remains a major complication. The Book of Kings is not only about kings. It is also about heroes, and about one hero in particular, Rostam the *tājbakhsh* or 'crown-bestower'. Rostam emerges as a major figure in Ferdowsi's *Shāhnāma*—and in Davidson's book as well. Paradoxically, this hero is a living challenge to the idea of kingship even though his whole epic life is dedicated to upholding it. This paradox, as Davidson argues, is a fundamental theme in Iranian oral epic traditions through the ages. Moreover, it can be traced further back as a mythological construct shared by other Indo-European language groups, including the Indic, the Celtic, and the Greek traditions. Davidson points to the Homeric narrative of the conflict of Achilles and Agamemnon, for example, as a distant cognate of the conflicts between Rostam and the succession of *shāh*s that he serves. This epic theme of a conflict between hero and king turns out to be an indispensable part of the larger story that is the Book of Kings.

Given that the poet authorizes the idea of kingship by virtue of being the author of the Book of Kings, we may ask whether he is also challenging that same idea by virtue of introducing the hero of the epic. Here the parallel Davidson draws between poet and hero becomes most telling. In this connection, she takes note of the story, accretively embedded in the *Shāhnāma* tradition, of Ferdowsi's having personally challenged his patron, the Sultan Maḥmud of Ghazna. Such an antagonism is of course a paradox: just as the hero ultimately upholds kingship while all along challenging it, so does the poet. Davidson sees as a symbol for this overarching theme the mythical paradox of eternal fire in water, as embodied in the *farr,* that mystical luminous halo of Persian kings which Rostam must ever safeguard.

In earlier Iranian traditions, the *farr* is pictured as hidden and inaccessible, lodged in the depths of a lake within the sacred space that was the homeland of Zoroaster, to be recovered some day in the fullness of time by an eschatological hero. Just as the sacred space of Zoroaster becomes a "shifter," a movable signifier, in the diachrony of Iranian traditions, so also the eschatological hero and the poet who glorifies him both await their own self-realization in future moments in time. In the world of the *Shāhnāma,* that hero is Rostam, that poet is Ferdowsi.

Acknowledgments

At various stages in the writing of this work, I have benefited from the advice and criticism of Margaret Alexiou, Deborah Boedeker, Jerome W. Clinton, the late Martin Dickson, the late Georges Dumézil, Jacques Duchesne-Guillemin, Richard N. Frye, András Hámori, William Hanaway, Joseph Harris, Mina Hedayati, Nicole Loraux, the late Albert B. Lord, Richard P. Martin, Stephen A. Mitchell, Sarah P. Morris, Roy Mottahedeh, Michael Nagler, Gregory Nagy, Joseph Nagy, Mark Nevins, Martin Schwartz, Prods Oktor Skjærvø, Laura Slatkin, Wheeler Thackston, Ali Vaezy, Abdo Azim Vaezy, and Brent Vine.

O. M. D.

POET AND HERO IN THE
PERSIAN BOOK OF KINGS

Introduction

There are two central figures in *Poet and Hero in the Persian Book of Kings*. The poet is Ferdowsi, native of Ṭōs, a renowned city of Khorāsān province in the eastern sector of medieval Iran, who is recognized as the creator of a monumental Persian epic poem known as the *Shāhnāma* 'Book of Kings', over fifty-thousand couplets in length and said to have been completed in the early eleventh century A.D.[1] The hero is Rostam, a preeminent character in the Book of Kings.

Rostam is the kind of figure that we would ordinarily associate with characters of epic and myth in other literary traditions—Achilles, for example, in the Homeric *Iliad*—and he is readily identifiable as what we would conventionally call a "hero." Yet the poem in which Rostam is so central is more difficult to reconcile with the expectations we

---

[1] The basic sources are reviewed and analyzed in Browne 1902–1924.2:130–141 and Shahbazi 1991. (Hereafter Browne 1902–1924 is cited as Browne plus vol. number.) To transliterate classical Persian words, I write long *i* and *u* without length-markers (thus *Ferdowsi*, not *Ferdowsī*), since I write the corresponding short vowels as *e* and *o* (thus *Ferdowsi*, not *Firdowsī*); also, the diphthongs are represented as *ey* and *ow*, not *ay* and *aw* or *ai* and *au* (thus *Ferdowsi*, not *Firdawsī* or *Firdausī*). Citations from the *Shāhnāma* are keyed to the Moscow edition of Bertels and his colleagues (1966–1971); the first such citation in the discussion that follows, VI 136.9–15, is typical of the format to be followed: the roman numeral designates the volume number of the Moscow edition, while the subsequent arabic numeral and the numerals after the decimal point give the page and line numbers respectively. Citations from other editions specify the name of the editor, as in the case of Mohl 1838–1878. All translations are my own unless otherwise specified.

hold about heroic epic. Like epic as we ordinarily understand it, the *Shāhnāma* is indeed poetry about heroes. But it is also much more: as the very name indicates, it is a "Book of Kings"—which suggests that we are witnessing recorded history, not epic or myth. The *Shāhnāma* presents itself as a book of kings chronicling the reigns of all the national *shāh*s of Iran, from the primordial founders all the way down to the last days of the Sasanian dynasty (A.D. 651). It is as if we were dealing with a combination of myth and history.

The key to understanding this apparent combination is the other central figure in this book, the poet. To understand the heroic essence of Rostam, as glorified by the Book of Kings, we must understand the poet's role in Iranian society. In both Ferdowsi and Rostam, we also seem to be dealing with a combination of myth and history. On the one hand, what Ferdowsi says about himself and his life as poet, elaborated in some detail throughout his colossal poem, looks on the surface like historical information, which scholars tend to supplement with texts extraneous to the *Shāhnāma* that record a vast array of further information, likewise purportedly historical, from various "Life of Ferdowsi" traditions.[2] On the other hand, as I shall argue, much of this information is derived from myths beneath the surface—myths that serve to explain the role of the poet and of his poetry in society. Some of these myths seem to be built into the poem while others are extrapolated from it, but in either case they amount to an ongoing reinterpretation of the role of poetry in an ever-changing society.[3] To that extent, not only the ascertainable facts but even the myths about the life of a poet like Ferdowsi constitute historical evidence about the poetry attributed to him.

By virtue of its sweeping range over the history of Iran, Ferdowsi's *Shāhnāma* seems destined to have become a centerpiece for scholarship in Iranian studies. For about a century, a prime concern of scholars working in this field has been to ascertain whether the information it contains about the kings of Iran can be verified—by way of actual

---

[2] Such information has been exhaustively collected in Shahbazi 1991.

[3] For comparative evidence, see the function of myth in "Lives of Poets" traditions discussed by Nagy 1979.304 paragraph 4 (with n4), 306–307, with special reference to ancient Greek evidence. On the Provençal genres of the *vida* 'life story' and *razo* (from Latin *ratiō*), see Nagy 1990a.80, n140.

historical evidence from the Sasanian dynasty (ca. A.D. 224 to A.D. 651) and before. Such preoccupations mark the relevant scholarly contributions of such prominent orientalists of the past as Theodor Nöldeke and Arthur Christensen, whose painstaking work goes a long way in showing that the *Shāhnāma* by and large preserves a vast body of lore that must have been gathered and stored primarily in the Sasanian dynasty.[4] More recent work by such scholars as Hasan Taqizāda and Moḥammad Qazvini has helped to clarify how the flow of authentic information into the *Shāhnāma* came about.[5] They have argued for the existence of a Persian prose version of a Book of Kings, slightly antedating Ferdowsi's poetic version and translated by Zoroastrian savants from a purportedly original Pahlavi text. The very idea of such an original text, written in Pahlavi, the official language of the Sasanian dynasty, imparts a sense of definitive authority. Iranists could thus feel confident if Ferdowsi's primary source was indeed a document stemming ultimately from the lost archives of the Sasanian dynasty. They could hope to have no better evidence to authenticate the memory of the past Ferdowsi preserved.

This circular assumption concerning the authenticity of what the poet says has encouraged a historicist perspective on the *Shāhnāma*. Such a perspective seems all the more "scientific" because the actual sequence of monarchs who ruled over Iran provides the narrative superstructure for all the stories that make up this monumental poem. The historicist perspective is further encouraged by the apparent realism that we shall see in the poet's numerous self-references within the poem.

The main concern of this book, however, is not the poet's "autobiography" or the "history" that can be reconstructed through the *Shāhnāma*. Rather, it is the poetry exemplified by the poet's life and the story that he tells. This poetry is a combination of history and myth, and understanding it requires careful study of both Ferdowsi's self-presentation and his focal portrayal of the hero Rostam.

In Rostam, we confront a character who, even superficially, strikes us as a poetic creation of mythological traditions, rather than a histor-

[4] Nöldeke 1930 [1879] and Christensen 1932.
[5] Taqizāda 1944 and Qazvini 1944.

ical reality. This impression is fostered by the very beginning of the story: according to the *Shāhnāma*, Rostam's father, Zāl, is rejected by his own father, Sām, because he was born with an old man's white hair.[6] Shunned by his parents, Zāl is raised in the wilderness by a magical bird called the Simorgh. Even these few details suffice to show the mythical heritage of the Rostam figure. As for Rostam himself, we shall be surveying a wealth of narrative traditions that follow in a similar mythical vein. Such a survey shows that Ferdowsi's narratives surrounding Rostam's exploits are clearly comparable with narratives about heroes as they appear in the epic traditions of other cultures.

Rostam is hardly peripheral to the *Shāhnāma*. His exploits dominate the overall narrative for vast stretches, and in fact the combined lifetimes of this hero and of his father overlap with the set chronology of a kingly succession covering a whole millennium. Given the centrality of both the *shāh*s and Rostam in the *Shāhnāma*, we may pose the question: how can we reconcile the book of kings with the epic of heroes?

The general attitude of recent Iranistic scholarship, as we see in the synthesis of Dhabihollāh Ṣafā or in such specialized studies as the dissertation of Marcia Maguire on Rostam, is to treat the "book of kings" aspect of the *Shāhnāma* as history, especially in light of Ferdowsi's purported Pahlavi "sourcebook," and to treat by default the "epic of heroes" as myth.[7] A corollary to this attitude is to assume that Rostam and his family are themselves an intrusion into the Iranian history of kings. This assumption is encouraged especially by Rostam's relationship, as portrayed in the *Shāhnāma*, to the national kings of Iran. Always a kingmaker but never a king, Rostam has as his main task in life the continual protection of the current national king and thereby of the nation itself; one of the hero's distinctive epithets is in fact *tājbakhsh* 'crown-bestower'. And yet, Rostam is also often at odds with the kingship and at times seems more of a menace to the *shāh* than a help. Moreover, he is an outsider to the national ways: he comes from Sistān, a region visualized in the *Shāhnāma* as a remote outpost in the eastern stretches of the empire. Recognizing the historically veri-

---

[6] For this theme, compare Hesiod *Works and Days* 181.
[7] Ṣafā 1944 and Maguire 1973.

fiable distinctness of Sistān from the centralized Iranian Empire, experts such as Ṣafā associate this distinctness with Rostam's idiosyncrasies. They assume that the epic stories of Rostam are regional traditions that have intruded on the central Iranian traditions as represented by the books of kings.

But there is a serious problem with this tendency to divide the *Shāhnāma* into two separable components, the "book of kings" and the "epic of heroes" aspects. The conjunction of the stories of kings with the stories of Rostam was already clearly attested in the Sasanian era.[8] Thus it cannot be attributed to an artistic invention of Ferdowsi's and must instead be considered a tradition in its own right. Another problem is that the stories of kings, in the era of the Sasanian dynasty and, even before that, in the era of the Parthian dynasty of the Arsacids (ca. 200 B.C. to A.D. 227), were transmitted not only by the records of the royal archives but also in oral performances by professional poets; and the same goes for the stories of heroes, Rostam in particular.[9]

My book juxtaposes such considerations with the internal testimony of the *Shāhnāma* itself. Ferdowsi claims as his source not only a single Book of Kings but also the multiple oral reports of learned men called *mōbad*s and *dehqān*s, whom he conventionally describes as masters of traditions that are specifically poetic in nature. What Ferdowsi is claiming, as we shall see, is that he is creating his Persian Book of Kings from a Pahlavi Book of Kings *and* from the Persian oral poetic tradition. Moreover, there is nothing in the poet's testimony that would suggest a clear delineation between the stories of kings as drawn from a book and the stories of heroes as drawn from the oral tradition. It is as if both kinds of stories came from both kinds of sources.

Thus my work takes issue with the prevailing idea of Nöldeke and other experts in Iranistic studies that the Rostam tradition is extrinsic or intrusive to the Book of Kings tradition. If there had been any intrusion at all, I argue, it would have happened at least as early as the era of the Parthian dynasty of the Arsacids. Whereas Ferdowsi implicitly presents his poem if it were the very first to combine a book of kings and oral poetic traditions as sources, the findings of Mary Boyce

[8] Boyce 1955, 1957.
[9] Boyce 1955, 1957.

suggest that, even in Sasanian times, the subject matter found in books of kings was just as much an aspect of oral poetry as that in epics of heroes.[10] As the discussion proceeds, we shall have reason to posit the existence of separate narrative traditions about kings and heroes, but I shall also be arguing that stories of kings were potentially just as much an inherited poetic form as the stories of heroes, and that the two kinds of story could also exist as one: an epic about kings *and* heroes.

Still, it is problematical to assume that the traditions about kings should have had a predominantly historical basis, while the traditions about heroes were grounded in myth. In this book, I propose that the poetic combination of themes concerning the hero Rostam and themes concerning the national kings is a tradition that goes back not only to Parthian Arsacid times.[11] Rather, they can be traced all the way back to the remotest Indo-Iranian and even Indo-European layers of the classical Persian language. My proposition is supported by the work of Georges Dumézil, who argues that the narrative traditions about the Iranian dynasty of the Keyānids, as transmitted by Ferdowsi's *Shāhnāma,* represent an authentic continuation of traditions that have a common Indo-Iranian and even Indo-European heritage.[12]

In particular, Dumézil shows that the traditions about the Indic hero Kāvya Uśanas and those about the Iranian *shāh* Key Kāus are cognate, both centering on the water of life and its magical powers in bringing the dead back to life.[13] My own results supplement those of Dumézil about the Keyānids: I find that the relationship between the Keyānid kings and the Sistanian heroes, namely, Rostam and his family, is in its own right an equally old mythical theme of Indo-European provenience, cognate with such themes as the relationship of Agamemnon and Achilles in the Greek epic tradition of the *Iliad.*

To argue, as Dumézil has done by way of the comparative method, that some of the main story patterns concerning the Keyānids have a mythical heritage, is a matter of controversy for experts in Iranistic

---

[10] Boyce 1955, 1957.

[11] Boyce did not concern herself over whether the oral poetry of the Parthian Arsacid era and thereafter dealt with matters historical or mythical, but it seems clear from her writings that she considered the poetic traditions about kings to be primarily historical in inspiration.

[12] Dumézil 1971; cf. Puhvel 1987.118–121.

[13] Dumézil 1971.137–238.

studies: such arguments contravene one of the most influential pieces of scholarship on Iranian subjects, Arthur Christensen's masterly book on the Keyānids, which had consistently defended the historicity of this dynasty.[14] In general, historicist assumptions have impeded the acceptance by Iranists of Dumézil's findings.[15] My work will have to confront the same sort of historicist viewpoint.

I shall argue, however, that we need not deny the existence of an element of historicity in epic. We need only affirm a discovery by such experts in oral poetry as Albert Lord, who notes that mythical patterns regularly absorb and then reshape historical patterns in the context of oral poetry.[16] In other words, the Iranian "book of kings" tradition can theoretically stem from a combination of history and myth. But if it is oral poetry, it must be a combination where the patterns of history are subordinated to the controlling patterns of myth.

Because we do have evidence, thanks to Mary Boyce's survey of the Arsacid period and beyond, for thinking that the "book of kings" tradition was indeed a matter of oral poetry, we have a sound theoretical basis for positing the continuity of Indo-European traditions up to Ferdowsi. But the impact of Boyce's work is blunted precisely at the point where the application of her findings would be most striking. Although she corroborates the flourishing of oral poetry from Arsacid times all the way to the era of Ferdowsi, we encounter a major obstacle in Ferdowsi. The consensus among Iranists is that, on the basis of internal and external evidence, the *Shāhnāma* of Ferdowsi draws its treasury of lore about kings from a prose Persian translation of a Pahlavi Book of Kings, not from a continuum of Persian oral poetic traditions about kings.[17] Boyce's work, however, suggests that even the Pahlavi Book of Kings is a repository of oral traditions. I in turn shall argue that the multiformity of the Arabic translations provides supporting evidence.[18] Thus my findings about Rostam, added to

[14] Christensen 1932.30.

[15] Still, some Iranists have followed in Dumézil's footsteps. For example, one study argues for the Indo-European provenance of the story of Rostam's inheriting his *gorz* 'mace' as described in the *Shāhnāma,* see Sarkārāti 1975.

[16] Lord 1970.29–30; cf. Nagy 1990b.7–9.

[17] Cf. Minavi 1973.5–8 and Shahbazi 1991.39–41.

[18] That Ferdowsi knew neither the Pahlavi nor the Arabic language is argued by Shahbazi (1991.39–41).

Dumézil's findings about the Indo-European heritage of Iranian heroic narrative, would still hold, even if it were true that the *Shāhnāma* of Ferdowsi is based on a prose Persian translation of a Pahlavi Book of Kings. It is just that we would then have to say that the Rostam narrative is an *indirect* continuation of Indo-European poetic traditions.

In this book, however, I propose that the Rostam narrative of Ferdowsi's *Shāhnāma* is in fact a direct continuation of Indo-European poetic tradition. There are two main lines of argumentation. First, I examine extensively what the *Shāhnāma* itself says about its own mode of composition, comparing this stylized testimony with the available external evidence about Middle and New Persian poetry. Second, I offer an internal analysis of Ferdowsi's New Persian poetry, with the purpose of trying to isolate traits that are characteristic of the workings of oral poetry. In considering such characteristics, I rely on the definitions of oral poetry as developed by Milman Parry and Albert Lord in the course of their fieldwork—and as reformulated in more recent theoretical work.[19]

I should note in advance that no single aspect of the evidence that I have assembled can prove, of and by itself, that the composition of Ferdowsi's *Shāhnāma* followed the principles of oral poetry. But this book does, I hope, present a persuasive constellation of evidence. My minimal position is that the Rostam narrative is a matter of oral tradition in Middle Persian poetry and that at least the themes of this narrative were accurately revived by Ferdowsi. My maximal position is that this narrative is not just oral tradition but also an oral poetic tradition, inherited directly in New Persian poetry and recorded permanently in the *Shāhnāma* of Ferdowsi.

Inspired by the linguistic terms "Old Persian" (as marked by the Achaemenid dynasty, 559 B.C. to 330 B.C.), "Middle Persian" (as marked by the Sasanian dynasty, ca. A.D. 224 to A.D. 651), and "New Persian" (as marked by the Islamic period, after ca. A.D. 642), with their implications of cultural continuity spanning the political vicissi-

---

[19] For an introduction to the work of Parry and Lord on South Slavic oral epic traditions and for the impact of their findings on the study of other poetic traditions, most notably the Homeric, see Lord 1960. The collected papers of Milman Parry have been published by his son, Adam Parry: Parry 1971. For an important application of speech-act theory to oral poetics, see Martin 1989.

tudes of the Iranian Empire in its historically attested phases, I shall frequently refer to the traditions studied in this book as *Persian* as well as *Iranian*. These traditions of poets and heroes transcend politics and even history. The classicism of these traditions deserves and demands scrutiny beyond the historicism of those specialists in Iranian studies who may not wish to concern themselves with the humanism inherent in Iranian traditions. Such an attitude on the part of experts only reinforces a lack of interest on the part of nonexperts, who may feel either threatened by or at least indifferent to whatever might be called "non-Western" values. Let the classicism inherent in the concept of "Persian" symbolize a resistance to any hostility or indifference on the part of such nonexperts, who would dismiss Iranian civilization because it seems alien to them.[20] And let the resistance extend to the parochialism of those experts in Iranistic studies who may foster such prejudice by treating their subject so narrowly as to exclude interested nonexperts.

While the concept of "Persian" helps us keep track of the continuum of traditions inherited by Ferdowsi's *Shāhnāma,* we must not lose sight of the diversity represented by the concept of "Iranian"—and realized in the actual history of the Iranian Empire. This diversity is brought to life in the very geography of Iran, as captured in the panoramic visualization of the empire in the *Shāhnāma:* we see a dazzling array of mountains, valleys, deserts, rivers, lakes, and oases framing a vast variety of peoples and cultures. Most dramatically, eastern and western Iran are divided by two salt deserts that run through the center of the country. This east-west division, as we shall see, figures prominently in the history that unfolds.

That history, the story of the Iranian Empire, is reflected in the narrative sweep of Ferdowsi's *Shāhnāma.* Granted, this colossal poem may not be history as we know it, but it was indeed considered to be history by the society that made it possible in the first place. For us it may be just a story, but we must also treat it as evidence for the study of history, to the extent that we wish to study the society for whom the *Shāhnāma* was indeed history. The *Shāhnāma* is a formal and traditional

[20] It should be noted that the nomenclature of "Old Persian" and "Middle Persian" masks some significant discontinuities. On the dangers of orientalism, see Saïd 1978.

expression of how Iranian society views itself and how it wishes to be remembered through the ages. Only from this point of view can the *Shāhnāma* be deemed history. Such a distinctly Iranian vision of history has been described as follows:

> The purpose of history was to maintain and promote the national and moral ideas of the state. . . . History was to teach the rulers and the ruling classes the virtues of abiding by the dictates of "the good religion," of rendering justice to the people and making the land prosper. To the people it taught the virtues of unswerving loyalty to the kings and observing "law and order." Innovations were to be mistrusted, unless they were beneficial ones instituted by a good king. History was, then, an educational instrument of social stability and cohesion. It was intended to strengthen the common heritage and promote a common ideal. It was to teach its readers love of their homeland and pride in their ancestry. It exalted the life of the heroes of the Iranian past before their eyes as models to be emulated.[21]

As a prelude, I offer here a brief overview of this majestic story or history as retold by the *Shāhnāma*. To trace what this monumental poem retells is to grasp the central interpretive challenge of the book, the concepts of poet and hero in Persian epic.

The *Shāhnāma* of Ferdowsi reflects the national history of the Iranian Empire before Islam by telling the stories, or *dāstān*s, of a canonical number of fifty pre-Islamic *shāh*s, beginning with the very first king of the world, the mythical Gayomars, who is the *shāh* at the time of creation, and ending with the last of the Sasanian *shāh*s, Yazdgerd (A.D. 632–651), who died only a few years after the Islamic conquest of Iran. The *Shāhnāma* divides these fifty *shāh*s into four dynasties: Pishdādians, Keyānids, Ashkānians, and Sasanians. The first two dynasties, especially the first, are grounded in myth, but the last two are "historical" to the extent that they do coincide closely with the history of pre-Islamic Iran as we know it.

Let us consider, briefly, the highlights of these four dynasties as narrated by the *Shāhnāma*, focusing on the first two inasmuch as they are the primary concern of this book and take up the bulk of Ferdowsi's colossal poem.

---

[21] Yarshater 1983.368–369.

The Pishdādians are traced back to primordial times and are said to last for 2,441 years. There are ten *shāhs*, the first being Keyumarṣ, the prototype of all humankind. He incurs the jealousy of Ahriman, the incarnation of evil, who attacks him and kills his son. Keyumarṣ is followed by Hushang, his grandson according to the *Shāhnāma*. Hushang bears the title Pishdād, whence the name of the dynasty. A culture hero, he introduces agriculture. The next *shāh* is Tahmuras, who subdues the archfiend Ahriman and the *div*s, demonlike figures who ally themselves with Ahriman in hopes of overthrowing the social order established by Ahura Māzda, the incarnation of Good.

Tahmuras is followed by Jamshid, who organizes society into four classes: (1) priests, (2) warriors, (3) farmers, and (4) artisans. He rules in peace and prosperity, but his good fortune makes him so arrogant that he likens himself to divinity. Jamshid is punished for his excess by losing his *farr* 'luminous glory', the visible sign of kingly grace that accompanies rulers and entitles them to reign with success. With no *farr*-bearing king, Iran falls into the hands of the evil oppressor, Zaḥḥāk. As a youth, Zaḥḥāk is seduced by a demonlike figure called Iblis, and he eventually becomes a three-headed monster, having two serpents growing out of each of his shoulders. He depopulates Iran by feeding young boys' brains to these serpents, and his reign is marked by darkness and chaos lasting for a thousand years. Faridun, with the aid of a smith called Kāva, overthrows Zaḥḥāk and chains him inside a mountain called Mount Alborz, where he must stay until the eschatological moment of reckoning is destined to arrive.

Faridun has three sons, Salm, Tur, and Iraj (in that birth order), and he divides his kingdom, ostensibly the world, among the three of them. Salm gets the western lands; Tur gets the north and east, namely China and Turān, the second of which is a mythical land that will figure prominently in the discussion that follows; and Iraj gets Iran, which is considered the center of the world and therefore the choice territory. Jealous because he inherited Iran, Salm and Tur murder Iraj. Manuchehr, the grandson of Iraj, avenges his grandfather by killing both Salm and Tur, thus becoming the next *shāh*.

During the reign of Manuchehr, Zāl, son of Sām, is born, and rejected by his father because of his white hair. Exposed on a mountain, Zāl is raised by a magical bird, the Simorgh. Sām later reclaims his son Zāl, who, after a long courtship, marries Rudāba, a descendant of the evil Ẓaḥḥāk himself; Rudāba and Zāl conceive Rostam, the primary heroic figure of the *Shāhnāma*. Manuchehr is succeeded by three other *shāh*s, but the interest is centered on the childhood deeds of Rostam in the *Shāhnāma*.

The second of the four dynasties in the Book of Kings, the Keyānid, consists of ten *shāh*s and lasts for 732 years. After a period with no *farr*-bearing *shāh* on the throne, the hero Rostam is sent out to fetch Key Qobād, who is said to be of princely origin. He finds Key Qobād in a beautiful wilderness setting, sitting on a throne by a stream under Mount Alborz. Seeing that Key Qobād has the bearings of *farr*, Rostam brings him back to Iran to be the *shāh*. Key Qobād begins the Keyānid dynasty. Key Qobād is succeeded by his son Key Kāus, phlegmatic, arrogant, unpredictable. The reign of Key Kāus is marked by rash and foolish exploits that lead him into all sorts of troubles, and many a time is Rostam compelled to come to his rescue. Though Rostam has as much difficulty in respecting Key Kāus as Achilles has with Agamemnon in the *Iliad,* he is loyal enough to sacrifice the life of his own son, Sohrāb, for the sake of the Iranian throne. During the reign of Key Kāus there is continuous warfare against Iran's arch-enemy, the land of Turān, led by Afrāsiyāb, king of the Turanians.

Key Kāus and Afrāsiyāb share a grandson called Key Khosrow, who becomes the next Iranian *shāh*. This Key Khosrow is thus of both Iranian and Turanian descent. Famed for his wisdom and nobility, Key Khosrow is the *shāh* who finally ends the fiendish Afrāsiyāb's life. Shortly after defeating Afrāsiyāb, he vanishes from public view, choosing the life of a hermit, having already left instructions that a distant relative, Lohrāsp, should succeed him as *shāh*.

The reign of Lohrāsp is followed by that of his son, Goshtāsp. This succession happens prematurely in that Goshtāsp, in his eagerness for the crown, had put pressure on his father Lohrāsp to abdicate before the fullness of time. Despite this characterization of rashness, Goshtāsp is treated with reverence in the *Shāhnāma* inasmuch as it is his reign that marks both the coming of Zoroaster and the prophet's acceptance by both king and empire. At a later point, King Goshtāsp is in turn threatened by his son Esfandiyār, who shows a similar impatience for the crown. Such impatience eventually leads Esfandiyār into an inevitable confrontation with Rostam the crown-bestower. Rostam is beset with the awkward situation of having to abandon his conventional role of defending the crown, as is always expected of him, and being forced either to kill Prince Esfandiyār or to lose face. Rostam does indeed kill the future *shāh* Esfandiyār. When it finally happens, however many earlier times Rostam may have been tempted to kill any of the *shāh*s that he had served, this killing of the king by the kingmaker is conceived by the *Shāhnāma* of Ferdowsi as a fundamentally unnatural act. This deed seals Rostam's own fate: he is to die prematurely, and in the end he is murdered by his half-brother.

With the death of Rostam, the *Shāhnāma* shifts into a narrative mode that becomes ever less mythical and more historical as the tales about the kings begin to coincide more and more with what the Persian and Arab chroniclers report—and with what we ourselves interpret as historical facts. After Goshtāsp, a series of successive *shāh*s culminates with Dārā the Second (Darius), who is overthrown by Sekandar, that is, Alexander the Great. Although the historical Alexander in fact posed a threat to the very fabric of Iranian society by overthrowing the authority of its kings, dividing the empire among feudal lords, and undermining all that is sacred to Zoroastrianism, he is nevertheless treated with sympathy in the *Shāhnāma*. Ferdowsi's colossal poem highlights the legendary life of Alexander and portrays him as a legitimate ruler of Iran, the true son of Dārā the First—the son that Dārā never knew he had. Here, then, is a clear example where epic mythmaking reshapes history to serve its own purposes.

The third of the four dynasties celebrated by the *Shāhnāma* is called the Ashkānian, which is described as lasting for 200 years—all under the reign of one single *shāh*. In this version of dynastic succession, there is no room for the historical reality of the Seleucid dynasty, descended from Seleucus, one of Alexander's generals; nor is there that much more room for the Arsacids, considered heirs to Alexander. The *Shāhnāma* merely focuses on one branch of the decentralized Arsacids, namely, the Ashkānians, inasmuch as they were the strongest of the Arsacid feudal principalities, ruling over western and central Iran and controlling Babylonia. In effect, the *Shāhnāma* collapses a succession of eleven historical Arsacid kings into one figure, King Ardavān, making him the successor of Alexander. The entirety of the Seleucid and Arsacid dynasties is attributed to him alone. This way, the narrative of the *Shāhnāma* maintains the flow of the Book of Kings as a succession of sovereignty without any interruption of centralized government. The very idea of such interruption would have been utterly alien to the Iranian social order.

The fourth and last dynasty that the *Shāhnāma* celebrates is the Sasanian, described as lasting for 501 years and comprised of a succession of twenty-nine *shāh*s. Ardavān the Ashkānian is overthrown by Ardashir Pāpagān, a vassal king from the House of Sāsān. Ardashir is the great-grandson of Shāh Goshtāsp, and he is therefore of Keyānid descent. He founds the Sasanian dynasty and is succeeded by twenty-eight *shāh*s, the last one being Yazdgerd.

With the death of Yazdgerd and the fall of the Sasanian House, historically dated at A.D. 651, the *Shāhnāma* comes to an end. Thus the poem stops precisely at the time of the Islamic Conquest, where the history of Islamic Iran begins. This beginning inaugurates the social milieu of the poet Ferdowsi himself.

With the Islamic Conquest, the historical Iran at first ceases to be an empire ruled by *shāh*s. Still, after a difficult period of Arab-centered rule by caliphs, the rudiments of empire return, albeit in strikingly different shapes and sizes. New dynasties appear, the major ones being the Buyids in the west (A.D. 932–1062) and the Ghaznavids in the east (A.D. 977–1186). Our interest centers on the Ghaznavids, a dynasty of newcomers descended from Turkic invaders, and on one particularly powerful ruler in this dynastic line, the Sultan Maḥmud of Ghazna (A.D. 998–1030). As we shall see, it was under the reign of this Maḥmud that Ferdowsi is said to have composed the *Shāhnāma*.

Though the *Shāhnāma* of Ferdowsi was created in the Islamic Iran of the early part of the eleventh century, both its narrative time-frame and even its orientation are pre-Islamic. This pre-Islamic orientation of the *Shāhnāma* reflects at least in part a Zoroastrian world-view, even though the audience of Ferdowsi was not just Muslim but also, ultimately, Shī'ite Muslim.

Zoroastrianism had been the primary religious structure of Iran before Islam. The most dramatic illustration of this heritage in the *Shāhnāma* is that Ferdowsi ordinarily expresses the concept of "God" not with the Islamic term *Allāh* but with a more generic term *Khodā*, usually translated into English as 'lord', which is compatible with a Zoroastrian world-view.

As we look back at this panorama that is the *Shāhnāma*, we cannot think of it simply as one of several sources for the true history of pre-Islamic Iran—a source to be treated on a par with the works of Persian and Arab chroniclers. Rather, we may appreciate it for its sheer monumentality: it is a majestically vast poem concerned with the very identity of Iran as a nation, as an empire. As we look ahead to the central issues of poet and hero in the *Shāhnāma,* their very greatness is a function of this identity that is Iran.

PART I

THE POET AND HIS POETRY

CHAPTER I

The Authority of
Ferdowsi the Poet

It is universally acknowledged that Ferdowsi, in composing the *Shāhnāma*, produced the authoritative national epic about the Iranian Empire. The most eloquent confirmation of Ferdowsi's poetic authority is that his poem precluded any subsequent poetic version of the narratives it treated. Jules Mohl, a nineteenth-century orientalist who translated the epic into French, makes an observation that captures the essence of the relationship between poet and hero: Ferdowsi, Mohl writes, has so well "celebrated" the life of Rostam "that no Persian author after him could have attempted to write on the same subject."[1]

This pattern of preclusion can readily be seen from the subject matter of the major epic nearest in time to the *Shāhnāma*, completed about A.D. 1010, namely, the *Garshāspnāma* of Asadi Ṭōsi, completed about A.D. 1056. The narrative here centers on an ancestor of Rostam, Garshāsp, an important figure in traditional Iranian lore who is barely even mentioned in the *Shāhnāma*.[2] Even though the poet of the *Garshāspnāma* considers himself a rival of Ferdowsi, the only way in which he can compete is to select something that Ferdowsi has not touched.

---

[1] Mohl 1838.lx: "[Ferdowsi] avait si bien célébré sa vie, qu'aucun auteur persan après lui n'a dû être tenté d'écrire sur le même sujet." (Citations from Mohl's introduction to the first volume: "Mohl 1838.[page number]"; citations from Mohl's comments in the other volumes: "Mohl [volume number] [page number].")

[2] For the importance of the traditions surrounding this figure, see Molé 1953.382.

The king who asks to be told the story of Garshāsp by the poet of the *Garshāspnāma* is represented as saying,

تو با گفتهٔ خویش گردانش جفت   گر ایدونک فردوسی اینرا نگفت

Although Ferdowsi has not re-counted this story	join them together with your own words.

Garshāspnāma 296[3]

As Mohl points out, even the *Garshāspnāma* never questions the poetic accuracy and quality of Ferdowsi's *Shāhnāma,* insisting instead on the superiority of its own central hero to Rostam (*Garshāspnāma* 264–281).[4] Ironically, Garshāsp's realm of heroic activities in the *Garshāspnāma* is restricted by—and therefore predicated on—that of Rostam and the *Shāhnāma.*[5] The rival poet could not claim to substitute a better version of the traditions already treated by Ferdowsi; he has to content himself with other stories and other traditions.[6]

The same pattern is in force with later national epics of the eleventh and twelfth centuries such as the *Borzunāma* and the *Farāmarznāma.* They consistently treat those traditions that have not been treated by Ferdowsi in the *Shāhnāma.*[7] From the testimony of all subsequent epics, then, we can conclude that Ferdowsi's *Shāhnāma* is the normative version of the epic traditions of medieval Persia.

Ferdowsi himself makes the claim that his version is the first as well as the best. His *Shāhnāma* presents itself as the first full poetic treatment of the entire Iranian heritage in the Persian language. The only poetic antecedent in Persian that he formally acknowledges is a section of a thousand-odd verses, attributed to a poet called Daqiqi, which Ferdowsi's epic actually incorporates (*Shāhnāma* VI 68–136.14–1022).[8] And except for Daqiqi, the claim of Ferdowsi's *Shāhnāma* is that there is no other poetic version.

---

[3] From p. 36 of the edition by Huart and Massé 1926.
[4] Mohl 1838.lvi–lvii.
[5] Ibid.
[6] Ibid. lvii, n1.
[7] See Molé 1953.386–390.
[8] For a definitive introduction to Daqiqi the poet, see Lazard 1964 I 32–36. Addenda in ibid. 184–187.

The next chapter examines in some detail Ferdowsi's account of a Pahlavi Book of Kings, which he described as an ancient prose text and claimed as the primary source of his *Shāhnāma*. This claim is a crucial aspect of the poem's authority. For now, however, since we are concentrating on the authority personally claimed by the poet himself, we shall consider Ferdowsi's references to the Pahlavi Book of Kings only to the extent that this "source" is supposed to reflect on the poet's authority *as poet*. Still, since Ferdowsi explicitly described the Pahlavi Book of Kings as a prose text that he was the first, except for Daqiqi, to transform into poetry, it is central to the poet's claim that he is the first authoritative poet of a Book of Kings.

Let us turn to some passages in which Ferdowsi expresses these two claims. In his introduction to the poem, he is already boasting that he alone is worthy to put the Book of Kings into verse:

بگفتار این مرمرا یار بود   ندیدم کسی کش سزاوار بود

بروآفرین از کهان و مهان   زنیکو سخن به چه اندر جهان

I saw no one worthy	of being my companion in discourse of this kind.
What in the world is better than eloquence?	Both great and small praise it.

Mohl I 18–20.161–162[9]

This conceit becomes most explicit in the confrontation of Ferdowsi's poetic skills with those of Daqiqi. When he criticizes Daqiqi's verses, Ferdowsi declares that no one before him, with the exception of Daqiqi, had ever tried to put the Book of Kings into verse:

سخنهای آن برمنش راستان   یکی نامه بود از گه باستان

طبایع ز پیوند او دور بود   چو جامی گهر بود ومنثور بود

گر ایدونک پرسش نماید شمار   گذشته برو سالیان شش هزار

پر اندیشه گشت این دل شادمان   نبردی بپیوند او کس گمان

که پیوندرا راه داد اندرین   گرفتم بگوینده بر آفرین

ز رزم و ز بزم از هزاران یکی   اگر چه نپیوست جز اندکی

که بنشاند شاهی ابر گاه بر   همو بود گوینده را راهبر

---

[9] The Moscow edition gives a variant wording at I 23.154.

There was a book [nāma] from ancient times,
It [the book] was like a goblet full of
pearls, and in prose.

Six thousand years had passed it by

No one had thought of stringing
[peyvand] them together.
I praised the singer [guyanda, i.e.,
Daqiqi]

although he did not string together
[peyvast] but a few [pearls]
It was he also, this singer's guide,

the words of which are noble and
just.
Men's dispositions were far from
stringing [peyvand] them [the
pearls] together.
if thus the inquiry shows [correct]
counting.
This glad heart became full of care.

who showed the way within this
[poem], for stringing together
[peyvand],
only one among thousands about
feasting and fighting.
who placed kingliness upon the
throne.

VI 136.9–15

Earlier in the same passage, Ferdowsi has declared that Daqiqi is an
inferior poet:

بسی بیت ناتندرست آمدم   نگه کردم این نظم سست آمدم

بداند سخن گفتن نابکار   من این زان بگفتم که تا شهریار

I glanced at these verses, and they
appeared to me weak.
I recited this [portion] from them so
that the ruler

Many of the lines [beyts] appeared
defective to me.
may know worthless speech.

VI 136.2–3

Despite such claims by Ferdowsi that his is the first and the best
poetic version of the Book of Kings, we know for a fact that there
were earlier poetic versions.[10] Even the critic Nöldeke, who consistently takes the words of Ferdowsi literally, as if the poet's claims were
ipso facto historical data, documents fragments of earlier heroic poetry, composed in Ferdowsi's heroic narrative meter, mutaqārib,[11] that

[10] For traces of earlier poets of the Book of Kings tradition, such as Mas'udi Marvazi
(early tenth century A.D.), see Shahbazi 1991.35–36. For an introduction to the traditions of Persian court poetry, see Meisami 1987.
[11] For background on this meter, see Elwell-Sutton 1976.180–183.

are attributed to Abu Shakur[12] and that have been preserved in the eleventh-century glossary of Asadi.[13] We also have independent evidence that Daqiqi himself was credited with poetic works beyond the thousand-odd lines incorporated in the *Shāhnāma*. There is, for example, a fragment attributed to Daqiqi that mentions such subjects as the prodigious bird known as the Simorgh, an unfeathered arrow, Rostam's wondrous horse Rakhsh, and the "magician" Zāl, father of Rostam.[14] Such subjects pervade Ferdowsi's *Shāhnāma*.

Why did Ferdowsi ostensibly incorporate only the poetry of Daqiqi, not that of other poets, and why these particular one thousand lines? The answer suggested by Nöldeke and now generally accepted is that Ferdowsi appropriated Daqiqi's poetry, despite his claims concerning its inferiority, in order to deal with a "rather ticklish subject" for Ferdowsi's Muslim context, namely, the coming of Zoroaster.[15]

I suggest that there is another and equally strong reason for Ferdowsi's appropriation of Daqiqi: he is seeking to make Daqiqi the representative of the preexisting poetic traditions, a single foil for and rival of his own version. In fact, we know that Daqiqi's Zoroastrian themes share the heritage of a Middle Persian epic tradition: there is a Pahlavi narrative poem, *Ayādgār ī Zarērān* "The Memorial of Zarēr," the themes of which converge with those in the verses of Daqiqi as incorporated in the *Shāhnāma*.[16] In this connection, it seems to be no accident that Daqiqi supposedly just happens to have composed only those thousand-odd lines incorporated in the *Shāhnāma*, and that these lines, in turn, just happen to coincide with the narrative framework of *The Memorial of Zarēr*.

Daqiqi himself is a Zoroastrian, and his own poetry boasts about it:

[12] For a definitive introduction to Abu Shakur, see Lazard 1964 I 27–30.

[13] Asadi, *Lughat-e furs* (ed. Horn 1987); see Nöldeke 1930.35. Addenda in Lazard 1964 I 181–184. Lazard 1975.606 observes: "The earliest extant Persian dictionary, the [*Lughat-e furs*] of Asadi, was compiled towards the middle of the [11th] century precisely with the object of explaining [East Iranian] words to readers belonging to Western Iran."

[14] Daqiqi fr. 126, in the edition of Lazard 1964; cf. Nöldeke 1894–1904 [1930].33, n4. (Cited hereafter as "Nöldeke 1930," with page numbers from the English version.)

[15] Nöldeke 1930.35.

[16] For a detailed survey of convergences, see Benveniste 1932a. For a discussion of the continuity of the narrative traditions as attested in *The Memorial of Zarēr* and in the *Shāhnāma*, see Boyce 1955.18, 36.

دقیقی چار خصلت بر گزیدست   بگــیــتــی در ز خوبیها و زشـتـی
لــب بــیــجــاده رنگ و نالهٔ چنگ   مـی خون رنگ و کیش زرد هشتی

Daqiqi has chosen four qualities	in the world from all that is beautiful and all that is ugly—
ruby-colored lips, the plaint of the harp,	blood-colored wine, and the religion of Zoroaster.

Daqiqi fr. 204, ed. Lazard 1964

In this light, it is indeed safer for Ferdowsi to present the orthodox Zo-roastrian doctrine from the mouth of a self-acknowledged Zoroas-trian. By supposedly quoting Daqiqi on the overall narrative of the coming of Zoroaster, Ferdowsi achieves a critical distance, being thus one step removed from his own Muslim context and thereby not personally responsible for anything that might be offensive to Muslim sensibilities. But he also achieves something that is even more impor-tant: with his gesture of quoting Daqiqi in the *Shāhnāma,* Ferdowsi appropriates, in one stroke, the cumulative poetic traditions of his Zoroastrian predecessors.

Such poetic traditions, I argue, are *oral* poetic traditions. I use the term "oral" in line with the investigations of living oral traditions by Parry and Lord.[17] As we know from evidence independent of Fer-dowsi's *Shāhnāma,* a lengthy history of Iranian oral poetic traditions stretches back many centuries. The most striking testimony, collected by Mary Boyce, centers on the New Persian and Middle Persian contexts of the Parthian word *gōsān,* roughly translatable as 'min-strel'.[18] Boyce sums up the essence of this testimony:

The *gōsān* played a considerable part in the life of the Parthians and their neighbours, down to late in the Sasanian epoch: entertainer of king and commoner, privileged at court and popular with the people; present at the graveside and at the feast; eulogist, satirist, storyteller, musician; recorder of past achievements, and commentator of his own times. He is sometimes an object of emulation, sometimes a despised frequenter of taverns and bawdy-houses; sometimes a solitary singer and musician,

[17] Parry 1971 and Lord 1960.
[18] See esp. Boyce 1957.

and sometimes one of a group, singing or performing on a variety of instruments. The explanation of such diversity is presumably that for the Parthians music and poetry were so closely entwined, that a man could not be professional poet without being also a musician, skilled in instrumental as well as vocal music. . . . As poet-musicians, in Parthian society as in any other, the *gōsān*s presumably enjoyed reputation and esteem in proportion to their individual talents.[19]

There is comparable evidence about singer-poets in the earlier Iranian traditions of the Medes (Athenaeus 633), Achaemenids (Xenophon *Cyropaedia* 1.2.1), and Sasanians (*Letter of Tansar*, Minavi 1932.12).[20]

The medium of the singer-poet was competitive. Particularly striking anecdotes concern competitions between Bārbad, traditionally the greatest Sasanian minstrel, and various rivals (cf. Thaʿālibī, Zotenberg 1900.704).[21] These traditions of poetic competition are prominently featured in the *Shāhnāma* of Ferdowsi (for example, IX 226–228.3610–3677).[22] These traditions help explain the tenor of Ferdowsi's competitiveness with Daqiqi.

In this connection, it is important again to draw attention to the way in which Ferdowsi presents Daqiqi as the sum total of previous traditions. Oral poets in most cultures appropriate all previous traditions of composition to themselves in the context of each poet's own performance/composition.[23] So too Ferdowsi claims that he is definitive by virtue of being the ultimate transmitter of the stories he tells. The poet figuratively owns the whole poem in the context of composition, which is presented as a stylized performance:

کهن گشته این داستانها زمن   همــــی نو شود بر سر انجمن

These stories, grown old,   will be renewed by me in all assemblies.

III 6.9

---

[19] Ibid. 17–18; for a comparative discussion of oral traditions in poetry *and* song, see Nagy 1990a.17–51.

[20] Cf. Boyce 1957.20–22.

[21] Cf. ibid. 23–25, 27, n6.

[22] Cf. ibid. 23, n7.

[23] See Lord 1960.102: "A song has no 'author' but a multiplicity of authors, each singing being a creation, each singing having its own single author."

In performance, the oral poet appropriates the song to himself at the expense of other oral poets.[24] A cross-cultural survey reveals that such a claim on the part of the performer/composer is typical of oral poetics.[25] In the *Shāhnāma,* Ferdowsi appropriates the poetry of his predecessors, as represented by Daqiqi, because they are long dead and removed from the realm of performance:

کـنــون من بگویم سخن کو بگفت   مــنــم زنده او گــشــت با خاك جفت

Now I will tell what he [Daqiqi] has told.	For I am alive and he has become joined with the dust.
	VI 66.13

Alternatively, Ferdowsi can present his predecessors as having lost control over the transmission of their poetry.[26]

بنقل اندرون سست گشتش سخن   ازو نـــونـــشـــد روزگــــار کهن

In transmitting, his words became weak.	Ancient times were not renewed by him.
	VI 136.18 (K variant)

Ferdowsi presents his composition as his "performance," *his own song.*

Some may think that the testimony of Ferdowsi about Daqiqi should be taken more literally, to the extent that Ferdowsi may be citing Daqiqi because the latter figure is truly his only significant predecessor in his use of poetic form. In this line of thinking, some might argue that, even if there were oral poetry in the time of Ferdowsi, this poetry would still be very different from that of Daqiqi and Ferdowsi. For example, if we take the obvious aspect of the formal features shared by Daqiqi and Ferdowsi, namely the *mutaqārib* meter, some would be inclined to think that the poetry of these two poets, as well as all New Persian poetry, results from the artificial literary adoption of Arabic poetic forms.[27] Why not, then, consider Daqiqi and Ferdowsi to be forerunners of a new literary form? After all, this

---

[24] Ibid.

[25] See Nagy 1990a. 54–56.

[26] In what follows, I draw attention to the expression بنقل 'in transmitting'.

[27] See, e.g., Qazvini 1953 I 35.

mutaqārib form, with its strict rules in quantitative meter, would seem to be in sharp contrast with what Iranists have considered to be the form of native Persian oral poetry.[28] Judging from the evidence of attested Avestan and Middle Persian poetry, Emile Benveniste in 1930 proposed that the basic native Persian metrical principle is a system of lines with equal syllable count,[29] while W. B. Henning posited a system of equal stress counts.[30]

But these evaluations of native Persian poetic forms have now been seriously challenged by L. P. Elwell-Sutton, who makes a strong case for quantitative meter as the basic principle of Middle Persian poetry, thereby directly linking it with the quantitative meter of New Persian poetry, like the *mutaqārib* lines of Ferdowsi's *Shāhnāma*.[31] Moreover, Elwell-Sutton argues convincingly that Ferdowsi's *mutaqārib* meter, as well as other meters related to it, is not derived from the corresponding Arabic meter, one that is unattested in pre-Islamic Arabic poetry, extremely rare in the Umayyad period (A.D. 661–750), and relatively frequent only in 'Abbāsid times (A.D. 750–1258); rather it is the Arabic *mutaqārib* that seems to be modeled on the Persian.[32] In fact, the New Persian *mutaqārib* seems to be derived from Middle Persian forms.[33] The thrust, then, of Elwell-Sutton's findings is that the attested fragments of New Persian poetry before Daqiqi and Ferdowsi consistently reveal the formal characteristics of Middle Persian poetry.[34] I cite Elwell-Sutton's illuminating survey of these New Persian poetic fragments, such as the three surviving lines attributed to the Sasanian minstrel Bārbad,[35] part of a hymn recited by the Zoroastrian priests at the fire-temple of Karkoy,[36] and a two-line lament for the ruin of Samarqand.[37]

[28] See the discussion of Lazard 1964 I 10.

[29] Benveniste 1930, 1932a.

[30] See, e.g., Henning 1942.51–56; 1950.641–648; Boyce 1957.39–40.

[31] Elwell-Sutton 1976, esp. 180–183. For the linguistic concepts of Old, Middle, and New Persian, see the Introduction.

[32] Elwell-Sutton 1976.172–173.

[33] Ibid. 172; cf. Marr 1944.

[34] Elwell-Sutton 1976.172–179.

[35] Ibid. 178; quoted in Lazard 1975.605. For the time-frame of Sasanian, see the Introduction. For more on Bārbad, see Boyce 1957.23–25.

[36] Attested in the *Tārikh-e Sistān:* see Elwell-Sutton 1976.176; also Lazard 1975.605, 614.

[37] See Elwell-Sutton 1976.173; also Lazard 1975.605.

Accordingly, I maintain that Ferdowsi's description of Daqiqi as his *only* predecessor cannot be taken literally. By appropriating his rival Daqiqi as the representative of Zoroastrian traditions, Ferdowsi implicitly declares himself heir to the Middle Persian epic traditions, and he does so with a gesture typical of oral poetics.

CHAPTER 2

The Authority of
Ferdowsi's *Shāhnāma*

Evidence shows that Ferdowsi's epic poetry cannot have been the
first of its kind. The question remains, however: why was his claim to
be the first poet of national epic implicitly accepted by later generations of poets? It will not suffice to assume that Ferdowsi's poetry came
to be considered the first of its kind simply because it was the best.
Ferdowsi's primacy is not just a matter of artistic superiority. As the
poet himself affirms, it is also a matter of authenticity and authority.
And authority is a matter of control over tradition.[1] For Ferdowsi,
moreover, such control is specified as control over both *oral* and *written*
traditions. The oral traditions, as we shall see, are represented as
stylized performances by figures called *mōbad*s and *dehqān*s, while the
written traditions take the form of an archetypal book, the Pahlavi
Book of Kings.

Ferdowsi's claimed control over both oral and written traditions, I
argue, is an expression of authority that is derived primarily from oral,
not written, poetic traditions. Ferdowsi's poetic tradition was an oral
tradition in its own right, and his *Shāhnāma* had survived as a living
oral tradition in the period following its composition. Ferdowsi's
poetry was an accretive medium that kept adapting itself to the society
for which it was composed and recomposed.

[1] For comparative evidence from Archaic Greece concerning the correlation of
political power with poetic authority and authorship, see Nagy 1990a.146–198, 339–
413.

As I proposed in the preceding chapter, Ferdowsi not only inherited the Middle Persian oral poetic traditions; he also re-created the New Persian oral traditions, composing a version of national epic meant to be both more comprehensive and better than any that preceded him. His version became canonical. And yet, ironically, this very fact of canonicity became a guarantee that the national epic tradition would not come to an end with Ferdowsi. Rather, the *Shāhnāma* of Ferdowsi went on regenerating itself all over the land. The key to this process was the oral poetic tradition that Ferdowsi had inherited and appropriated from his predecessors. In his extensive study of medieval Western European literary traditions, Paul Zumthor describes as *mouvance* the phenomenon in which the act of composition is regenerated with each act of copying a manuscript; we may expect such a process to be ongoing in any tradition where the act of composition is still part of a living process of composition-in-performance.[2] With the passage of time, as we shall see, the national epic of Ferdowsi even became a focus for the accretion of extraneous oral poetic traditions.

It is not necessary to apply our own modern poetic criteria in order to determine whether or not the poet Ferdowsi was indeed superior to all other poets of national epic. A clear sign of Ferdowsi's poetic superiority from his own society's point of view can be found in the very fact that it was Ferdowsi's *Shāhnāma,* not some other poet's Book of Kings, that survived, and that its survival precluded any subsequent treatment of the narratives that the *Shāhnāma* has treated. This is a matter of authority as well as artistry, and that authority, I propose, is conferred by the continuum of oral poetic traditions.

With its authority, Ferdowsi's *Shāhnāma* became perceived as the only *Shāhnāma*. It survived Ferdowsi's formative social context, as defined by the patronage of the Sunni sultanate of Maḥmud of Ghazna (A.D. 998–1030), founder of the Ghaznavid dynasty,[3] and it continued through the centuries, prevailing as the national epic of Shīʿite Iran.[4]

---

[2] Zumthor 1972.40–41, 65–75.

[3] For a valuable collection of references to this patronage, both internally in the *Shāhnāma* and externally, see Shahbazi 1991.2, 52, 83–103. My interpretation of these references, as the following discussion makes clear, differs in some respects from his.

[4] On later traditions that represent Ferdowsi himself as a Shīʿite, see Browne II 134 and the general discussion in Shahbazi 1991.

Ferdowsi's *Shāhnāma* has carried such weight and prestige that, even down to the present century, the recitation of oral prosaic traditions of the Book of Kings is conventionally attributed by the reciters to Ferdowsi.[5]

The survival of the *Shāhnāma* from Sunni to Shīʿite contexts raises the possibility that there were shifts in the actual orientation of the poem as it kept on being reshaped in performance over the course of time. Such shifts seem to be reflected in the "Life of Ferdowsi" tradition, both what is built into the *Shāhnāma* and what is extraneously supplied from the prefaces and other sources. Here I interpret the "Life of Ferdowsi" lore not simply as raw data about the real life and times of the poet but as a traditional discourse that merges factual details with an ongoing mythical reinterpretation of the poem's role in society.[6] A salient example is the tradition that tells of Ferdowsi's supposedly having composed a poem of blame, that is, a satire or invective, against the Sunni sultan Maḥmud of Ghazna.[7] The essential themes of this poem of blame attributed to Ferdowsi are accretively built into the *Shāhnāma* proper.[8] The purpose of such accretions in the *Shāhnāma* may well have been to acclimatize the poetry of Ferdowsi to a Shīʿite audience at large. In terms of my interpretation of the "Life of Ferdowsi" tradition, instances of praise for Sultan Maḥmud reflect the requirements of Sunni listeners, whereas instances of invective reflect those of Shīʿites. Thus there is no need to reject the authenticity of the blame passages, as a strictly biographical reading requires on the grounds that the blame itself seems to undermine any impression of sincerity that we may read into Ferdowsi's words of praise elsewhere.[9] Since the praising of Maḥmud is centrally and pervasively reflected by the *Shāhnāma* itself, while the blaming of this sultan is represented

[5] Page 1977.224; discussed further later.

[6] For comparative evidence on the function of myth in "Lives of Poets" traditions, see Nagy 1979.304 paragraph 4 (with n4), 306–307, and 1990a.80, n140.

[7] See Browne II pp.134–139 and Shahbazi 1991.2–8.

[8] For examples of built-in references to Ferdowsi's satire within the *Shāhnāma*, see Nöldeke 1930.46. For the opposite view, that such built-in references must consistently be explained as textual interpolations, see Shahbazi 1991.13.

[9] Here I disagree with Shahbazi. On the appropriateness of assigning poetic words of praise or blame, whichever is required, in the poetic traditions of languages cognate with the Persian, especially Greek and Irish, see Nagy 1979.222–242.

more marginally and sporadically, it seems reasonable to infer that the Sunni orientation of the poet's patronage was dominant in the most formative phases of the poem, while the Shīʿite orientation may have developed only over time, accretively. In any case, it seems to me fruitless to discount the patronage of Maḥmud's Ghaznavid dynasty in considering the historical formation of the text that we know as Ferdowsi's *Shāhnāma*. There is also a related problem concerning the historical attribution to Ferdowsi of a work known as *Yusof and Zoleykhā*.[10]

Ferdowsi's appropriation of all previous poetic traditions in his *Shāhnāma* goes beyond the formal gesture of incorporating the poetry of his main rival Daqiqi. On another level, the poet is making a colossal effort to establish his poetry as the text of a definitive *book,* and in fact the entire *Shāhnāma* is pervaded by references to this effort. On the surface, such references to the *Shāhnāma* as a book seem to contradict the argument that Ferdowsi's poetry is the product of an oral tradition. As we shall see, however, the idea of a book, in Ferdowsi's medieval Persian context, is not at odds with the dynamics of the oral poetic traditions that he inherited.

A basic question arises: should we assume that oral poetry is basically incompatible with literacy? The cross-cultural evidence of social anthropology suggests that no universalized formulation can be made about the phenomenon of literacy: in some societies, literacy erodes the traditions of oral poetry, whereas in others, these traditions may remain unaffected.[11] There is therefore no justification in assuming a priori that the poetry of Ferdowsi is not oral poetry, or that it is some kind of "semi-oral" poetry, solely on the grounds that the *Shāhnāma* refers to itself as a book in the making.[12] Moreover, the act of writing, of creating a book, can be assumed to be a factor merely in the *recording,* not necessarily in the *composing,* of Ferdowsi's poetry. In other words, whatever we may ultimately conclude about the ques-

[10] On which see Shahbazi 1991.11, 13–14, who disputes the authenticity of this attribution, on the grounds that the world-view of this work is "anti-Iranian and fiercely pro-Arab" (p. 14).

[11] For an admirable survey see Zumthor 1983.

[12] There is no ethnographic basis for such categories as "semi-oral" poetry: see Zumthor 1983.34 (cf. also Nagy 1990a.8, 17–18).

tion of deriving the *Shāhnāma* from oral traditions, it cannot simply be taken for granted that the actual composition of the *Shāhnāma* depended on writing. We can be certain about the factor of literacy only to the extent that writing had played a part in the recording of the poem, and that the factor of literacy is a prerequisite for the reading of any recording in the form of a book. It does not necessarily follow that literacy was a prerequisite for the composition that resulted in such a book. Moreover, according to the account of Neẓāmi ʿAruḍi Samarqandi in his *Chahār Maqāla*,[13] the *Shāhnāma* was dictated by Ferdowsi to one ʿAli Daylam and performed on behalf of Ferdowsi on specific occasions by one Abu Dulaf, described as a *rāwi* 'repeater'.[14]

In the first chapter, we saw that the medium of Ferdowsi's *Shāhnāma* talks about itself both as a stylized performance and as a stylized book. The *Shāhnāma* talks about its sources in the same way: it refers to them in terms that suit either stylized performances or a stylized book.

Let us examine, then, the claim made by the *Shāhnāma* to two basic sources. The first is a Pahlavi "Book of Kings" that Ferdowsi says he acquired through "a friend":

بشهرم یکی مهربان دوست بود   تو گفتی که با من بیك پوست بود
مرا گفت خوب آمد این رای تو   به نیکی گراید همی پای تو
نبشته من از این نامه پهلوی   به پیش تو آرم مگر نغنوی
گشاده زبان و جوانیت هست   سخن گفتن پهلوانیت هست
شو این نامهٔ خسروان باز گوی   بدین جوی نزد مهان آبروی
چو آورد این نامه نزدیك من   بر افروخت این جان تاریك من

In my city a congenial [*mehrbān*] man was my friend.

You might say that he and I were in one skin.

[13] Qazvini and Moʿin 1953.76.

[14] On the meaning of this term *rāwi* in Arabic usage as "performer" of oral poetry, see Zwettler 1978.85 and following. As for the reference in the *Chahār Maqāla* of Neẓāmi to the scribe ʿAli Daylam, we may compare an internal reference to Abu Naṣr-e Warrāq, a scribe described in *Shāhnāma* IX 381.n18 as having written down what Ferdowsi composed *at a specific stage of his overall composition* (on the chronology, see Shahbazi 1991.73–74; I disagree, however, with Shahbazi's inference that Abu Naṣr-e Warrāq achieved the master copy of an incomplete "first edition").

He said to me: "This idea of yours is
good.
This book [*nāma*] written down in
Pahlavi,
You have lucid language and youth.

Go, render anew this book [*nāma*]
of kings!
When he brought this book [*nāma*]
to me,

Your feet indeed tend to goodness.

I will present to you so that you
may not slumber!
You have the words for heroic composition.
With it seek honor among the
great!"
it inflamed my dark soul.

I 23.156–161

In previous scholarship, this passage has been interpreted literally as
a piece of historical information, and some have gone so far as to
claim, on the basis of external lore about the life of Ferdowsi, that the
man here described as a *mehrbān* 'congenial' friend of the poet can be
identified as one Moḥammad Lashkari.[15]

I suggest, however, that it is more productive to exhaust first the internal evidence of the *Shāhnāma* itself. Specifically, this passage should
be compared with the passage that leads into the Story of Bēzhan and
Manēzha, *Shāhnāma* V 6–9. 1–37, a description of a mystical nighttime
encounter between Ferdowsi and an unnamed figure who is, again,
described as a *mehrbān* 'congenial one' (lines 15, 16, 29). Most commentators infer that the "congenial one" is in this case meant to be
understood as a concubine.[16] This *mehrbān* proceeds to recite from a
nāma 'book', said to be written in Pahlavi, the love story of Bēzhan and
Manēzha, which Ferdowsi is then to put into verse.

---

[15] See Nöldeke 1930.40 (cf. Mohl III p. iv); also Shahbazi 1991.68–71, who in
general extrapolates a historicized account of Ferdowsi's poetic career on the basis of
the Bāysonghor preface and various passages of the *Shāhnāma*, which will be interpreted later in a different way. I stress that my goal is not to deny the likelihood that
some of the declarations by the poet within the poem, especially concerning such
details as his precise age at various stages of his composing the *Shāhnāma*, are based on
historical fact (Shahbazi's book is particularly valuable in offering a rich collection of
such details). Rather, I see such details not as raw data about the life and times of the
poet but as part of a traditional discourse that incorporates factual details into an
ongoing reinterpretation of the poem's role in society. Such reinterpretation operates
on the principles of myth, provided we understand *myth* in the sense of a given society's
codification of its own truth-values. For a pertinent theoretical discussion of myth in
contexts of authorial self-definition, see Nagy 1990a.436.

[16] Further discussion and references in Shahbazi 1991.65.

It seems that both passages, *Shāhnāma* I 23.156–161 and V 6–9.1–37, are variants of an integral type-scene where a "dear one" gives Ferdowsi a prose rendition of a part of the *Shāhnāma*, supposedly taken from a book written in Pahlavi, and where it is Ferdowsi's task to convert the given rendition from prose to verse. In the second passage, we are told explicitly that Ferdowsi has difficulty falling asleep, whereupon the *mehrbān* consoles him by reading out loud from this Pahlavi book the story of Bēzhan and Manēzha. We can compare this theme of a sleepless night in the second passage with the *mehrbān*'s words in the first passage, where he is pictured as exhorting Ferdowsi not to sleep.

I draw attention to a detail from the second passage, where the *mehrbān* is pictured as setting for Ferdowsi a spread-out feast [*khwān*]; in the mode of a *dehqān*, this *mehrbān* sets the spread *in order to tell a story* (*Shāhnāma* V 167.25).[17] In this image, we see a stylized reference to performance in oral poetic traditions—a reference that is fused in the same context with a reference to the alleged acquisition of a Pahlavi book from this *mehrbān*.

Use of the word *dehqān* in this passage brings us to the important subject of the second of the two primary sources adduced by the *Shāhnāma*. As the inspiration for the *Shāhnāma*, the poet not only receives a Pahlavi book from the mysterious *mehrbān*: he also actually "hears" the poetic traditions spoken by what are called *mōbad*s and *dehqān*s, and references to their spoken words pervade the whole *Shāhnāma*. The first term, *mōbad*, means 'priest' or 'wise man', and the second, *dehqān*, 'landowner'. The latter meaning, however, masks the actual function of the *dehqān*: as a chief owner of property in a particular locale, he is the "authority" not only in the narrow sense that he has administrative powers but also in the broader sense that he actually validates the traditions of that given locale.[18] In other words, the *mōbad*s and *dehqān*s are performers of the oral tradition. In fact, Nezāmi ʿAruḍi Samarqandi in his *Chahār Maqāla* reports that Ferdowsi himself was a *dehqān*.[19]

In the poetic diction of the *Shāhnāma*, as the following passages show, the words *mōbad* and *dehqān* are in fact the functional equivalents of each other, inasmuch as they both designate performers of the oral

---

[17] The passage is quoted later in this chapter (passage 14).
[18] Cf. Mohl 1838.viii–x.
[19] See Qazvini and Moʿin 1953.74.

tradition, validators of tradition itself. In example 1, the words are even synonymous. In example 3, the *dehqān* is the son of a *mōbad,* while in example 4, the *mōbad* is a descendant of a *dehqān*. Moreover, the *mōbad*s and *dehqān*s are characterized as validators of a specifically *poetic* oral tradition. In fact, the word *sarāyanda* 'singer' is synonymous with both *mōbad* and *dehqān* in example 1.[20]

بگـفـتـار دهقان کنون باز گرد   نـگـر تـا چـ گوید سراینده مرد ۱.

چنین گفت موبد که یك روز طوس   بدانگ که بر خاست بـانـگ خروس

Consider what the singer [*sarā-yanda*] says.	Now turn back to the words of the *dehqān*.
at the time when the cock crowed . . .	Thus the *mōbad* said, that, one day Ṭōs
III 7.19–20	

نبـاشی بدیـن گفته همداستان   که دهـقـان همـی گوید از باستان ۲.

خردمـنـد کین داستان بشنود   بـدانـش گـرایـد بـدیـن نگـرود

ولیـکن چـو معنیش یاد آوری   شـود رام و کـوته کـنـد داوری

تو بشنو ز گفتار دهقان پیـر   گر ایـدونـك بـاشد سخن دلپذیـر

سخن گوی دهقان چنین کرد یاد   کـ یـکروز کیـخـسـرو از بامداد

that the *dehqān* continuously recites about ancient times.	Perhaps you do not agree with this account
chooses knowledge and does not accept it.	A wise man who hears this story
he complies and cuts short his quarrel.	But when you remind him of the meaning
if now the words are agreeable,	Listen to the words of the old *dehqān,*
That one day, at daybreak, Key Khosrow . . .	the *dehqān* who thus recalled the spoken words [*sokhan guy*].
IV 302.16–20	

ازیـن داسـتـانم چـنیـن داد یاد ۳.   سـرایـنده دهـقـان مـوبـد نـژاد

20 Cf. also examples 3, 7, 8.

A singer [sarāyanda], a dehqān, son of a mōbad,

thus taught me this story.

Mohl V 424.8

هم از گفت آن پیر دهقان نژاد ‖ ز موبد بدین گونه داریم یاد ۴.

From the mōbad, in this manner we know

also from the speech of that old man of dehqān descent.

Mohl II 4.1

که بر خواند از گفتهٔ باستان ‖ زدهقان کنون بشنو این داستان ۵.

Now listen to this story from the dehqān,

who recites it from ancient discourse.

VIII 146.1559

نگر تا چه گوید جهاندیده مرد ‖ بگفتار دهقان کنون باز گرد ۶.

Now turn back to the words of the dehqān.

Consider what the experienced man says.

Mohl III 6.19

نگر تا چه گوید سراینده مرد ‖ بگفتار دهقان کنون باز گرد ۷.

Now turn back to the words of the dehqān.

Consider what the singer says.

III 169.2587

ز گشتسپ وز نامدار اردشیر ‖ چه گفت آن سراینده دهقان پیر ۸.

What did that singer say, that old dehqān

about Goshtasp and famous Ardashir?

VI 373.6

چه گفت اندر این گردش روزگار ‖ جهانجوی دهقان آموزگار ۹.

What did the teacher, the ambitious *dehqān*, say about the passage of time?

VIII 303.4268

که نام بزرگی بگیتی که جست   سخن‌گوی دهقان چه گوید نخست   .10

What did the reciting [*sokhan guy*] *dehqān* say first? Who in the world sought the name of greatness?

I 28.1

که دهقان همی گوید از باستان   چو باشی بدین گفته همداستان   .11

... while you are in accord with the story that the *dehqān* keeps on reciting about ancient times.

IV 208.5

سخنها همه یک بیک یاد گیر   کنون بشنو از مرد دهقان پیر   .12

Now listen to the old *dehqān* and learn all his stories, one by one.

Mohl IV 276.3200

که یاد آرد از گفتهٔ باستان   زدهقان تو نشنیده آن داستان   .13

Did you not hear the story from the *dehqān* who calls to mind the ancient times?

VI 312.1518

یکی داستان راند از هفتخوان   سخن‌گوی دهقان چه بنهاد خوان   .14

The *dehqān*, when he set the spread for feasting,[21] knowing the tradition [*sokhan*], recited a story about the *Haft Khwān*.

VI 167.25

[21] See further discussion in Chapter 9.

Thus the *mōbad*s and the *dehqān*s represent for Ferdowsi the equivalent of oral poetry, and it is their traditions that he appropriates in the manner of an oral poet:[22]

15. تو بر خوان و بر گوی با راستان   ز گفتار دهقان کنون داستان
     همـــــی نـو شـود بر سـر انجمن   کهـن گشته این داستانها زمـن

From the spoken words of the *deh-qān* recall now | the stories and recite to the Truth-ful.
These stories, having become old, | will on account of me be renewed before all assemblies.

III 6.8–9

16. بدین خویشتنرا نشان خواستم   چو گفتار دهقان بیاراستم

When I put into verse the spoken words of the *dehqān* | I wanted some sign of my own self in it.

VIII 97.763

There is even an instance where two variants of one distich explicitly refer to the aspect of oral poetry on one hand and to the aspect of Ferdowsi's appropriating this oral poetry on the other:

17. نگـر تـا چـه گوید سراینده مرد   بگفتار دهئقـان کنون باز کرد

Now turn back to the spoken words of the *dehqān*. | Consider what the singer says.

II 170.15 (ms. VI)

بپیوندم از گفتـئ باستان   ز گفتار دهقان یکی داستان

From the spoken words of the *deh-qān* | I will join together a story from what was said in ancient times.

II 170.15 (other mss.)

[22] See Chapter 1.

Such testimony about the authenticity of the poetry as both written and oral tradition, offered by the poetry itself, is essentially accepted as valid by Jules Mohl, one of the first editors and translators of the *Shāhnāma*. He interprets the acquisition of a Pahlavi Book of Kings as the written aspect of Ferdowsi's sources[23] and the hearing of the stories from *mōbad*s and *dehqān*s as the "oral" aspect.[24]

Since the work of Mohl, however, there has been a decided movement away from his interpretation, under the aegis of Nöldeke, who has been followed by succeeding generations of European, American, and native Iranian scholars.[25] Although Nöldeke was an admirer of both the literary and the editorial judgment of Mohl, and in fact concedes that he became increasingly so with each consultation,[26] he stresses his disagreement with his predecessor in this particular case. I agree with Nöldeke by treating the reference to *mōbad*s and *dehqān*s not literally but as narrative gestures; still, I disagree with him by treating the references to writing likewise as narrative gestures.

Nöldeke was an exponent of what he called the "scientific method," grounded in the European heritage of textual criticism and *Quellenforschung*.[27] Oriented toward finding the textual sources of the *Shāhnāma*, Nöldeke rejected Mohl's idea that Ferdowsi's sources included "oral" traditions.[28] In Nöldeke's time, the empirical study of living oral traditions, later perfected by Parry and Lord, had not yet taken shape, so that the very term "oral" did not as yet have "scientific" status.[29] As we shall see, there are indeed empirical techniques available in applying our knowledge of living oral traditions to poetic evidence that happens to be preserved only in "dead" textual traditions. For now, however, let us pursue Nöldeke's line of thinking, based purely on the textual evidence.

Ferdowsi's ubiquitous conceit of hearing the stories from a *mōbad* or

---

[23] Mohl 1838.x, n2. For evidence that Ferdowsi knew neither Pahlavi nor Arabic see Shahbazi 1991.39–41.

[24] Mohl 1838.ix.

[25] Most notable of the latter group are Ḥasan Taqizāda, Moḥammad Qazvini, Dhabihollāh Ṣafā.

[26] Nöldeke 1930.126.

[27] Ibid.

[28] Ibid. 62.

[29] See Chapter 1.

a *dehqān* was discounted by Nöldeke as a stylized way of expressing the consultation of texts:

> It is a delusion when he [Ferdowsi] speaks in such a way as if relating from an oral narrative of some *dehqān* or the like. When he says . . . that he brings into verse "what had been related of the antiquity" it only means the same thing that is meant by "the book of old times." In the next verse he addresses the reader as a listener: "O son, lend me thy ear!" . . . which is a similar case.[30]

Nöldeke's reasoning was obviously based on the assumption that the *Shāhnāma* is a *text* that is meant to be *read*. For him, Ferdowsi's frequent exhortations that the audience listen are simply a matter of stylization.

The major impetus for the confidence of Nöldeke and his followers in the notion of a purely textual basis for the composition of the *Shāhnāma* had been the cumulative evidence, gathered for the most part after the time of Mohl, of narratives in Arabic and Persian prose that retell the Book of Kings:

(1) Abū Ḥanīfa Aḥmad Ibn Dāwūd Dīnawarī, *Al akhbār aṭ-ṭiwāl* (ninth century, Arabic)

(2) Abū al-Faẓl Balʿamī, *Tarīkh-e Balʿamī* (tenth century, Persian)

(3) ʿAlī Ibn Ḥusayn Masʿūdī, *Murūj aẓ-ẓahab* (tenth century, Arabic)

(4) Ḥamza Ibn al Ḥasan Iṣfahānī, *Tārīkh sinī mulūk al-arẓ wa 'l anbiyā* (tenth century, Arabic)

(5) Anon., *Mujmal at-tawārikh wa 'l qiṣaṣ* (eleventh century, Persian)

(6) Abū Manṣūr ʿAbd al-Malik Ibn Muḥammad Ibn Ismāʿīl Thaʿālibī, *Ghurar akhbār mulūk al furs wa siyarihim* (eleventh century, Arabic)

(7) Abū Rayḥan Muḥammad Ibn Aḥmad al Bīrūnī, *Al āthār al bāqiya ʿan al qurūn al khāliya* (eleventh century, Persian)

(8) Abū Saʿīd ʿAbd al Ḥayy Ibn aẓ Ẓaḥḥāk Gardīzī, *Zayn al akhbār* (eleventh century, Persian)

(9) Anon., *Tārikh-e Sistān* (eleventh century, Persian)

---

[30] Nöldeke 1930.67.

(10) Malik Shāh Ḥusayn Sīstānī, *Iḥyāʾ al mulūk* (sixteenth century, Persian)

It has been suggested that these Arabic and Persian texts are based ultimately on sources written in Pahlavi, the official language of the Sasanian dynasty. There is thought to be one such source in particular, the Pahlavi *Khwatāy-nāmak,* the equivalent of the Persian *Khodāynāma* 'Book of Lords', originally commissioned by King Yazdgerd (A.D. 632–651) and compiled by his vizier, a *dehqān* called Dāneshvar,[31] covering a period that extends from Keyumarṣ to Khosrow Parviz.[32] In this line of reasoning, then, Ferdowsi's immediate textual source would have been a Persian translation of the Pahlavi *Khodāynāma.*

In what is known as the "older preface" to Ferdowsi's *Shāhnāma,* there are reports of a translation of the *Khodāynāma* into Persian prose. This translation was commissioned by a figure with strong Zoroastrian connections, the "Lord of Ṭōs" Abu Manṣur-e ʿAbd al-Razzāq, and compiled by his secretary, Abu Manṣur Maʿmari; the project was reportedly completed in 346/April A.D. 957.[33] By "preface," what is meant are the varied prose accounts that precede the actual text of Ferdowsi's *Shāhnāma* in the surviving manuscripts. These accounts can be grouped into different families on the basis of differing contents. A systematic edition of all these varied accounts is at present wanting,[34] but one such account, known as the "older preface," as it emerges from one family of manuscripts, has drawn particular attention since the days of Mohl.[35] In this "older preface," then, we find the

---

[31] The name may be generic, not historical: *dāneshvar* means 'skilled, intelligent, learned'.

[32] This information is provided in the preface of Bāysonghor to the *Shāhnāma* (cf. Mohl 1838.vii, n4 and Nöldeke 1930.23); this preface is characteristic of most post-fifteenth-century manuscripts of the *Shāhnāma* (cf. Minorsky 1964.261, n4; also Shahbazi 1991.6).

[33] The information concerning this prose *Shāhnāma* is provided in the "older preface" of the *Shāhnāma.* The text of the "older preface" is published by Qazvini 1944 and translated by Minorsky 1964.263–273. On the confirmation provided by the "most reliable" Bīrūnī, see Nöldeke 1930.27. For other instances of such translations from Pahlavi into Persian prose, see Lazard 1971.387, n19; cf. also Lazard 1975.625. On the Zoroastrian (and possibly Shīʿite) connections of Abu Manṣur-e ʿAbd al-Razzāq, see Shahbazi 1991.31–32 (esp. n54).

[34] Cf. Minorsky 1964.261.

[35] Cf. Mohl 1838.xv–xvi. Later, an attempt was made by Qazvini (1944.123–148) to establish its text. On an earlier attempt, by Jacques de Wallenbourg, to establish the

report about a commissioning of a prose *Shāhnāma* written in Persian and translated from the Pahlavi Book of Kings, presumed to be the one mentioned in Ferdowsi's account. This Persian prose text, no longer extant, extended the Book of Kings all the way down to the reign of Yazdgerd, a terminus that in fact coincides with that of Ferdowsi's *Shāhnāma*.[36] Some go so far as to argue that the "older preface" had originally served to introduce this prose *Shāhnāma,* now lost, rather than Ferdowsi's poetic *Shāhnāma.*[37]

It is commonly inferred by modern commentators that Abu Manṣur's prose *Shāhnāma* is the "source" for Ferdowsi's poetic *Shāhnāma.*[38] There are, however, serious problems with such an inference. To begin with, we have already seen that the "ancient book" given by the unnamed *mehrbān* 'congenial one' to Ferdowsi in the *Shāhnāma* is stylized to such an extent that it seems more generic than specific.[39] The book is described not as Persian but more vaguely as Pahlavi:[40]

نبشته من این نامهٔ پهلوی   به پیش تو آرم مگر نغنوی

| This Pahlavi book [*nāma*], written down, | I bring before you so that you may not slumber. |

I 23.158

There is a striking parallel in the most ancient attested Zoroastrian text composed in New Persian, the *Zarātoshtnāma* (ca. A.D. 978; Dabir-Siyāqi 1959). In the proem of his composition, the poet speaks of his source in the following words (line 14):

یکی دفتری دیدم از خسروی   به خطی که خوانی ورا پهلوی

| I saw a book [*daftar*] from the time of the empire | in a writing which is called Pahlavi. |

---

text of this preface, see Minorsky 1964.262, n2. Note the reservations expressed already by Mohl 1838.xvi on the accuracy of Wallenbourg's translations.

[36] Minorsky 1964.266.

[37] Qazvini 1944, followed by Shahbazi 1991.132–133.

[38] See, for example, the survey of views collected by Shahbazi p. 40.

[39] See discussion earlier in this chapter.

[40] On the latitude inherent in this term, which can refer both to the newer Persian and to the older Pahlavi diction, see Lazard 1971.364–369.

Later on a *mōbad* urges the poet to translate the book into Persian verse
(lines 23–25):

کـز او یـاد نارد کسی اصل و بن | همـی بـیـنـی این قصّهای کهن
بـتـرسـم کـه گردد بـه یـك ره تباه | ندارد بدین خطّ کسی دستگاه
به پـاکـیـزه گفـتـار و خطّه دری | همان به که اینرا به نظم آوری

You see these ancient stories	of which no one recalls the beginning or the end.
No one understands this writing.	I fear it will disappear altogether.
It is better that you put it in verse,	in beautiful language and in *dari* [= Persian] writing.[41]

I conclude that it is unjustified to posit a specifically Persian prose
archetype for Ferdowsi's poetry merely on the basis of his references to
an authoritative book of prose as his source.[42]

A similar argument can be made concerning a Pahlavi version,
produced in the reign of Khosrow I Anushirvān (A.D. 531–579), of the
Indic corpus of fables known as the *Pañcatantra;* the Arabic version of
Ibn al-Muqaffaʿ, apparently based on the Pahlavi version, is known by
the title *Kalīla and Dimna* (names of two jackals who are characters in
one of the stories). There was a version of *Kalīla and Dimna* in Persian,
composed in verse by the poet Rudaki and commissioned by Abu'l-
Faẓl Balʿami, vizier to the Sāmanid king Naṣr II Ibn Aḥmad; this
poem is not extant, except for some fragments.[43] Ferdowsi himself
draws a parallel between his own *Shāhnāma* and Rudaki's *Kalīla and
Dimna,* stressing that the uniqueness of both compositions depends on
what is described as the turning of prose into poetry (*Shāhnāma* VIII
655.3460–3464).[44] Here again it is unjustified to posit a Persian prose
archetype for the Persian poetry of the *Kalīla and Dimna* merely on the
basis of references to an authoritative book of prose as source. The

[41] Ibid. 365–366.
[42] We may compare the Old French *Guiron le courtois,* composed about 1235, where
the author tells of the many French books resulting from what is described as a
translation of a mythical Latin book of the Holy Grail: see Huot 1991.218–221.
[43] Background in Lazard 1975.622–623.
[44] Ibid. 626.

implicit equation of "prose" with Pahlavi documents conveys an authority that is comparable to the medium of Ferdowsi's poetry. In this medium, as we have seen, both the Pahlavi book *and* oral poetic traditions are visualized as the basis for a poem's authority.

Moreover, it is impossible to establish with certainty that the Pahlavi *Khodāynāma,* as commissioned by Yazdgerd, was even the ultimate source of Ferdowsi's *Shāhnāma.* We come back to the parallel retellings of the Book of Kings in Arabic and Persian prose, cited by Nöldeke as proof of the existence of a Pahlavi archetype, the *Khodāynāma.* These retellings are so often at variance with Ferdowsi's *Shāhnāma,* and with each other, that a stemma leading back to a single archetypal *Khodāynāma* simply cannot be constructed.[45] It is pertinent here to cite the anecdote, recorded in Ḥamza 24, that one Mōbad Bahrām had to use twenty "copies" to establish the "correct" chronology of the *Khodāynāma.*[46]

Yet Nöldeke, who wants to believe that there is an archetypal version of the *Shāhnāma,* is in fact the first to despair of establishing, by way of Arabic and Persian prose sources, a textual stemma for Ferdowsi's *Shāhnāma.* Even the *Ghurar* of Thaʿālibī, a contemporary of Ferdowsi,[47] is disappointing in this regard. Although Nöldeke believes that the *Ghurar,* unlike the other Arabic sources, was based directly on the Persian prose *Shāhnāma* commissioned by Abu Manṣur, he is forced to posit, on the basis of the textual divergences, that Thaʿālibī and Ferdowsi must have used different copies of this Persian prose *Shāhnāma,* copies that varied considerably one from the other:

> The text used by Thaʿālibī was, however, not exactly the same as used by our poet. We have here to do with two somewhat different copies of the Book of Kings. . . . The Persian copyists have, and always have had, the tendency of "correcting" at least in minor details quite arbitrarily or guided by their supposed discernment the originals on hand, and the number of such disfigurements made on purpose is further increased by mistakes made out of sheer carelessness. In that way there appear also in

---

[45] Nöldeke 1930.25.

[46] Ibid.; cf. Lazard 1975.624–625.

[47] The traditional dates for Thaʿālibī are 350–429/A.D. 961–1057. For the standard edition and translation of Thaʿālibī, see Zotenberg 1900.

those portions which take their origin in a common source and cannot
be traced to any of the other Arab authors certain divergences between
the *Ghurar* and our Epic.[48]

Nöldeke rationalizes even further the divergences between
Thaʿālibī and Ferdowsi. Since Ferdowsi is after all a poet, so Nöldeke
reasons, he may allow his imagination to elaborate and make more
beautiful those things that the "elegant rhetoric" of the scholar
Thaʿālibī would have left alone.[49] The same sort of reasoning emerges
in a monograph by Kurt Heinrich Hansen that systematically com-
pares the parallel narratives of Thaʿālibī and Ferdowsi.[50] Whenever
Hansen deems something gratuitously present in Ferdowsi's *Shāhnāma*
while it is absent in Thaʿālibī's *Ghurar,* he infers that Ferdowsi has filled
the gap in the traditional narrative by unleashing his poetic "Phantasie."[51] But Hansen's reasoning can be replaced by a more satisfactory
explanatory model. For example, in Ferdowsi's *Shāhnāma,* when the
hero Sām, Rostam's grandfather, goes to war against Māzandarān and
the Gorgsārs, there is an elaborate description of his handing over the
crown and kingdom to his son Zāl, who is destined to be Rostam's
father (I 154.281–285). Later, however, after Zāl marries Rudāba,
Rostam's mother-to-be, Sām again goes to war against the Gorgsārs—
and again there is an elaborate description of his handing over the
crown and kingdom to Zāl (I 243–235.1459–1464).[52] By contrast, the
corresponding narrative of Thaʿālibī has Sām hand over his kingdom
to Zāl *as his representative* the first time and then *as his successor* the
second time. Hansen thinks that the version of Thaʿālibī is closer to the
"original" version, and that the version of Ferdowsi is by contrast a
misunderstanding of the same hypothetical original: not understanding the difference between representative and successor, the poet supposedly executes an awkward duplication of scenes and then fills in the
gaps with his imagination.[53]

Such a doublet in Ferdowsi's narrative, deemed gratuitous by Han-

[48] Nöldeke 1930.63–64.
[49] Nöldeke 1930.64.
[50] Hansen 1954.
[51] Ibid. 116.
[52] Ibid.
[53] Ibid.

sen, can be explained as a typical feature of "oral" traditional narrative patterns as described by Albert Lord in *The Singer of Tales:* a traditional scene A can be doubled in the pattern A_1BA_2 by way of an interposed scene B.[54] For example, a certain South Slavic "oral" traditional singer, Avdo Mededović, at one point of a performance seems to contradict himself when narrating the sequence of events concerning the receiving of a letter and the rewarding of a messenger (pattern A). Avdo has the letter delivered, the recipient open it and read it, and the head of the assembly ask about the letter (pattern A_1). Only after he has shifted to the next stage of his narrative (pattern B) does Avdo realize that he has not mentioned the rewarding of the messenger, a theme that proves to be important for a later part of the song. So Avdo repeats the theme of reading the letter, this time mentioning the reward (A_2), thereby leaving a minor violation in the sequence.[55] It can be argued, then, that Ferdowsi's *Shāhnāma* here reveals a feature typical of "oral" poetry, and that it is Thaʿālibī's account that may reflect innovation here, namely, the undoing of a doublet by way of making the two variants complementary rather than redundant.

The factor of oral poetry, especially as it was investigated by Parry and Lord well after the time of Mohl's writing, can help account for this and for many other aspects of Ferdowsi's *Shāhnāma*. Thus we will be moving back toward the position represented by Mohl, who—as has been previously noted—believed that the *Shāhnāma* of Ferdowsi was built on "oral" as well as written sources. For the moment, however, we shall not insist, as Mohl did, that references to *mōbad*s and *dehqān*s are to be taken literally to mean that Ferdowsi heard oral poetry from them. By the same token, however, we also cannot say for sure, as Nöldeke did, that Ferdowsi literally acquired an ancient book from a friend. In both cases, I suggest, we are dealing with poetic conventions that are expressing the authority and authenticity of the traditions that are being told. Thus we come back to our point of departure: not only does the *Shāhnāma* present itself as both stylized performance and a stylized book, but it also presents its sources in the same way.

The fusion of themes is so complete that *performance* and *book* can be

[54] Lord 1960.96–98.
[55] Ibid. 103.

interchangeable concepts.[56] Thus, as we have seen, the book of Ferdowsi is presented as preempting the book of Daqiqi, just as an oral
poet's performance might preempt the performance of another oral
poet. And yet, we know that we are dealing with rival fixations of the
text. The preemption is presented as it might happen in oral poetry,
but the poetry of Daqiqi is not presented as merely a performance or
oral poem, but also as a book like that of Ferdowsi.[57]

So the poetry of Daqiqi is seen as more than oral poetry, just like the
poetry of Ferdowsi. As for the oral poet, he is stylized in a different
way, as a *mōbad* or *dehqān* from whom Ferdowsi hears tradition. It
would be tempting for some to assume that the poetry of the *mōbad*s
and *dehqān*s, if it is poetry, would be different from that of Daqiqi. But
we have already seen that the arguments assembled by Elwell-Sutton,
concerning the native Persian heritage of Daqiqi's and Ferdowsi's
mutaqārib poetics, suggest otherwise.[58] The major difference established by the *Shāhnāma* between the likes of Daqiqi and the *mōbad*s/
*dehqān*s is that his poetry has become a fixed text, though the mode of
rivalry and the mode of appropriating is that of oral poetry.

That the *mōbad*s and *dehqān*s do represent oral *poetic* traditions, not
just any kind of oral traditions, becomes clear from Ferdowsi's own
description of the genesis of the Pahlavi Book of Kings that he claims
as his source. In this description, we have what amounts to a myth-
made stylization of oral poetry. A noble and wise *pahlavān,* born of the
*dehqān*s, assembles *mōbad*s from all over Iran, each possessing a "fragment" of a preexisting ancient book. Each *mōbad* recites his portion
and, in this way, this ancient but once "fragmented" book is won-
drously reassembled:

یکی نامه بود از گه باستان   فراوان بـدو انـدرون داسـتـان
پراگنده در دست هر موبدی   ازو بهرهٔ نـزد هـر بخردی

---

[56] For a study of cases where writing becomes viewed by society as an alternative to
the speech-act of performing poetry, see Nagy 1990a. 171–172, 219–220.

[57] The background of patronage in the case of Daqiqi is evidently quite distinct from
what we see in the case of Ferdowsi, whose connections with the Ghaznavid dynasty
have already been discussed. A passage from Ferdowsi's *Shāhnāma,* I 9.152, refers to
Daqiqi as situated in Bokharā, capital of the Sāmānid dynasty; see Shahbazi 1991.68 and
70. I do not agree with Shahbazi's historicizing inferences concerning the archetypal
Book of Kings, as supposedly used by Daqiqi at Bokharā, to which Ferdowsi refers in
this passage.

[58] See Chapter 1.

یکی پهلوان بود دهقان نژاد
پژوهندهٔ روزگار نخست
ز هر کشوری موبدی سالخورد
بپرسیدشان از کیان جهان
که گیتی به آغاز چون داشتند
چه گونه سر آمد بنیك اختری
بگفتند پیشش یکایك مهان
چو بشنید ازیشان سپهبد سخن
چنین یادگاری شد اندر جهان

دلیـر و بـزرگ و خردمند و راد
گذشتـه سـخنها همه باز جسـت
بیـاورد کاین نامه را یـاد کرد
وزان نامـداران فـرخ مـهـان
که ایدون بمـا خـوار بگذاشتند
بـدایشان همـه روز کنـدآوری
سـخنـهـای شاهان و گشت جهان
یکـی نامـور نامـه افکـنـد بن
بـرو آفـریـن از کهـان و مهـان

There was a book [nāma] from ancient times

in which there was an abundance of stories.

It was dispersed into the hands of every mobad.

Every wise one [of the mobads] possessed a portion of it.

There was a pahlavān, born of the dehqāns,

brave, powerful, wise, and noble,

one who inquired into the earliest days.

He sought anew all the past stories.

From every region an aged mobad

he brought, since he [= the mobad] remembered this book [nāma].

He asked them about kings of the world

and about the famed and glorious heroes,

when and how they held the world in the beginning

that they should have passed it down to us in such a wretched state,

how, with a lucky star

every day completed a heroic exploit for them.

The great ones, one by one, recited before him

the stories [sokhanhā] about kings and the turnings of the world.

When the lord heard their words from them

he began to compose a renowned book [nāma].

Thus it became his memorial in the world.

The small and the great praise him.

I 21.126–136

It is implicit in this passage that the authority of the unified empire and the unified Book of Kings are one. The key to this essentially Zoroastrian concept of the empire is to be found in the traditional role of the *mōbad*. In a Zoroastrian document known as the *Selections of Zātspram* (23.5), the idealized Iranian Empire of the supreme god Ohrmazd is visualized as one in which every village has a true-speaking witness,[59] every district has a judge who knows the law, and every province has a *moγbad* 'high priest' [Pahlavi for *mōbad*] who is the guarantor of truth.[60] It appears that the "truth" of the *mōbad* is a foundation for the structure of the empire just as it is a foundation for the structure of the poetry that glorifies the empire.

With regard to this passage in the *Shāhnāma* about the *mōbad*s and their "book," Mohl comments in passing that such a story parallels the myths of other societies about their respective national poetic traditions.[61] But he does not go further in thinking of Ferdowsi's source "book" as anything other than a "book."[62] In this case, then, Mohl makes no inferences about possible stylized reference to performance of oral traditions, as he has done with other passages involving *mōbad*s and *dehqān*s.

One may be tempted to reject the idea of a reference here to oral traditions on the grounds that, according to the "older preface" to the *Shāhnāma*, the story of what happened to the Pahlavi Book of Kings can theoretically be followed all the way down to the time of Ferdowsi himself, with the commissioning of a Persian prose *Shāhnāma* translated from the Pahlavi book.

The identity of the man who commissioned this prose *Shāhnāma*, Abu Manṣur, has already been considered.[63] This person not only had a Zoroastrian background but also claimed to trace his genealogy all the way back to Gōdarz, a hero of the Keyānid court.[64] The details of this prominent nobleman's distinguished career have been carefully reconstructed,[65] and I limit the discussion here to the part of the narrative that describes the constitution of the Book of Kings. The passage from the "older preface" must be quoted in its entirety.

---

[59] Cf. the Persian concept of *dehqān*, discussed earlier in this chapter.
[60] For a translation of *Selections of Zātspram* 23.5, see Molé 1963.338.
[61] Mohl 1838.xi.
[62] Ibid.
[63] See discussion earlier in this chapter.
[64] Minorsky 1964.263; references updated in Shahbazi 1991.30–33, esp. 32.
[65] Minorsky 1964.263–264; see also Shahbazi 1991.

Therefore he [Abu Manṣur-e ʿAbd al-Razzāq] commanded his minister [*dastur*] Abu Manṣur Maʿmari to gather owners of books from among the *dehqān*s, sages, and men of experience from various towns, and by his orders his servant (the said) Abu Manṣur Maʿmari compiled the book: he sent a person to various towns of Khorāsān and brought wise men therefrom [variant and from elsewhere?], such as Mākh, son of Khorāsān, from Herāt; Yazdāndād, son of Shāpur, from Sistān; Māhōy Khorshēd, son of Bahrām, from Bishāpur; Shādān, son of Borzin, from Ṭōs. He brought all four and set them down to produce those books of the kings, with their actions, their life-stories, the epochs of justice or injustice, troubles, wars, and the (royal) institutions, beginning with the first king [*key*] who was he who established the practices of civilization in the world and brought men out of (the condition of) beasts—down to Yazdgerd Shahriyār, who was the last of the Iranian kings.[66]

This passage has led to the assumption that the book in question must have been Ferdowsi's own source.[67] Moreover, such convergences as the fact that Abu Manṣur is "Lord of Ṭōs" while Ferdowsi himself is a native of Ṭōs prompts the inference that "Ferdowsi, in his early years, did certainly know the Lord of Ṭōs and could have met him."[68] And yet, the description of the "older preface" is strikingly parallel to Ferdowsi's narrative, which we have just considered, concerning the genesis of the Book of Kings. It is also parallel to a story that tells how King Anushirvān (531–579) commissioned a collection, from all the provinces in his empire, of popular stories concerning ancient kings (حکایت ملوك), a collection which he then deposited in his library.[69] Finally, it is parallel to a story of the commissioning, by Yazdgerd the last Sasanian king, of the *dehqān* Dāneshvar to reassemble the Book of Kings.[70]

[66] Translation by Minorsky 1964.266. For a variant reading of *Bishāpur*, see Shahbazi 1991.36, n96.

[67] Even Jules Mohl (1838) thinks so.

[68] Minorsky 1964.264.

[69] This information comes from a preface to the *Shāhnāma* in the manuscripts (see Mohl 1838.vii, n3). This version is different from the one in the "older preface," where the acquisition made by Anushirvān is not a primordial Book of Kings but rather the story of *Kalīla and Dimna*; see Mohl 1838.xi–xii.

[70] See Mohl 1838.vii, n4 (also Nöldeke 1930.23 and n39); this information likewise comes from the preface to the *Shāhnāma*, but not from the "older preface" as reconstructed by Qazvini 1944.

In view of all these parallelisms that exist between the story of the prose *Shāhnāma* and the stories of earlier forms of the Book of Kings, it becomes clear that the version of the "older preface," even if it has a historical basis, conforms nevertheless to a mythmaking pattern that keeps revalidating the Book of Kings by way of explaining its "origins."[71] The greater density of historical information in the "older preface" version does not take it out of consideration as a variant.[72] Cross-cultural studies of interaction between myths and historical events that are independently known to have taken place show that myths tend to appropriate and then reorganize historical information.[73] As for Ferdowsi's version of the story, it is more versatile because it is more stylized and therefore generic. Ferdowsi's version of how the Book of Kings came about can usurp more specific versions because it is so generic. His version acknowledges the variation of these stories by *not* identifying the persons, places, or time involved in the genesis of his own source "book" for the *Shāhnāma*. And by acknowledging this multiformity, Ferdowsi is in effect transcending it.[74] His *Shāhnāma* does not depend on any one version for the estab-

[71] In terms of the "older preface" as we have it, it cannot even be assumed that the primary authority belongs to the earlier prose *Shāhnāma* instead of the later poetic *Shāhnāma* of Ferdowsi. Shahbazi (1991.132–133) draws attention to the sequence of narration in the "older preface" as edited by Qazvini (sections 50–51): "Before we proceed to describe the words of the kings and their history, we mention the descent of Abu Manṣur-e ʿAbd al-Razzāq, who ordered this chronicle to be collected in prose writing"; at this point, we find this additional remark in the preface: "And after it had been made into a prose work, Solṭān Maḥmud-e Sebüg-Tegin ordered Ferdowsi to reduce it into the *dari* language in the form of poetry." I question whether it is justifiable to assume, in Shahbazi's formulation (p. 132), that this remark was added by "a later copyist using the older preface as the introduction to the *Shāhnāma* of Ferdowsi." Given Ferdowsi's own conventional claims concerning the superiority of Persian poetry over Persian prose, I find it questionable to assume that the author of the "older preface" would have considered the prose *Shāhnāma* superior in prestige to the poetic *Shāhnāma* of Ferdowsi.

[72] Of the four wise men credited in the "older preface" with producing the Persian prose *Shāhnāma*, some are mentioned as independent authorities by the poetic *Shāhnāma* of Ferdowsi himself. It is interesting that such mentions take place with reference to specific narrative traditions; the clearest cases are the poet's reference to Mākh of Herāt, in the story of Hormazd (VIII 316.15–16), and to Shādān of Ṭōs, in the story of Kalila and Dimna (VIII 247.3337). See Shahbazi 1991.133–134, n87 (where a misprint of the citation for the Hormazd story is to be corrected to the numbers given here).

[73] Lord 1970.29–30; cf. Nagy 1990b.7–9.

[74] In this connection, I stress that the *mehrbān* or "congenial one" who gave Ferdowsi the ancient *nāma* 'book' written in Pahlavi (discussed earlier) is left unnamed. In

lishment of a text. The myth gives validity to the text by making the assembly of wise and pious men in the community the collective source of the text.

In this sense, of the three multiform stories concerning the constitution or reconstitution of the Book of Kings, the one in the "older preface" is the least essential for the purposes of understanding the composition of Ferdowsi's *Shāhnāma*. To motivate the constitution of a prose *Shāhnāma* is to motivate something less prestigious, and from hindsight, less enduring. In the end this version can after all survive only as an intrusion in the text of the poetic *Shāhnāma*. Ferdowsi's *Shāhnāma* needs no prose introduction, because it introduces itself poetically. By contrast, the prosaic *Shāhnāma* requires an equally prosaic introduction. It seems to me ironic that this unattested prosaic *Shāhnāma*, of which we know only by way of its attested prosaic preface, should be treated in current scholarship as the source of Ferdowsi's poetry.

I conclude, then, that the tradition of oral poetics, as reflected in the references to performances by *mobad*s and *dehqān*s, accounts ultimately for the authoritativeness of Ferdowsi's *Shāhnāma*. Ferdowsi's claim, that he received an old Pahlavi Book of Kings, written in prose, and that he turned it into poetry—the first, the best, and therefore the only *Shāhnāma*—could not have been made without the authority of the oral *poetic* traditions that he had mastered. The idea of the book contains, like a time-capsule, not only an idealized composition-in-performance but also, cumulatively, an idealized sum total of all oral poetic traditions as they were performed before Ferdowsi and as they continue to be performed after Ferdowsi. As such, the book is both a concrete object and a symbol, expressing the authority and authenticity of the oral poetic traditions that are being performed.

---

this way, the poetry makes it even possible to picture the *nāma* as the original *nāma* of the *dehqān* Dāneshvar, so that the poet's ultimate *mehrbān* may be viewed as Dāneshvar himself. In an earlier work I suggested that the poetic imagination in this passage conjures up an archetypal Dāneshvar as a "mysterious nocturnal reciter" (Davidson 1985.125, n70).

CHAPTER 3

Ferdowsi's Oral
Poetic Heritage

The composite picture of an assembly of *mōbad*s, whose coming together literally constitutes Ferdowsi's "sourcebook" by way of their collective recitation, can be supplemented by individual pictures, recurring throughout the *Shāhnāma*, of individual recitation. Here too, as in the composite picture, the idea of an archetypal book can be combined with the idea of performance, wherever Ferdowsi claims that he heard a given story from a reciter, who in turn got it from an "ancient book":

سـوی گـاه اشکـانـیــان بــاز گرد   کنون ای سراینده فرتوت مرد

کـه گویــنــده یــاد آرد از باستان   چه گفت اندر آن نامهٔ راستان

Now, O aged singer,	return to the time of the Ash-kanians.
What did the book of the Truthful say	that the reciter recollected from ancient times?

VII 115.46–47

In one case, the reciter is described as having special affinities not only with the archetypal book but also with the family of the main hero of the *Shāhnāma*, Rostam. The hero Sām, Rostam's grandfather, is described as an ancestor of the family of the reciter himself, so that the source of the oral tradition, the performer, is directly linked to the subject of that same tradition, the hero:

که با احمد سهل بودی بمرو   یکی پیر بود نامش آزادسرو

زبان پر ز گفتارهای کهن   دلی پر ز دانش سری پر سخن

تن و پیکر پهلوان داشتی   کجا نامهٔ خسروان داشتی

بسی داشتی رزم رستم بیاد   بسام نریمان کشیدی نژاد

سخن را یک اندر دگر بافتم   بگویم کنون آنچ ازو یافتم

روان و خرد باشدم رهنمای   اگر مانم اندر سپنجی سرای

بگیتی بمانم یکی داستان   سرآرم من این نامهٔ باستان

There was an old man whose name was Āzādsarv,
who was in Marv with Ahmad son of Sahl.

His heart was full of wisdom, his head full of words,
and his speech full of ancient traditions.

Who had the Book of Kings,
who had the images and portraits of *pahlavān*s.

He traced his ancestry back to Sām, son of Narimān
and knew much about the battles of Rostam.

I will now say what I found out from him;
I will weave the words together, one to another.

If I remain in this fleeting world,
and if my soul and intellect guide me,

I will finish this ancient book
and leave to this world a story.

VI 322.1–7

With reference to the second of these two examples, it has been argued on chronological grounds that Ferdowsi could not actually have heard his predecessor perform epic.[1] We have already seen, however, that the medium of performance, as an authority, is just as stylized in the *Shāhnāma* as is the medium of the book. What is essential, therefore, in the reference to Āzādsarv is that his authority is envisaged as a performance that was heard, just as any living oral performance can be heard. Such a stylized reference to authority, then, affirms that the medium of performance is intrinsic to Ferdowsi's own poetry, which presents itself as part of a continuum in oral tradition.[2]

[1] See Shahbazi 1991.133.

[2] I therefore disagree with Shahbazi's inference, ibid., on the basis of such examples as the anachronism just mentioned, that Ferdowsi was literally copying from earlier

The point remains that the Book of Kings, where it is described as the possession of a performer heard by Ferdowsi, is a visible sign of that performer's authority, parallel with other visible signs such as an ancestry actually shared with the lineage of a principal hero. The final authority is not in the book itself but in the actual *performance* of the poem. Even the preface of the prose *Shāhnāma* acknowledges the authoritativeness of performance, which is then immediately tied in with the concept of "book."

> Whatever we discuss of this book must be told from statements of the *dehqān*s, for this kingdom was in their hands and they know the affairs and proceedings, whether good or bad, and whether more or less. Therefore we must go by what they say. Consequently, whatever we learn concerning them has been collected from their books.[3]

Till recent times, in fact, the *Shāhnāma* has survived by way of performance in oral tradition—albeit indirectly, since it has assumed the format of prose. Mary Ellen Page has made a study of the professional storytelling, *naqqāli,* of the *Shāhnāma* as it is performed in the Iran of recent times.[4] The word for the professional storyteller is *naqqāl,* meaning literally 'transmitter'.[5] Granted, the format of this transmission of the *Shāhnāma* is prose, but the ubiquitous conceit of the *naqqāl* is that he is indeed performing Ferdowsi's *Shāhnāma.*[6]

The traditional social context for such performances was a setting of coffee- and tea-houses. Adam Olearius describes such a coffee-house in his account, dated A.D. 1631–32, of the main square in Iṣfahan.

---

sources in earlier books whenever he introduces a narrative with such phrases as "So I have heard from the aged *dehqān.*" Such an inference simply displaces to a previous poet what Ferdowsi is doing in the present, that is, claiming a previous performance as the authority for what is "now" written in his book. Even in terms of the inference, the hypothetical previous poet would still be doing exactly the same thing. I maintain that, even if Ferdowsi follows the tradition of earlier books when he bases the authority of his written word on the authority of a continuum of performances that precede him, we have no reason to doubt that he could have direct access to that same continuum—and in fact that he could be part of it.

[3] Minorsky 1964.269.

[4] Page 1977.

[5] Ibid. 4. For a survey of the contexts of the root *naqala,* see ibid. 16.

[6] Ibid. 224. She adds at p. 2, paraphrasing Maranda and Maranda 1971.12: "Once the reworking of the tradition ceases to be meaningful to the audience, the tradition will disappear despite written versions."

Kahweh chane is ein Krug in welchem die Tabackschmäucher and *Kah-weh* Wassertrincker sich finden lassen. In solchen drenen Kruegen finden sich auch Poeten und Historici welche ich mitten im Gemache auff hohen Stuelen sitzen gesehen und allerhand Historien Fabeln und er-dichtete Dinge erzehlenhoeren. Im erzehlen phantasiren sie wie mit einem Stoecklein gleich die so aus der Taschen spielen.

The coffee-house is an inn in which smokers of tobacco and drinkers of coffee-water are found. In such inns are also found poets and historians whom I have seen sitting inside on high stools and have heard telling all manner of legends, fables, poeticized things. While narrating they con-jure up images by gestures with a little wand, much as magicians play tricks.[7]

A typical performance by a *naqqāl* lasts for about ninety minutes.[8] He uses a *ṭumār* 'prompt-book' which contains highly compressed the-matic summaries of his own repertoire. A study of such a *ṭumār* shows that it is not a text to be adhered to but rather a skeletal outline of a story—a story that the *naqqāl* may expand or compress, even shift around with variations of theme; the decision is up to the performer, whose primary need is to keep his hold over the audience.[9] The *ṭumār*s of different *naqqāl*s covering a parallel stretch of narrative vary in much the same way.[10] The *naqqāl* can of course diverge from his *ṭumār* as he or his audience wishes.[11]

There are of course profound variations between Ferdowsi's verse *Shāhnāma* and the prose retellings of the *Shāhnāma* tradition. For example, whereas the reign of Bahman is covered in about two hun-dred distichs in Ferdowsi's *Shāhnāma*, it takes up forty-eight pages in one *naqqāl*'s *ṭumār* and roughly a month's length of actual retelling in successive daily performances.[12] Yet the conceit of the *naqqāl*, as we have noted, is that he is indeed performing the *Shāhnāma* of Ferdowsi.

There is a comparable conceit among the South Slavic poets, the

[7] Olearius 1656 [1971].558.
[8] Page 1977.55.
[9] Cf. also the work of Smith 1979 on Indian oral epic traditions where pictures are used to prompt as well as explain the narrative.
[10] Page 1977.134–151.
[11] For examples, see ibid. 140, 142, 146, 277.
[12] Ibid. 143.

*guslar*s studied by Parry and Lord. The *guslar* will say that he performs
the song that he has learned exactly as it has always been performed.
For example, Lord quotes from an interview with the *guslar* Suleyman
Makić:

> *Interviewer*: "Could you still pick up a song today?"
> *Suleyman*: "I could."
> *I*: "For example, if you heard me sing a song, let's say, could you pick
>   it up right away?"
> *S*: "Yes, I could sing it for you right away the next day."
> *I*: "If you were to hear it just once?"
> *S*: "Yes, by Allah, if I were to hear it once to the *gusle*."
> *I*: "Why not until the next day? . . . What do you think about in those
>   two days? Isn't it better to sing it right away than later, when you
>   might forget it after so long a time?"
> *S*: "It has to come to one. One has to think . . . how it goes, and then
>   little by little it comes to him, so that he won't leave anything
>   out. . . . One couldn't sing it like that all the way right away."
> *I*: "Why couldn't you, when it is possible the second or third day
>   afterwards?"
> *S*: "Anybody who can't write can't do it."
> *I*: "All right, but when you've learned my song would . . . you sing it
>   exactly as I do?"
> *S*: "I would."
> *I*: "You wouldn't add anything . . . nor leave anything out?"
> *S*: "I wouldn't . . . by Allah I would sing it just as I heard it. . . . It isn't
>   good to change or add."[13]

This conceit notwithstanding, the fieldwork of Parry and Lord has
established that no two performances, even of the "same" song by the
same *guslar,* are ever identical.

In the case of Persian poetic traditions, it is important to note that
the narratives of Ferdowsi and of any given *naqqāl* can converge point-
for-point—as well as diverge. And such thematic convergences between Ferdowsi and a *naqqāl* are in effect no different from the convergences between any two different *naqqāl*s. It is as if Ferdowsi too
were a *naqqāl*—the definitive *naqqāl*—of the *Shāhnāma* tradition.[14]

---

[13] Lord 1960.26–27.
[14] Cf. Page 1977.150, where she describes Ferdowsi's *Shāhnāma* as "one recension of
a work which continues being told today."

Occasionally a *naqqāl* will recite some of Ferdowsi's actual verses.[15] Again this may be a matter of convergence, not derivation. After all, there can be found, in a given *naqqāl*'s *ṭumār*, verses in *mutaqārib* meter that are not even attested in the canonical version of Ferdowsi's *Shāh-nāma*.[16] In fact, when the *naqqāl* introduces his story, he can use rhymed prose or a combination of poetry and rhymed prose,[17] and sometimes there is even a melody.[18] Thus the traditional format of a *naqqāl*'s introduction may reveal vestigial aspects of an earlier stage in the art-form of the *naqqāl* when his medium was indeed all poetry.[19]

But the crucial indication of the *naqqāl*'s independence from Fer-dowsi's *Shāhnāma* lies in the fact that there is much narrative material attested in the *naqqāl*'s oral traditions that is not attested in any of the literary epics so far known.[20] Many of the themes found in later literary epics such as the *Garshāspnāma* appear as an integral part of the *naqqāl*'s narrative repertoire.[21] For example, the Garshāsp stories will be included in the *naqqāl*'s story-line where it would have been chrono-logically appropriate for the *Shāhnāma* to include it. Nöldeke con-demns these later epics as not folklore but invention: "It is a common opinion that a great deal of popular epic has been preserved in those poems. It might sound a little bold if I flatly deny that and declare the contents of those narratives to be essentially a free fancy of the respec-tive authors."[22] Similarly, Mohl claims that the epics after Ferdowsi's *Shāhnāma* are not only artless but also simply a matter of filling in lacunae left by Ferdowsi, with no pride in authorship.[23] There can only be a limited number of ultimate poets, however, and what is worthy of special note is the sheer mass of poetic compositions that deal with material beyond Ferdowsi and which usually take a verse from Ferdowsi as a point of departure.

[15] Ibid. 67.

[16] See, e.g., ibid. 73.

[17] See ibid. 67.

[18] Ibid. 118, n1. For comparable forms of expression in other cultures, where song, poetry, and prose are combined, see, e.g., Nagy 1990a.47, esp. n47.

[19] Cf. Zumthor 1972.99–100 on the phenomenon of *dérimage* in Old French poetic traditions.

[20] Page 1977.128; see, e.g., the details of the Sohrāb story at pp. 135–139.

[21] Ibid. 128.

[22] Nöldeke 1930.209.

[23] Mohl 1838.liv.

These considerations bring us to one of the major problems confronting the "scientific method" of editing Ferdowsi's *Shāhnāma*. The manuscripts seem to be full of "interpolations," sometimes massive ones, from other literary epics; at other times it is impossible to establish the provenience of the "interpolation." But it can now be seen, from the perspective of studies centering on the *naqqāl* traditions of the *Shāhnāma,* that such interpolations may correspond to actual conventions of *performance.* In other words, the divergences of manuscripts in this regard may be parallel to divergences in performance, since the *ṭumār* allows the *naqqāl* to expand or compress during any performance in patterns of thematic variations that are clearly parallel to those of the manuscripts. And, as noted, the *naqqāl* can diverge from his *ṭumār.*

Thus the *Shāhnāma* tradition has survived till recent times, albeit indirectly, as a medium still dynamic, still alive. It could theoretically generate an infinite number of performances—provided that the *naqqāl* is still there to perform and the audience is there to listen. In this light, we may call into doubt the theory that there were gaps in the story-line of the Book of Kings—gaps that had to be filled with Ferdowsi's "Phantasie."[24] From what we can see even from the *naqqāl* traditions, there was a seemingly endless reservoir of narrative traditions standing ready to be filled in at any point in the retelling of the Book of Kings. And just as the *naqqāl* testifies that he is indeed performing Ferdowsi's *Shāhnāma,* so also Ferdowsi himself testifies that he is "translating" the Pahlavi Book of Kings.

After comparing what the poem says about itself with the external evidence about Middle and New Persian poetry, we may now isolate characteristics of oral poetry as formulated in current scholarship. The fieldwork on oral poetics by Parry and Lord corroborated Parry's earlier work on the crystallized traditions of ancient Greek epic as they survived in the Homeric *Iliad* and *Odyssey.* For our present purposes, the most important aspect of the findings of Parry and Lord is their observation that the formal building blocks of oral poetry consists of what they call *formulas.*

Parry's working definition of the formula had been as follows: "A

[24] Hansen 1954.116.

group of words which is regularly employed under the same metrical conditions to express a given essential idea."[25] This definition, devised by Parry on the basis of his work on Homeric poetry, before he even started work on the living poetry of the South Slavic tradition, has proved enduring despite the need of one small adjustment. Ironically, this adjustment has been prompted at least partly by the evidence of Homeric poetry itself: it has recently been shown that the metrical conditions of the formula can vary, although this variation itself is systematic.[26] Thus it may be useful to revise the phrase "under the same metrical conditions" to read instead "under fixed metrical conditions." The phrase "to express a given essential idea" is crucial, since this aspect of Parry's definition has often been undervalued or even missed altogether. It is important to stress that, for Parry, the formula is not simply a phrase that is repeated for its metrical utility.[27] Rather, the formula is the expression of a traditional *theme*. To quote Parry, "The formulas in any poetry are due, so far as their ideas go, to the theme, their rhythm is fixed by the verse-form, but their art is that of the poets who made them and of the poets who kept them."[28] The word "theme," according to Lord's working definition is "a subject unit, a group of ideas, regularly employed by the singer, not merely in any given poem, but in the poetry as a whole."[29] In other words, the Parry-Lord definition of oral poetry is founded on the proposition that the traditional formula is a direct expression of the traditional theme; in oral poetry, there is a formulaic *system* that corresponds to a thematic *system*.[30]

In a 1977 book by Ruth Finnegan, however, which purports to present the overall subject of oral poetry to the general reader, this basic aspect of the Parry-Lord definition of the formula goes unmentioned.[31] She consistently treats formula as if it were merely a repeated phrase,

[25] Parry 1971.272.

[26] See Nagy 1990b.18–35.

[27] Cf. Parry 1971.304.

[28] Ibid. 272.

[29] Lord 1938.440; see also Lord 1974.206–207.

[30] For a useful survey of recent scholarship on the interrelationship of formula and theme, see Cantilena 1982.41–73. On p. 56, he offers this summary: "Ogni formula, dalla più stereotipa alla più consapevolmente usata, è motivata semanticamente."

[31] Finnegan 1977.

repeated simply for its metrical utility. In discussing Homeric epithets, for example, she writes that they "are often combined with other formulaic phrases—repeated word-groups—which have the right metrical qualities to fit the [given] part of the line."[32] In the same context, she quotes Parry for support: "In composing [the poet] will do no more than put together for his needs phrases which he has often heard or used himself, and which, grouping themselves *in accordance with a fixed pattern of thought* [emphasis mine], come naturally to make the sentence and the verse."[33] We see here that Parry is saying much more than Finnegan, however; the formula is not just a phrase that the poet is free to choose according to his metrical needs,[34] since the formulas are regulated by the traditional themes of the poet's composition. By contrast, Finnegan seems to assume that *formulas* and *themes* are separate ingredients in the poet's repertoire: "*As well as* formulaic phrases and sequences [emphasis mine], the bard has in his repertoire a number of set themes which he can draw on to form the structure of his poem."[35] Working on the assumption that formulas are simply stock phrases repeated to fill metrical needs, Finnegan offers the following criticism of the Parry-Lord theory of oral poetry: "Does it really add to our understanding of the style or process of composition in a given piece to name certain repeated patterns of words, sounds or meanings as 'formulae'? Or to suggest that the characteristic of oral style is that such formulae are 'all-pervasive' (as in Lord 1960, p. 47)?"[36] In light of what I have adduced from the writings of Parry and Lord, I find this criticism unfounded; if the formula is the building-block of a system of traditional oral poetic expression, then I cannot find fault with Lord's observation that the formulas are "all-pervasive" in oral poetry.

Another important point of disagreement between Finnegan and Lord is her insistence that, on the basis of what we know of oral poetry in such cultures as that of the Bantu of South Africa (both Zulu and

[32] Ibid. 59.
[33] Parry 1971.270.
[34] Cf. Finnegan 1977.62: "He can select what he wishes from the common stock of formulae, and can choose slightly different terms that fit his metre . . . and vary the details."
[35] Ibid. 64.
[36] Ibid. 71.

!Xhosa), the oral poet can both *compose* poetry and *write it down*.[37] It is tempting, of course, to extend such findings to medieval European poetry, where the fundamentals of what is freely acknowledged as oral poetry are preserved and transmitted by *literati* in the context of a vigorous scribal tradition. Finnegan's point of contention with Lord provides ammunition for medievalists who have argued that an Old English poem like the *Beowulf* cannot be considered oral poetry on the basis of the formulas that we find as its building-blocks, simply because we can find comparable levels of formulaic behavior in other Old English poems which were clearly written compositions and some of which were even translations from Latin originals. As one expert concludes, "To prove that an Old English poem is formulaic is only to prove that it is an Old English poem, and to show that such work has high or low percentage of formulas reveals nothing about whether or not it is literate composition, though it may tell us something about the skill with which a particular poet uses tradition."[38]

An important challenge to such a position has been proposed by Michael Zwettler: applying the work of the medievalist H. J. Chaytor,[39] Zwettler suggests that, even when an Old English poem is written down, it is not meant to be read by an individual but performed before an audience.[40] In other words, as Zwettler points out, there is no such thing as an "audience of readers" in medieval European poetry.[41] To quote Chaytor: "The whole technique . . . presupposed . . . a hearing, not reading public."[42] The rules of this poetry, written or not, are those of oral poetry. Zwettler extends this principle to pre-Islamic Arabic poetry, and I for my part hope to extend it here to the New Persian poetry of Ferdowsi. So long as I can argue that the building-blocks of his *Shāhnāma* are functional formulas, I can also argue that his poetry is based on the rules of oral poetry.

In the appendix to this book, using as a test case a randomly selected passage, I show that every word in this given passage can be generated

---

[37] Ibid. 70, citing the work on Bantu oral poetry by Opland 1971.
[38] Benson 1966.336.
[39] Chaytor 1967.10–13 and chapters 4 and 6.
[40] Zwettler 1978.15–19.
[41] Ibid.
[42] Chaytor 1967.13.

on the basis of parallel phraseology expressing parallel themes. The degree of regularity and economy[43] in the arrangement of phraseology is clearly suggestive of formulaic language. Moreover, the regularity extends to the actual variation of phraseology. This factor may well be an important additional clue to the formulaic nature of Ferdowsi's *Shāhnāma*. As Parry and Lord had noticed in their South Slavic field-work *each new performance/recomposition of a song involved variation in the deployment of formulas.* This principle has been applied successfully by Michael Zwettler in his study of classical Arabic poetry.[44] He extends the observations of the Romance philologist Ramón Menéndez-Pidal, who has drawn attention to the fact that three of the earliest manuscript versions of the *Chanson de Roland* do not share a single identical verse with each other.[45] He had inferred from this and other such facts that this kind of poetry, which Zwettler rightly equates with oral poetry, is "a poetry that lives through variants."[46] "How ironic," Zwettler writes, "that scholars of Arabic poetry have so often cast doubt upon the 'authenticity' or 'genuineness' of this or that verse, poem, or body of poems, or, sometimes, of pre-Islamic poetry in general, because they have found it impossible to establish an 'original version'."[47] The same irony, as we shall see, applies to scholars of Persian poetry. Zwettler goes on to say that

> the multiplicity of variants and attributions and of formulaic phrases and elements attested for the great majority of classical Arabic poems may undermine our confidence in ever establishing an "author's original version"—as indeed it should! But they ought to convince us that we do have voluminous record of a genuine and on-going oral poetic tradition (even if in its latest stages), such as no other nation can match in breadth of content and scrupulosity of collection and documentation.[48]

The conscientiousness of those who preserved all these variants in their editions is a reflection of an attitude that we also witness in the

[43] For this concept, see Lord 1960.53.
[44] Zwettler 1978.
[45] Menéndez-Pidal 1960.60–63; cf. Zumthor 1972.40–41.
[46] Zwettler 1978.189.
[47] Ibid.
[48] Ibid. 212.

context of Islamic oral transmission, or *ḥadīth,* and Zwettler insists that the editors' quest for authenticity by way of examining and collecting all variants was due not so much to any need of determining the author but to the desire of recovering the authentic poetic traditions of Bedouin poetry.[49]

An analogous principle of variation, I propose, can also be applied to the text tradition of the *Shāhnāma.*[50] A systematic and exhaustive application, of course, is at this point impossible, since there is no available centralized collection of all the variants as could be collected from the entire textual tradition. Such a collection would be a monumental task indeed. Still, the limited experiment of formulaic analysis that I present in the appendix illustrates the principle of compositional variation as reflected by textual variation. The examples could be multiplied by the hundreds, even thousands, and by then we would start to see clearly that there are legitimate formulaic variants attested for vast portions of the *Shāhnāma.* We may postpone for later any questions about how these considerations may affect our evaluation of the standard Moscow edition. What is important is that even a preliminary test reveals such patterns of variation in the text of the *Shāhnāma*—the surest available sign that we are dealing with the heritage of oral poetry.

We must note, however, an essential difference between the patterns of variation in the textual tradition of the *Shāhnāma,* as revealed by its textual transmission, and in the Arabic poetry studied by Zwettler. In the case of the Arabic evidence, the variants seem to have been collected *while* the given poem was evolving into a fixed text in the process of continual performance/recomposition. In the case of the *Shāhnāma,* on the other hand, the variants seem to have gone on accumulating even *after* the composition had become a fixed text by way of writing. This fact alone suggests that, side by side with the

[49] Ibid. 203.
[50] Cf. Pearsall 1984.126–127, with reference to fifteenth-century English manuscript production: "The surviving manuscripts of a poem like *Beves of Hamptoun* make it clear that each act of copying was to a large extent an act of recomposition, and not an episode in a process of decomposition from an ideal form." On the notion of *mouvance,* where the text is reconstituted with the production of each new copy, see Zumthor 1984.160. For an editorial application of this principle, see the exemplary work of Pickens 1978.

written transmission of the text, the oral transmission of poetry continued as well. Each new performance must have entailed recomposition, and the oral poetry must have continually influenced the text.

This means that we cannot reconstruct with any absolute certainty the original composition of Ferdowsi, because of its susceptibility to recomposition with each new performance in a living oral tradition. All we can say about the original is that, if it is capable of being recomposed, it too must be a product of oral composition. And the continual recomposition on the level of form was matched by recomposition on the level of content, leading to new accretions that are anachronistic to the patterns of earlier layers.[51] We may even compare the accretion of Muslim elements in the Arab pre-Islamic poetic traditions studied by Zwettler:

> We must consider the alleged "inconsistencies," "anachronisms" and "Islamic emendations" that do crop up in our received texts and have so frequently been adduced as proof of the "corruption" of the tradition. Such phenomena as the introduction of post-Islamic expressions or neologisms into archaic poems, elimination of pagan theophoric names or substitution of the name *Allāh,* allusions to Qur'ānic passages or Islamic concepts or rituals, and so on, can all legitimately be seen as a natural result of the circumstance that versions of those poems were derived from oral renditions performed by Muslim renderants conditioned now to the sensibilities of Muslim audiences.[52]

Similarly, we find the accretion and eventual dominance of Shī'ite elements in the poetry of Ferdowsi, which seems to show traces of an earlier Sunni patronage.[53] But even if we cannot reconstruct the original composition, its authority or authenticity as tradition could survive the countless accretions and reshapings of each recomposition in performance. That is the true nature of oral poetry.

Let us imagine going back in time to a point where the oral tradition of the *Shāhnāma* was still in *mutaqārib* verse. At such a point, the formal and thematic variations of performance/composition in oral poetry

[51] Such a possibility is emotionally and sarcastically resisted by Minavi 1972.110.
[52] Zwettler 1978.221.
[53] Cf. Shahbazi 1991.52.

would surely have affected the manuscript tradition of Ferdowsi's
Shāhnāma. Even as late as in the era of Bāysonghor Mirza (died A.D.
1433), it seems that no definitive edition was possible, because the
extant manuscripts were clearly no better than *ṭumārs* would be in recent times for the purpose of deciding what is definitive and what
is not. The song must have existed in performance. Even though
Nöldeke yearns for the attestation of the original "critically revised"
copy of the *Shāhnāma* commissioned by Bāysonghor in A.D. 1425,[54] he
realizes that he would be disappointed if it suddenly came to light:
"How," he asks, "could the Persian bel-esprit in those times—only
such can be thought of, if it were not simply copyists—have managed
to accomplish a great and purely philological work somewhat critically?"[55] The point is, if no copy could be definitive and preemptive
even as late as 1425, it may be that each copy was, at least in part, a
reflection of traditions in *performance.*

Nöldeke says that redactors in the era of Bāysonghor could not be
"scientific" about consulting other manuscripts, for they had no Aris-
tophanes, no Zenodotus, no Aristarchus in the Timurid court.[56] The
princely libraries were full of manuscripts of the *Shāhnāma* such as the
one described as "a fine looking, beautifully written, and very defective copy" (to quote from a contemporary evaluation).[57] How, we
may ask, were such copies of the *Shāhnāma* "defective"? Is there a trace
here of a contemptuous attitude on the part of those better versed than
others in the performance of poetry? In Nöldeke's own words, there
exists no "final touch" for Ferdowsi's *Shāhnāma.*[58]

As if to console himself, Nöldeke adds: "We are not really worse off
than with the text of Homer."[59] But the Homeric analogy in fact leads
back to the factor of performance in the constitution of the text of any
poetry that is built on an oral tradition. Since Nöldeke's days, new
discoveries have emerged about the factor of performance as it affects
the canonical text of Homer. It now appears that even the Homeric

[54] Nöldeke 1930.125–126.
[55] Ibid. 126.
[56] Ibid.
[57] Testimony by way of M. Lumsden, appendix 5, Nöldeke 1930.126.
[58] Ibid.
[59] Ibid. 127.

text is replete with variants that are to be attributed not to textual inconsistencies but rather to actual formulaic alternatives.[60] So also with the textual tradition of Ferdowsi's *Shāhnāma* in its present form: as even Nöldeke concedes, it is replete with "various genuine versions" of given passages.[61] In other words, a given passage may have two or more textual variants that are not a matter of one genuine reading and one or more corrupt or interpolated readings, but rather of two or more traditional alternatives, either or any of which would be acceptable to the discerning audience of Ferdowsi's *Shāhnāma*.

It is now possible to imagine how Ferdowsi's *Shāhnāma* could survive and prevail, albeit with accretions and modifications, if we allow that everything in it is traditional. In his own lifetime, Mohl had an ever-growing intuition that Ferdowsi invented nothing, and he says so most forcefully: "The more one studies the work of Ferdowsi, the more one is convinced, I believe, that he invented nothing and that he was content to restore in brilliant hues the traditions that formed the popular stories of Persia."[62]

For Ferdowsi, the writing down of his composition would make permanent his appropriation of living poetic traditions. For a typical oral poet, by contrast, appropriation could ordinarily be achieved only in the context of performance. But even if Ferdowsi's book, *his* Book of Kings, constitutes a more lasting way of establishing appropriation of his composition, it is nevertheless not a frozen text, like some Pahlavi book. To put it schematically, we could say that the survival of Ferdowsi's *Shāhnāma* depends not so much on the writing down of the composition as on the Persian nation's general approval of the writing down of the performance of the composition. And the approval of Persian audiences through the ages could happen only if the *Shāhnāma* were traditional, that is, if it conformed to the rules of composition-in-performance. It could even be claimed that the survival of the *Shāhnāma*, in the context of countless performances for countless audiences steeped in oral poetry, is the best argument for its own essence as oral

[60] Cf. Muellner 1976.57–62.
[61] Nöldeke 1930.125.
[62] Mohl IV p. ii: "Plus on étudiera l'oeuvre de Firdousi, plus on se convaincra, je crois, qu'il n'a rien inventé, et qu'il s'est contenté de revêtir de son brillant coloris les traditions qui formaient l'histoire populaire de la Perse."

poetry. It is also, of course, the best argument against the notion that the poetic form and overall content of the *Shāhnāma* were in any sense an invention of Ferdowsi.

If, however, we accept the idea that the medium of the *Shāhnāma* is that of traditional oral poetry, we should expect that it will be subject to accretions and modifications in the context of each new performance. Thus the recording of an original composition by Ferdowsi, in the process of its textual transmission, would be continually subject to interference from the concurrent process of oral transmission in performance, since each performance in oral poetry entails recomposition. Thus the *Shāhnāma* really could not ever become a completely fixed text until the oral tradition died altogether. The manuscripts of the *Shāhnāma* seem to reflect a period when oral poetry had not yet died, so that editors are left to struggle with the textual variants that are not just a matter of textual transmission. As we have seen, it seems that some variants are also a matter of oral transmission.

The archetypal fixed text of Ferdowsi's *Shāhnāma* can never be re-created, since it would be impossible to decide in any given instance which of, say, two "genuine" variants was actually composed by Ferdowsi. To understand the full creative range of the *Shāhnāma* tradition, it would be more important to have an edition that lists all variants, since many of these will be a matter of *composition/performance*, not *text*.

If indeed textual variants arise from the perpetuation of the *Shāhnāma* in performance, we need just the opposite of the so-called critical Moscow edition (1960–1971) of Y. E. Bertels and his colleagues.[63] This edition strips Ferdowsi's *Shāhnāma* to its bare bones (50,000-odd distichs), selecting variants essentially on textual grounds by comparing "superior" and "inferior" manuscripts. It is based essentially on five manuscripts:

(1) L. = ms. Add. Or. 21103 of the British Museum, London, dated A.D. 1276, the oldest extant ms. at the time that the work on the Moscow edition was proceeding; contains the preface of Abu Manṣur.

---

[63] For a brief history of this edition, see Yarshater 1988.viii–ix. On the principles governing the new edition of Khaleghi-Motlagh (1988), see Yarshater 1988.x–xi.

(2) I = ms. 329 of the National Public Library of St. Petersburg, dated A.D. 1333 and the second oldest ms. after L.

(3) IV = ms. S.1654 of the Oriental Institute of the Academy of Sciences, St. Petersburg, dated A.D. 1445; contains the preface of Abu Manṣur.

(4) VI = ms. S.822 of the Oriental Institute of the Academy of Sciences, St. Petersburg, dated A.D. 1450.

(5) K = ms. S.40 of the Dār al-Kutub al-Miṣrīya, Cairo, dated A.D. 1394,[64] utilized only in volumes IV–IX of the Moscow edition; contains the preface of Abu Manṣur.

In view of the fact that there are about 500 extant manuscripts of Ferdowsi's *Shāhnāma*,[65] and especially in view of all the variations in manuscript readings, the restriction of the editorial field of vision to five manuscripts is a bold move indeed. The Moscow editors' confidence in this particular 1 percent of manuscript evidence was based primarily on two facts: that this particular manuscript family was singularly old and that this family inherits the "older preface," that is, the preface of Abu Manṣur.

But we have already seen that the "older" preface of Abu Manṣur, no matter how valuable it is for understanding the history of early Persian prose, cannot be directly linked to the composition of Ferdowsi's *Shāhnāma*. Even on textual grounds, there is a contextual gap between the poetry of Ferdowsi and this particular preface, in marked contrast with the preface of the recension of Bāysonghor.[66]

The latter recension of Bāysonghor, transmitted in a vast family of manuscripts, represents our "vulgate": the Calcutta edition (Macan 1829) follows it closely, and this edition, collated with the eclectic Paris edition of Mohl (1838–1878), is the basis for the incomplete Leiden edition of Vullers (1877–1884) and the completed Tehran edition of Nafisi-Vullers (1934–1936). But the recension of Bāysonghor is late: the preface is dated A.D. 1425, in marked contrast to the preface of Abu Manṣur, dated A.D. 957. In view of this contrast, the Moscow editors

---

[64] On the problems in dating this manuscript, see Yarshater 1988.ix.

[65] See Piemontese 1980.11–12, n27.

[66] See ibid. 32–34.

of the *Shāhnāma* considered the Bāysonghor recension inferior, as opposed to the recension represented by the family of manuscripts L, I, IV, VI, and K, a recension that seems to have had affinities to the preface of Abu Manṣur. Guided by the reasoning that a more recent recension must be inferior to an older recension, the Moscow editors as a matter of policy rejected variant readings stemming from the Bāysonghor recension. They also eliminated readings that could not be verified from the collective testimony of the old family of manuscripts that they had isolated, thereby reducing the corpus of the *Shāhnāma* to 48,617 distichs, to which are added in the appendix another 1,486 distichs, deemed probably spurious. We may appreciate the extent of this textual reduction by comparing the number of distichs in the Calcutta edition, 55,204.

But the basic principle of the Moscow edition, that the older group of manuscripts is by necessity closer to the "original," is open to question. If, as I claim, the many variations in the textual transmission of the *Shāhnāma* are due at least in part to the rich repertoire of concurrent oral poetic traditions, then each attested variation must be judged on its own merits, regardless of its textual provenience.

Moreover, the Moscow edition's dependence on the manuscript family L, I, IV, VI, and K, *to the exclusion of others,* must now be brought in line with the discovery of yet another manuscript of the *Shāhnāma:*

F = ms. Cl.III.24 (G.F.3) of the Biblioteca Nazionale Centrale, Florence, dated A.D. 1217.

Here, then, is a document considerably older than L, which in turn is dated A.D. 1276 and which had been for the Moscow editors the oldest extant manuscript of the *Shāhnāma*. As Angelo Michele Piemontese, the discoverer of F, has demonstrated, this manuscript, two centuries away from the traditional date of the completion of Ferdowsi's *Shāhnāma,* is replete with valuable new readings that are not to be found in the manuscript family of L;[67] there are also about two hundred "new" distichs attested—distichs that have not been known to exist before.[68]

[67] See ibid. esp. 218–221.
[68] Ibid. 222–226.

This is not to say that F is closer to the "original" than L simply by virtue of being older than L. Moreover, this is not to discredit L and its family, as opposed to F. Rather, the point is simply that the editorial field of vision cannot be restricted to the family of L.

In fact, the preface of F is clearly in the same tradition that we find attested in the much later preface of the Bāysonghor recension.[69] Even more important, the actual variants that we find in F correspond far more closely to those of the Bāysonghor recension than to those of L and its family.[70] Thus, ironically, the Calcutta edition and its off-shoots, most notably the Paris edition of Mohl and the Tehran edition of Nafisi-Vullers, contain "genuine" aspects of the *Shāhnāma* tradition that have been neglected by the "critical" Moscow edition.[71] What we need is an edition of the *Shāhnāma* that accounts for all the variants, each of which may be a reflex of variation in the oral tradition. In addition, we need a concordance that would include all variants that are demonstrably not just a matter of textual corruption or editorial tampering. With the aid of such an ideal edition and ideal concordance, we could demonstrate more rigorously both the power and the flexibility of the oral tradition as it was kept alive in Ferdowsi's *Shāhnāma*.

Even without such ideal aids, however, we can already begin to appreciate the qualities of oral tradition in the poetry of the *Shāhnāma*. As I hope I have demonstrated, there is enough evidence, both in the *Shāhnāma* and in the history of Persian poetry before and after this monumental composition, to show that the creative power of a rich oral tradition produced and then maintained the authority of the national poem of the Persians.

[69] Ibid. 31–34; cf. Shahbazi 1991.4, n9 (paraphrase of this preface at 5–6).

[70] Piemontese 1980.218–219.

[71] Ibid. 194, 219. In n145 of p. 219, for example, Piemontese cites cases where the readings of the Florence manuscript vindicate the adopted readings of (1) the Calcutta edition as against the Moscow and Tehran editions, (2) the Paris edition of Mohl as against the Moscow and Tehran editions, and (3) the Paris edition and the Manuscripts I, IV, VI of the Moscow edition as against the Tehran edition and the preferred manuscript L of the Moscow edition. Khaleghi-Motlagh (1988) takes into account the evidence of the Florence manuscript. See also Yarshater 1988.viii–xi.

PART II

THE HERO

CHAPTER 4

Book of Kings,
Epic of Heroes

At the beginning of the preceding chapter, we saw an example where a performer of the Book of Kings tradition, ostensibly heard by Ferdowsi, is described as having an ancestral claim not only on the archetypal book but also on the family of the main hero of the *Shāhnāma*, Rostam. On the authority of such an ancestral claim, the source of the oral tradition, the performer, is being directly linked to the subject of that same tradition, the hero. It is clear that the Book of Kings, described as the ancestral possession of the performer heard by Ferdowsi, is a visible sign of that performer's authority, so also is the ancestry actually shared with the lineage of the hero Rostam of Sistān, arguably the most prominent character in all the *Shāhnāma*.

I propose that these two kinds of authority, one based on the Book of Kings, and the other based on the essence of heroes like Rostam, represent a dichotomy between what may be called a "book of kings" and an "epic of heroes" tradition. This is not to say that we are dealing with two separate kinds of narrative tradition. I contend rather that such a dichotomy between "book of kings" and "epic of heroes" can exist within a single kind of narrative tradition, which actually combines lore about kings and heroes. If I succeed in making this case, then the *Shāhnāma* can be seen not as an innovative conflation of a "book of kings" and an "epic of heroes" but rather as a traditional combination of these distinct and sometimes conflicting elements. The central figure in the argumentation is the hero Rostam of Sistān.

This hero Rostam has been perceived as an "outsider" to the *Shāh-*

75

nāma. Such a perception, as we shall see, is in part inspired by the poem itself. For scholars like Nöldeke, who take as a given the historicity of the Keyānids, the dynasty with which Rostam and his father, Zāl, coincide in the *Shāhnāma,* the qualities and actions that characterize Zāl and Rostam are evidence enough that they must be considered essentially unlike their royal contemporaries.[1] The story of Zāl's being born with white hair and raised by a giant bird called the Simorgh, and also the many stories of Rostam's extraordinary feats, led Nöldeke to the conclusion that these heroes, unlike the kings they served, were mythical rather than historical.[2] Thus, the argument goes, if the Keyānids are historical, then surely Zāl and Rostam are intrusive.

Then there is the matter of chronology, which again suggests at first glance that Zāl and Rostam are exceptional in the Book of Kings.[3] Between the two of them, Zāl and Rostam live over a millennium, covering the reigns of kings extending from Manuchehr all the way to Goshtāsp.[4] This stretch of narrative takes up the first six volumes of the nine-volume Moscow edition of the *Shāhnāma.* No king that they served rivals the span of roughly five hundred years allotted to Zāl and Rostam each: the closest is the *shāh* Key Khosrow, whose own span is 150 years.[5] As Georges Dumézil has observed, the parallel narratives of the kings on the one side and of these heroes on the other reveal distinctly different "rhythms."[6]

It even seems as if the *Shāhnāma* itself were emphasizing the anomaly of Rostam and his ancestors. He is, after all, descended on his mother's side from the archdemon or *div* Zaḥḥāk, the monstrously cruel tyrant with snakes growing from his shoulders, and, as such, Rostam qualifies as part *div* 'demon' himself. In reference to Rostam's maternal grandfather Mehrāb, the *mōbad*s, who have been consulted by *Shāh* Manuchehr, have this to say:

بدانست کز گوهر اژدهاست   و گر چند بر تازیان پادشاست

[1] Nöldeke 1930.16–20. Another prominent believer in the historicity of the Keyānids is Arthur Christensen (1932).

[2] Ibid.

[3] Cf. Pagliaro 1940.248.

[4] Cf. Wikander 1950.324.

[5] Ibid.

[6] Dumézil 1971.231; cf. the theme of the longevity of the Indic hero Bhiṣma, as discussed by Dumézil 1968.176–190.

It is well known that his [Mehrāb's] roots are from the dragon [Zaḥḥāk],

although he has been the ruler over the Arabs for some years.

I 177.634

Sām, Rostam's paternal grandfather, questions the feasibility of the marriage of Rostam's parents-to-be, Zāl and Rudāba,

ازین مرغ پرورده وان دیوزاد   چه گوئی چگونه بر آید نژاد

From this bird-nursling and that *div*-born one

What say you, what kind of child will come?

I 180.693

Shāh Manuchehr also has doubts, saying,

چنین گفت با بخردان شهریار   که بر ما شود زین دژم روزگار

چو ایران زچنگال شیر و پلنگ   برون آوریدم برای و بجنگ

فریدون ز ضحّاك گیتی بشست   بترسم که آید ازان تخم رُست

نباید که بر خیره از عشق زال   همال سر افگنده گردد همال

چو از دخت مهراب و از پور سام   بر آید یکی تیغ تیز از نیام

اگر تاب گیرد سوی مادرش   ز گفت پراگنده گردد سرش

کند شهر ایران پر آشوب و رنج   بدو باز گردد مگر تاج وگنج

Thus spoke the monarch to the wise men,

saying: "Evil times will fall upon us from this."

When, from the claws of lions and leopards,

I have rescued Iran by wisdom and combat,

Faridun delivered the world from Zaḥḥāk,

but I fear what will grow from that seed.

It must not be that by negligence concerning Zāl's love,

the shamed one [Zaḥḥāk] become an equal,

when from the daughter of Mehrāb and the son of Sām

a sharp sword is drawn from the scabbard.

If he inclines toward his mother

his head will become confused from discourse.

He will fill the country of Iran with terror and pain

if by chance crown and throne come back to him."

I 192.867–873

Marcia Maguire suggests that this genetic heritage of Rostam does not affect the hero's character and his actions.[7] Still, she and others are ready to build from such details the inference that Rostam belongs to a "pre- or extra-Zoroastrian climate."[8]

Thus, when Rostam confronts the Zoroastrian prince and hero Esfandiyār, whose character and actions are in certain episodes strikingly parallel to those of Rostam,[9] Maguire is led to interpret the confrontation of the two heroes as a conscious juxtaposition of differing poetic traditions—a fading pre-Zoroastrian poetic mode on one side and the prevalent Zoroastrian mode on the other.[10] I shall argue, however, that (1) the figures of Rostam and his ancestors cannot be separated from the Zoroastrian traditions, and (2) the homeland of Rostam can in some traditions be identified with the "sacred space" of Zoroastrianism.[11]

The anomalous nature of Rostam and his ancestors in the *Shāhnāma* has led scholars to focus their attention on Sistān, the hero's homeland. The consensus, as reflected in Maguire's dissertation on Rostam, is to attribute the hero's anomaly in the Book of Kings to the native traditions of Sistān. The reasoning is that these native traditions would naturally be at variance with the national traditions of the Book of Kings, especially if Sistān were a remote outpost of the empire—an impression fostered by the *Shāhnāma* itself. According to this theory, a remote Sistān would surely reflect an outlook that is different conceptually—and maybe even politically—from that of the central power of the empire under the rule of the *shāhanshāh* 'king of kings'.

A notable example of such reasoning is the position taken by Nöldeke on the war of Rostam against the Turanians after the murder of Siyāvosh,[12] son of Key Kāus, who, unjustly driven out of Iran by his father, takes refuge with Afrāsiyāb and marries his daughter, and

[7] Maguire 1973.77, n4, as opposed to Zajączkowski 1970.683.

[8] Maguire 1973.116.

[9] See ibid. 158–170 for further discussion of the parallel seven deeds of Esfandiyār and Rostam.

[10] Ibid. 116. For a warning against the extreme position of interpreting the confrontation of Rostam and Esfandiyār as a juxtaposition of conflicting *ideologies*, see Boyce 1954.

[11] See Chapter 6.

[12] Nöldeke 1930.76.

then is treacherously murdered by Afrāsiyāb himself. Once he had defeated the Turanians, Rostam rules over them for seven years before leaving their country (III 191–193.2919–2950). Yet, as Nöldeke points out, there is no apparent trace of Rostam's undisputed reign over the Turanians after he withdraws.[13] The ensuing narrative seems to take it for granted that the archenemy Afrāsiyāb, king of the Turanians, is still in power; moreover, "the Iranian prince Khosrow, the son of Siyāvosh, was quietly growing up in Turān under the reign of Afrāsiyāb exactly at the same time when that country was supposed to be in the hands of Rostam."[14] Nöldeke goes on to conclude that there must have been two versions in conflict here, a local and a national one. In the hypothetical local Sistanian version, it was Rostam who was presented as primary avenger of Siyāvosh and conqueror of Afrāsiyāb, whereas in the national version the credit for the final defeat and killing of Afrāsiyāb was reserved for the Shāh Khosrow, the son of Siyāvosh who had grown up in obscurity in Turān under his archenemy's reign. It is the latter version that of course takes precedence in Ferdowsi's *Shāhnāma*, but the hypothetical local Sistanian version has left its trace in the detail about Rostam's seven-year reign over the Turanians.

For Nöldeke and Christensen and others who believe that Ferdowsi's *Shāhnāma* is based on the text of an earlier Pahlavi Book of Kings or *Khodāynāma*, it follows that the traditions about Rostam and his family, which seem so distinct from the Book of Kings, should in turn be based on a separate text, of Sistanian provenience.[15] Indeed, Christensen can point to the report of Masʿūdī (*Murūj* II p. 118) about a book called السكيسران (*'lskysr'n*), concerning such events as the combat of Rostam and Esfandiyār and the death of Rostam at the hands of Bahman, the son of Esfandiyār.[16] Christensen interprets the reported book title السكيسران as Pahlavi *Sagēsarān*, which would mean "The Chiefs of the Sakas," that is, "The Chiefs of Sagastan [= Sistān]."[17] This book, which was reportedly translated into Arabic by Ibn al

---

[13] Ibid.
[14] Ibid.
[15] Cf. Christensen 1932.142–143.
[16] Ibid.
[17] Ibid.

Muqaffaʿ, could then have supplemented the national *Khodāynāma*, also translated by Ibn al Muqaffaʿ, to constitute the general history of the Keyānid period as we find it represented by writers like Ṭabarī.[18]

The problem is that there is no indication, in Masʿūdī's description of the contents of this Book of Sistān, that its narratives actually veered from the traditions glorifying the national *shāh*, glorifying instead the heroes of Sistān at the expense of the *shāh*. Such references as there are, indeed, reflect a variant that seems perfectly appropriate to a national tradition that primarily glorifies the *shāh*s of Iran: the national king Bahman is shown killing Rostam, thus taking vengeance against the local hero of Sistān.[19] In this case it is the *Shāhnāma* of Ferdowsi that veers in the direction of what seems to be a local variant, in which Rostam is slain not by King Bahman but rather by his own treacherous half-brother Shaghād. The poet introduces the variant with these words:

There was an old man whose name was Āzādsarv,
who was in Marv with Ahmad son of Saḥl.

His heart was full of wisdom, his head full of words,
and his speech full of ancient traditions.

Who had the Book of Kings,
who had the images and portraits of *pahlavān*s.

He traced his ancestry back to Sām, son of Narimān
and knew much about the battles of Rostam.

I will now say what I found out from him;
I will weave the words together, one to another.

If I remain in this fleeting world,
and if my soul and intellect guide me,

I will finish this ancient book
and leave to this world a story.

VI 322.1–7[20]

I see no justification for positing a local Sistanian textual tradition as the primary source for the Rostam stories in the *Shāhnāma*. No doubt

---

[18] Ibid.

[19] Masʿūdī II 127; cf. Ṭabarī I 687. See Nöldeke 1930.29.

[20] For the Persian text, see my discussion in Chapter 3, citing this passage as an illustration of the poetic device where the poet's authority is based not only on his claim to have heard a previous performer but also on the genealogical connections of the performer with the hero of the story.

there were Sistanian traditions about Rostam that differed from the national tradition, and no doubt there were written versions of these. But the authority of these traditions rests ultimately upon the spoken word, as the *Shāhnāma* makes clear. From all of Ferdowsi's references to the testimony of *mōbad*s and *dehqān*s about the stories of Rostam, it seems clear that the poet was free to choose versions that would or would not be at variance with the stories of kings.[21] Thus the local Sistanian traditions about Rostam need not necessarily impose anomalies upon the traditions of kings.

We may conclude, then, that the anomalies in the Rostam stories of the *Shāhnāma* cannot be explained away simply by attributing them to the provincial lore of Sistān. The time has come to propose another, more comprehensive, explanation: the Rostam stories may be anomalous in the *Shāhnāma* simply because the "epic of heroes" and the "book of kings" represent two distinct aspects of poetic tradition. Instead of stressing, along with Nöldeke and others, a dichotomy between national and local (Sistanian) traditions, or between Zoroastrian and pre-Zoroastrian traditions, I want to make a case for a dichotomy along the lines of two different levels of narrative, one concerning heroes and the other, kings.

The problem with Nöldeke's approach is that he takes literally the testimony of the *Shāhnāma,* which presents itself as a direct descendant of a Pahlavi Book of Kings. The temptation, in light of this testimony, is not to treat the stories of kings as a poetic tradition in its own right. My working hypothesis, by contrast, is that both the "book of kings" and the "epic of heroes" components of the *Shāhnāma* are a matter of poetic tradition. The parallel but consecutive actions of Rostam and King Khosrow against the Turanian Afrāsiyāb represent a juxtaposition of parallel themes in two different poetic forms.

Nöldeke's sense of verisimilitude is violated by the tactical pointlessness of Rostam's conquering and ruling Turān only to withdraw from it.[22] Rostam's actions may be tactically pointless in military strategy—but not in poetic strategy. Rostam's conquest, followed by his withdrawal, sets the stage for glorifying the subsequent conquest by King Khosrow—an act that seems to receive priority over the "epic

[21] E.g., *Shāhnāma* III 169.2587.
[22] Nöldeke 1930.76.

of heroes" in the overall plan of Ferdowsi's *Shāhnāma*. So it is not a matter of Ferdowsi's inserting a contradictory local Sistanian version about Rostam's defeat of Afrāsiyāb and then having to distort it in order to make room for a rival national version about King Khosrow's defeat of Afrāsiyāb. Instead, the roles of Rostam and Khosrow in the defeat of Afrāsiyāb may be complementary—a traditional function of their roles as hero and king.

Even if the anomalous nature of the Rostam tradition in the *Shāhnāma* is due to its heritage as epic poetry and not to its provenience from Sistān, an explanation must still be found for why it is specifically Rostam of Sistān who became a focal point of the heroic level of the *Shāhnāma*. One possible solution is available from the researches of Mary Boyce on the Parthian oral poetic traditions. In a well-known article, Boyce makes it clear that the Pahlavi documents of the Sasanian dynasty draw on the heritage of a vigorous oral poetic tradition that flourished under the earlier Parthian dynasty.[23] In another article,[24] Boyce also shows that the Parthians, who are North Iranians, were in close political and cultural contact with Northeast Iranians, such as the Sakas.[25] Thus the Parthians hypothetically absorbed the epic traditions of Rostam that were native to the Sakas, and these epic traditions as appropriated by the Parthian oral poets were then "nationalized," spreading throughout the empire in the era of the succeeding dynasty, the Sasanians.[26] In this way, the hero of Sistān, "the land of the Sakas," became part of a national epic tradition, alongside the royal line of Keyānids. Supposedly, then, both the story of Rostam and the history of the Keyānids were transmitted by way of Parthian poetry.[27]

Moreover, the Rostam tradition has now been discovered in yet another branch of the Northeast Iranian family. Fragments of a text composed in Sogdian, a language closely related to that of the Sakas, tell of the adventures of *rwstmy* 'Rostam' and his wondrous horse *rgšy* 'Rakhsh' as they confront murderous demons or *dywt* 'divs'.[28] These

---

[23] Boyce 1957.
[24] Boyce 1955; not cited by, e.g., Maguire 1973.
[25] Boyce 1955.475.
[26] Ibid. 476.
[27] Ibid. 474.
[28] Published by Reichelt 1928–1931 II 62; republished, along with another fragment, in Benveniste's *Textes Sogdiens* (1940.134–136). Dresden 1970.36 divides all

narratives correspond to those found in the *Shāhnāma* about the war of Rostam against the *div*s 'demons' of Māzandarān (II 106–110.562–634), but the Sogdian version is clearly independent of the Persian.[29] For example, the demons fought by Rostam are described in the Sogdian version as riding on otherworldly animals, details missing in the *Shāhnāma*. Though such details in this particular Sogdian episode have no direct parallel in the *Shāhnāma* of Ferdowsi, the *themes* of the episode are nevertheless typical of the general characterization of Rostam in the *Shāhnāma,* where he is conventionally portrayed as single-handedly fighting off any attack on Iran with only the help of Rakhsh, his horse.

The same Sogdian episode describes Rostam's removing the saddle from his horse, cooking himself a repast, and then falling asleep. If we compare this narrative type-scene with parallel type-scenes found in the *Shāhnāma* of Ferdowsi we have grounds for understanding the Sogdian Rostam fragment to be part of a larger Iranian *Shāhnāma* tradition, composed in a poetic tradition that is cognate with the one inherited by Ferdowsi. In other words, the very manner in which Rostam goes about preparing his solitary feast in the Sogdian version is built on a traditional sequence of activities that closely matches the sequence of activities in corresponding scenes to be found in Ferdowsi's *Shāhnāma*. If the built-in rules of sequence can be shown to be as traditional as the narrative themes that enter into the sequence, the case for a common Iranian poetic heritage would be considerably strengthened. Let us briefly examine, then, not only the themes but also the actual organization of these themes in the Sogdian Rostam fragment, with special attention to the question of how they relate to similar themes that are found in the *Shāhnāma* of Ferdowsi.

The Sogdian Rostam fragment begins with the description of the hero's routing the horde of *div*s, forcing them to retreat back into their

---

attested Sogdian documents into three categories based on their religious sources of inspiration: Buddhist, Manichean, and Christian. After discussing the scholarship on each of these three categories of Sogdian sources, he proceeds to make room for a default category, containing some "secular" documents that are not restricted to any period or area. We can assign to this secular category Fragment 13 of Benveniste's *Textes Sogdiens,* to which I refer here as *The Tale of Rostam*. For a reassessment of the textual problems occasioned by this fragment, see Sims-Williams 1976, who also edits, translates, and comments afresh on the whole piece.

[29] Cf. Benveniste 1940.134.

city. Following that, starting with line 5 of the fragment, Rostam's actions are described as follows:

5. *rwstmy zywr't prw RBkw šyr'nm šw kw šyr'kh*
   Rostam turned back in great glory, went to a good
6. *wyšgwrt mnc'y pyrdnn sygw'y 'spw prw wyš w'c*
   meadow, stopped, unsaddled his horse, then sent it out to graze.
7. *gwty mnšpn gwrt gwr' š'twgw wb' 'nsp'kh pr'yštrn*
   He himself rested, ate food, was satisfied, spread out a rug,[30]
8. *nypd "g"z 'wbt . . .*
   lay down and began to sleep.

This visualization of Rostam "at ease," so to speak, is a very familiar one to the *Shāhnāma* of Ferdowsi. We see here the conventional theme of Rostam's being "off his guard": he lets Rakhsh roam free without a saddle or bridle, eats a substantial meal and then falls asleep, oblivious to danger that awaits him. Four scenes from the *Shāhnāma* each contain elements directly comparable to the Sogdian *Tale of Rostam*. The first example is taken from the episode known as the first *Haft Khwān* of Rostam. We join the action as Rostam sets out to rescue Key Kāus from the White Div of Māzandarān. Before his exploit, we find the hero engaged in a series of activities closely parallel to those in the Sogdian Rostam fragment.

همین بود دیگ و همین بود خوان   بخورد و بینداخت زو استخوان

چرا دید و بگذاشت در مرغزار   لگام از سر رخش برداشت خوار

در بیمرا جای ایمن شناخت   بر نیستان بستر خواب ساخت

He ate and threw the bones away.

He slipped off the bridle from Rakhsh's head,

Upon a reed-bed he made a bed for sleep.

It was both a stew and a platter.

saw some pasture, and sent [him] out into the meadow.

He considered the gates of fear a safe place.

II 91.290–292

The second example is taken from the episode known as the third of Rostam's *Haft Khwān*. Before his exploit, the killing of a dragon that

---

[30] This reading *'nsp'kh* 'rug' is offered by Sims-Williams (1976), acknowledging Martin Schwartz, as an improvement on Benveniste's reading *'nšp'kh* 'equipment'.

attacks him while he sleeps, we see Rostam acting in a comparable manner:

ز رخش تگاور جـدا کرد زین   روانش چو پرداخته شد زآفرین

بکردار خورشید شد تابناك   همه تن بشستش بران آب پاك

کمر بست و ترکش پراز تیر کرد   چو سیراب شد ساز نخچیر کرد

جدا کرد ازو چرم پای و میان   بیفگندگوری چو پیل ژیان

برآورد ز آب اندر آتش بسوخت   چو خورشید تیز آتشی برفروخت

بخاك استخوانش سپردن گرفت   بپرداخت ز آتش بخوردن گرفت

چو سیراب شد کرد آهنگ خواب   سوی چشمهٔ روشن آمد بر آب

When his recitation of praise was finished	he took the saddle off from good-gaited Rakhsh.
He also washed his [Rakhsh's] body with clean water,	and he became resplendent as the sun.
When he had quenched his thirst, he prepared for the hunt;	he fastened his belt and filled his quiver with arrows.
He struck down an onager that was as fierce as an elephant	and removed its hide, hooves, and entrails.
He lit up a fire, blazing like the sun,	brought it [the onager] from the water and roasted it in the fire.
This done, he took it from the fire to eat,	and he buried the bones.
He went to a shining source of water.	When he quenched his thirst, he prepared for sleep.

II 94.335–341

The third example is from the beginning of the celebrated story of the fight between Rostam and Sohrāb. The narrative begins with a scene describing Rostam hunting. He stops for a rest and, once again, lets Rakhsh loose, eats a large dinner, and falls asleep, oblivious to any danger:

درختی بجست از در باب زن   چو آتش پرا گنده شد پیلتن

که در چنگ او پرّ مرغی نسخت   یکی نره گوری بزد بر درخت

ز مغز استخوانش برآورد گرد   چو بریان شد ازهم بکندو بخورد

چمان و چران رخش در مرغزار   بخفت و برآسود از روزگار

When the fire was dispersed, the elephant-bodied one	found a tree for a spit.
He impaled a male onager upon the tree—	it weighed in his hand like a bird-feather.
When it was roasted, he tore it apart	and drew forth the marrow of the bones.
He slept and rested for a while	and Rakhsh pranced and grazed in the meadow.

II 171.23–26

The last example is from another well-known story, about Rostam's fight with Esfandiyār. We see Bahman, Esfandiyār's brother, watching Rostam as the hero takes some time out while hunting, again eating a substantial meal, while Rakhsh roams free:

نــهــاده بر خویش گوپال و رخت   یکی نرّه گوری زده بر درخت

پرسـتـنـده بر پای پیـشش پسر   یکی جام پر می بدست دگر

درخت و گیا بود و هم جـویـبـار   همی گشت رخش اندران مرغزار

He impaled an onager on the tree.	An iron mace and harness lay beside him.
He had a cup full of wine in his other hand;	a serving boy was standing before him.
Rakhsh wandered in the meadow	where there were trees, brush, and streams.

VI 237.318–320

Clearly, all four of these examples from the *Shāhnāma* of Ferdowsi are parallel on the level of theme to lines 6–8 of the Sogdian Rostam fragment. In each instance, including the Sogdian version, we see Rostam letting Rakhsh roam free to graze, unharnessed. In other words, Rakhsh is in a state of unreadiness for his master to leap on his back and charge into combat. As for Rostam, he enjoys such a substantial feast that it causes him to fall asleep, a state of unreadiness for combat. Note, however, the exception of the last example, where something happens before Rostam can fall asleep; the logic of this exception will be taken up presently. Needless to say, Rostam and Rakhsh in all these instances become the perfect targets for ambush, and this is exactly what happens each time, though the circumstances may vary.

Let us return to the Sogdian fragment. While Rostam sleeps, the *divs*, furious that they have been routed by him single-handedly, plan to attack him in full force. They leave their city, riding on their otherworldy mounts in search of Rostam. In lines 24–28 of the Rostam fragment there follows this description of the hero's reaction:

24. *wytr'nt γ'gy rwstmy prwyd'k rtyms "ys 'gw*
    They went to search for brave Rostam. And also then came
25. *βwδ'βr'nn rgšy ZKw rwstmy wygr'ys mnspt 'yw*
    perceptive Rakhsh (and) he woke up Rostam. Rostam
26. *rwstmy MN gwbn' zg'rt ptymynč ZKw pwrdnkh*
    tore himself from sleep, quickly put on again his leopard
27. *črm ngwdnh drwnšth nyb'ynt b'zgd prw rgšw*
    skin garment, attached his quiver, mounted Rakhsh,
28. *p'db'r kw dywt*
    and dashed toward the *divs*.

Rostam is so off guard that he needs his horse, Rakhsh, to wake him up. He then needs to rearm himself quickly before he charges off to fight his attackers. Let us now look at how the events in this chain reaction compare to the already-selected four passages from Ferdowsi's *Shāhnāma*. In our first passage, when a lion comes to attack the sleeping Rostam, his horse Rakhsh rushes out to fight and kill the lion himself while Rostam remains asleep. Rostam then wakes up on account of the noise and rebukes Rakhsh for doing something that he himself should have done. In the second passage, Rakhsh tries three times to wake the sleeping and ill-tempered Rostam as the dragon attacks. Rostam, not seeing the impending danger on account of the darkness, becomes irritated with his horse, who keeps trying to awaken him. When Rakhsh tries to wake him the fourth time, Rostam finally sees the dragon in the darkness, jumps up, and proceeds to fight it to the death. In the third passage, Rakhsh does not wake up Rostam but is himself stolen by some enemy Turanians while Rostam sleeps. Rostam finally gets Rakhsh back from the Turanians after he impregnates a princess, Tahmina, with Sohrāb, his future son. Finally, in the fourth passage, as Rostam roasts his onager and Rakhsh roams free,

Bahman hurls down a huge boulder; Rostam manages to kick the boulder far away, all along continuing to roast his onager.

The first two passages seem particularly close to the Sogdian Rostam fragment. As in the Sogdian version, Rakhsh wakes the sleeping Rostam in order to protect him from harm, causing Rostam to get up quickly and take action. In the third passage, Rostam is pushed into action on account of the disappearance of Rakhsh, stolen while the hero slept. Even here the horse reacts to being stolen in a manner that resembles what he does in the first two passages, where he is waking up Rostam at the prospect of danger: he tries to fight off, however unsuccessfully, the Turanians as they steal him, and the commotion awakens Rostam, forcing him into action. Finally, in the fourth passage, Rostam has not quite yet fallen asleep, though it takes the shouting of Zawāra, his brother, to warn him of the impending disaster.

To sum up: in the Sogdian and Persian examples of a type-scene we may call "Rostam-at-Ease," the hero goes off into the wilderness, entering a life-threatening situation, all alone, only to make himself totally vulnerable to mortal danger by unsaddling his war-horse and then gorging himself with a hearty meal that sends him into the deepest slumber. We see that the Sogdian example operates along lines of narrative technique that are clearly paralleled by the Persian examples, even in details of description and sequencing of events. These parallelisms appear to be the result of cognate patterns in a common Iranian heritage of storytelling, which culminated in Ferdowsi's reworking of the *Shāhnāma* tradition.

The evidence of this Sogdian version of the Rostam tradition can be used to support Boyce's claim that Rostam "was truly a Saka hero, and not a hero of the indigenous pre-Saka population [of Sistān]."[31] The Sakas, it seems, invaded Sakastān = Segistān = Sistān, the country that was to be named after them, toward the end of the second century B.C.[32] If, then, the opinion advanced by Boyce is correct, it must be assumed that the Rostam stories of the Sakas from that point on developed into a national Iranian epic tradition, through Parthian

[31] Boyce 1955.475; cf. also Yarshater 1983.455–456.
[32] Nöldeke 1930.19, n2; see now Tarn 1951.494–502.

intermediacy. By the beginning of the seventh century A.D., it is clear that this national tradition was already in effect: in Mecca itself, according to a report by Ibn Hishām (Wüstenfeld 1858.191, 235), the citizens of that city were entertained with the stories about Rostam and Esfandiyār as narrated by one Naṣr Ibn al Harīth, who learned them in the course of commercial travels along the Euphrates.[33]

Boyce leaves us with the impression that the aspect of the *Shāhnāma* that I have called "epic of heroes" was originally a provincial Northeast Iranian tradition that eventually evolved into a national Iranian tradition through Parthian intermediacy. Once this tradition became widespread among the peoples of the Iranian Empire, it could be grafted on to a preexisting national tradition as reflected by the aspect of the *Shāhnāma* that I have called the "book of kings."

A major problem arises in Boyce's historical scheme, however. She presupposes that the coexistence of Rostam and his father Zāl with the dynasty of the Keyānids results simply from an artificial merger of an "epic of heroes" tradition with a "book of kings" tradition. Such a merger is then supposed to account for the disparities in chronology: as already mentioned, the thousand-year life-span of the two Sistanians Zāl and Rostam exceeds the combined life-span of the entire Keyānid dynasty. These disparities suit the views of Christensen, who believes that the Keyānid kings are a matter of history while conceding that the Sistanian heroes are a matter of myth.[34]

Christensen's theory of a historical Keyānid dynasty, however, should be modified on the strength of a single fact: the life of Afrāsiyāb is long enough to span a succession of kings ranging from the generations that followed the primordial King Faridun himself, before the dynasty of the Keyānids, all the way to the reign of Key Khosrow. Throughout the *Shāhnāma*, Afrāsiyāb is primarily the enemy of the Keyānid kings, only secondarily that of the Sistanian heroes. Afrāsiyāb

---

[33] See Nöldeke 1930.19 for this and other pieces of evidence for the presence of the Rostam tradition in West Iran by the seventh century A.D. It is important to note that the report of Ibn Hishām specifies that the stories about Rostam and Esfandiyār are narrated in the general context of stories about "the kings of Persia." That is, the specific narrative about Rostam and Esfandiyār is being highlighted in a general "Book of Kings" narrative tradition, which is here represented as an oral tradition.

[34] Christensen 1932.30. Implicitly, Boyce agrees (1954.46).

is clearly a mythical figure, corresponding to the Frāsiyāp of the earlier Pahlavi texts and the demonic Fraŋrasiian of the even earlier *Avesta*.[35] There is no way that even Christensen could consider Afrāsiyāb to be historical, and yet his enmity with the national kings of Iran is a unifying theme in the "book of kings" traditions about the Keyānids, from Key Qobād to Key Apiva to Key Kāus to Siyāvosh to Key Khosrow. It stands to reason, then, that the Keyānids, like their enemy Afrāsiyāb and their paramount hero Rostam, are compatible with traditional figures in Iranian myth.

In fact, Dumézil's comparative studies establish in detail that the story patterns concerning the Keyānids are a heritage of Indo-Iranian and even Indo-European mythmaking traditions. The titular *Key* of the Keyānid dynasty (Key Qobād, Key Apiva, Key Kāus, Key Khosrow), attested in the earlier Avestan tradition as *kauui,* is cognate with the Indic word *kaví-*, which in the diction of the Vedas designates a priestly or at least hieratic figure endowed with special supernatural knowledge bordering on the magical. The ultimate *kaví-* in the Vedas is one Kāvya (derivative of *kaví-*) Uśanas, smith of Indra's thunderbolt (with which the god kills the demonic Vṛtra/Ahi); this theme is comparable with that of the Iranian Kāva, the smith who helped Faridun smite the dragonlike usurper Ẓaḥḥāk in the aetiological story about the banner of the Keyānid dynasty (*Shāhnāma* I 61–67.183–277). The narratives about one of the Keyānids in particular, Key Kāus, are closely parallel to those about the Indic Kāvya Uśanas: both build a magnificent castle on a high mountain, both have affinities with demons, and both possess a magical elixir that can bring the dead back to life. Such parallelisms bear out the argument that the Iranian and Indic traditions are cognate.[36] Moreover, the stories about Key Kāus and Kāvya Uśanas in the Indo-Iranian traditions are cognate with those found in the Old Irish tale known as the *Second Battle of Moytura*.[37] In this Celtic narrative, a wondrous smith called Goibniu has at his disposal the waters of life, over which the gods (Tuatha Dé Danann) and the demons (Fomoire) contend. The figure of Goibniu is parallel

[35] See Dumézil 1971.231.
[36] Ibid. 137–238.
[37] Ibid. 186–190.

to the Iranian Kāva, ancestor of the Keyānids, who is likewise a smith, and also to the Indic sorcerer Kāvya Uśanas, who stands between the gods and demons contending over the waters of life, which he controls.

It is beyond the scope of this book to exhaust all the details of the relevant comparisons that can be found in the work of Dumézil[38] and his predecessors, notably Stig Wikander,[39] Hermann Lommel,[40] and Friedrich von Spiegel.[41] It suffices to say that, on the basis of these comparisons, the traditions about the Keyānids can be ascribed to the narrative patterns of Indo-European myth, which could have reshaped the narrative patterns of history.[42]

In proposing that the Keyānids are reshaped by myth, my aim is not to discredit Boyce's argument that the Rostam stories were transmitted into Sasanian times by way of a Parthian oral poetic tradition—or even that these stories were ultimately the heritage of Northeast Iranians. Rather, the point is simply that the "epic of heroes" tradition about Rostam is organically linked to the "book of kings" tradition about the Keyānids, and that the interrelationship between these two traditions did not result from an arbitrary historical merger. Again, what I call the "book of kings" tradition about the Keyānids is ultimately a *poetic* tradition, through Parthian intermediacy.[43] Like the stories of Rostam, the "histories" about the Keyānids are fundamentally a matter of poetry. In fact it is possible to go even further than Boyce, who posits that the provenience of this poetry is specifically Parthian: as Wikander's studies have shown, the stories about the Keyānids themselves are a product of early Parthian and Northeast Iranian mythmaking traditions, which are in many ways alien to the Zoroastrian orthodoxies prevalent in the *Gāthās* of the *Avesta*.[44] Thus the poetry about the Keyānids and the poetry about Rostam may actually share a common Parthian and Northeast Iranian heritage.

[38] Ibid. esp. 147–157; see also p. 144 for a discussion of Christensen's polemics against James Darmesteter.
[39] Wikander 1950.
[40] Lommel 1939.
[41] Spiegel 1887.281–287.
[42] See now also Kellens 1976.
[43] See Boyce 1954.
[44] Wikander 1938, esp. 107–108; his work is not cited by Boyce (1954, 1955, 1957).

In the Pahlavi documents that preserve fragments of the Iranian poetic traditions in Sasanian times, we can actually witness convergences between the poetry about Rostam and the poetry about the Keyānids. In the *Draxt Asūrik*, for example, a text that has been shown to be composed in a Parthian dialect of Northwest Iran *and in verse*,[45] there is a passing reference to the saddles upon which *Rotastaxm* 'Rostam' and *Spendadāt* 'Esfandiyār' had been seated.[46] In the case of the battle between Rostam and Esfandiyār, which we have already noted is attested as the topic of an entertaining narrative performance in seventh-century Mecca and is one of the most important episodes of Ferdowsi's *Shāhnāma*, the Zoroastrian prince Esfandiyār, a prime character in the Keyānid tradition, is consciously juxtaposed with Rostam, a prime character of the "Sistanian" or heroic tradition. Already in Sasanian times, these characters were counterposed as parallel poetic figures, much as the *Shāhnāma* parallels the seven deeds of Esfandiyār with the seven deeds of Rostam.

There has been over the years much debate over which of the seven deeds served as a model for the other—those of Esfandiyār or those of Rostam.[47] As we shall see (Chapter 9), that debate is pointless if indeed we are dealing here with two multiforms of an oral poetic tradition. In any case the poetic device of fully treating both sets of seven deeds in the *Shāhnāma* establishes ipso facto a large-scale opposition of the two heroes involved, and the seed for this poetic device is already evident in the small-scale juxtaposition of the two heroes in the *Draxt Asūrik*.

In this sense, of course, the actual combat between Rostam and Esfandiyār—or more precisely, the poetic rendition of this combat—serves as the ultimate juxtaposition. In the course of this combat, Esfandiyār at one point compliments Rostam by comparing him to Zarēr:

که یزدان سپاس ای جهان‌پهلوان   که دیدم ترا شاد و روشن‌روان

سـزاوار بـاشد سـتـودن تـرا   یـلان جهـان خـاک بـودن تـرا

خنک آنك چون تو پسر باشدش   یـکـی شاخ بیند که بر باشدش

[45] Benveniste 1930.
[46] Paragraph 41, Unvala 1923.657–658.
[47] Esfandiyār: e.g., Nöldeke 1930.72–73. Rostam: e.g., Molé 1951.133.

بود ایمـن از روزگـار درشـت   خنك آنك اورا بود چون تو پشت

بگـیـتـی بمـانـد ترا یادگار   خـنـك زال كش بگـذرد روزگار

سپـهـدار اسپ‌افگن و نرّه شیر   بـدیـدم ترا یـادم آمـد زریـر

. . . saying: "thanks be to God, O world champion,	for I see you, contented and enlightened.
It is just to praise you	[and for] the heroes of the world to be dust before you.
Happy is he who has a son like you,	for he sees a branch upon which there is fruit.
Happy is he who has a descendant like yours,	for he has protection from bad times.
Happy is Zāl, who, when his time passes,	will leave you in the world as a memorial.
When I see you I am reminded of Zarēr,	the horse-overturner and lion-like leader."

VI 247.482–487

Zarēr, a Keyānid prince and Esfandiyār's uncle, is attested already in the *Avesta* (Zairiwairi in *Yašt* 5.112 and *Yašt* 13.101). He is celebrated as a heroic paragon of the Zoroastrian way: in an attested Pahlavi poem known as the *Ayādgār ī Zarērān* "Memorial of Zarēr,"[48] he is presented as a pious warrior who was instrumental in a key victory of the Iranians over King Arjāsp and his Turanians, and who lost his own life in that battle. This Pahlavi poem is strikingly parallel in both form and content to the later narrative about the death of Zarēr in the *Shāhnāma* that is attributed to that self-confessed Zoroastrian himself, Daqiqi (VI 66–119.39–787). It is worth pointing out that, in this story of Zarēr, the victory of the Iranians over the Turanians is described as worthy of Rostam:

همـه شب نخفتنـد زان خرّمی   که پـیـروزی بودشـان رستمی

They slept not for the whole night on account of joy,	for a "Rostamian" victory was theirs.

VI 118.769

[48] On which see esp. Benveniste 1932a; on p. 245 this poem is characterized as one of two rare instances of epic to survive from the Sasanian period. See also Lazard 1975.625.

In other words, the Keyānid tradition is comparing itself here to the Rostam tradition within the poetry, whereas earlier we have seen the Rostam tradition comparing itself to the Keyānid tradition by way of Esfandiyār's compliment.

To conclude: I have argued against the commonly held notion that the Rostam of Ferdowsi's *Shāhnāma* is historically an extrinsic and intrusive figure. The notion rests on five overlapping components:

(1) The qualities and actions of Rostam seem characteristic of what we find in myth, whereas the qualities and actions of the national (Keyānid) kings he serves should be situated in the context of history.

(2) The chronology of Rostam and his father Zāl is out of synchronization with that of the Keyānid kings.

(3) The genealogy of Rostam suggests that he is at least in part alien to the national traditions of Iran.

(4) The ideas that lie behind the Rostam figure seem non-Zoroastrian in nature, and as such they too would be alien to the national traditions of Iran.

(5) Finally, Rostam's provenience from the remote region of Sistān establishes him as a figure who is likewise remote from the national kings of Iran. This factor accounts for the other four factors already listed, in that Rostam could be considered an outsider to the national traditions of the *Shāhnāma* on the grounds that he was originally a regional, not a national, hero.

In regard to this last point, I propose an alternative explanation for the anomalous nature of Rostam in the *Shāhnāma*. On the basis of what survives from the regional traditions of Sistān about Rostam, we have found no radical differences between Rostam as a regional hero and Rostam as a national hero of the *Shāhnāma*. I therefore suggest that Rostam's Sistanian heritage is actually part of the national traditions about this hero, and that these national traditions combine narratives about heroes with narratives about kings. In other words, the Iranian concept of a "book of kings" is not incompatible with an "epic of heroes."

CHAPTER 5

King and Hero,
Shāh and *Pahlavān*

My proposal that the Iranian concept of a "book of kings" meshes with an "epic of heroes" has been built on the arguments presented by Mary Boyce, who shows that the combination of narratives about kings and narratives about heroes, specifically Rostam, was already a national tradition in Sasanian and, even before, in Arsacid times. For Boyce, as we have seen, this combination resulted from an absorption of the regional narratives of Northeast Iranians about the hero Rostam by the national Iranian narratives about kings. In this chapter I argue that it is actually an even earlier, pre-Arsacid, narrative tradition, going back to Indo-Iranian and even Indo-European times. In terms of this argument, Ferdowsi's narrative scheme concerning national heroes and kings stems from an Indo-European mythmaking tradition. Adding to Dumézil's arguments, adduced earlier, that the narratives associated with the Keyānids follow the patterns of Indo-European myth, not Iranian history, I propose that not only the Keyānid narratives, but also the juxtaposition of narratives about the Keyānids and Rostam, follow an Indo-European mythmaking tradition.[1]

Let us begin, then, with the narrative patterns juxtaposing the royal line of Keyānids with heroes or *pahlavān*s like Rostam and his father Zāl in the *Shāhnāma*. This pattern, clearly, reaches further back than the poetic heritage of the Parthians and Northeast Iranians. It is inherited from Indo-European mythology, centering on the theme of the

[1] Boyce 1954, 1955, 1957; Dumézil 1971.137–238.

95

coexistence and the conflict between the king who rules and the hero who serves him.[2] This Indo-European theme has been studied in some non-Iranian contexts by Dumézil, with a focus on three different heroes in three different Indo-European traditions: Starkaðr in the Old Norse, Śiśupāla in the Indic, and Herakles in the Greek.[3] Each of these heroes is not only in the service of but also in conflict with his respective king(s). As I argue, a close parallel can be found in the Iranian traditions about Rostam and the other Sistanian heroes.

In presenting this argument, I add a further detail from ancient Greek myth, with reference to the relationship between Eurystheus as king and Herakles as hero. This relationship is explicitly drawn into a parallel, by the Homeric *Iliad* itself (19.95–133), with the relationship between Agamemnon as king and Achilles as hero.

Let us turn, then, to the myths surrounding three heroes in three completely independent mythic structures: the Germanic Starkaðr, the Indic Śiśupāla, and the Greek Herakles. Dumézil shows that these three heroes share characteristics so strikingly parallel in sequence and in detail that they must have a common Indo-European basis. In his treatment of Herakles, however, Dumézil views only the overall *myth* rather than specific traces in *epic*. The value of his contribution should not be underrated on this account: Dumézil still manages to demonstrate that the sequence and details of the Herakles story as presented by Apollodorus and Diodorus match, from the standpoint of comparative mythology, the sequence and the details of the Starkaðr and Śiśupāla stories.

In order to supplement Dumézil's demonstration, I shall examine not only the Herakles myth per se but also the Herakles myth as attested in Greek epic, particularly the *Iliad*. First, let us look at the parallels linking Starkaðr, Śiśupāla, and Herakles on Dumézil's terms, without the *Iliad* in mind.[4]

All three heroes are abnormal at birth. In the case of Herakles, however, this abnormality is stylized. He is not a monster who needs

---

[2] Of course I do not mean to suggest that such a theme is to be found only in Indo-European mythology: cf., e.g., Moorman 1971. See also Davis 1992, following Jackson 1982.

[3] Dumézil 1971.17–132.

[4] The following is a summary of the extended analysis by Dumézil 1971.25–124.

Starkaðr	Śiśupāla	Herakles
1. He is born monstrous, with excess arms.	1. He is born monstrous, with excess arms and eye.	1. He is born with an excess of strength after an excess of procreation.
2. The god Thor "normalizes" him by ridding him of his excess arms.	2. The god Viṣṇu "normalizes" him by ridding him of his excess arms and eye.	2. —
3. The gods Odin and Thor are conflicting forces in his life. Odin is benevolent toward him, Thor is antagonistic.	3. The gods Śiva and Viṣṇu are conflicting forces in his life. Śiva is benevolent toward him, Viṣṇu is antagonistic.	3. The gods Zeus and Hera are conflicting forces in his life. Zeus is benevolent toward him, Hera is antagonistic.
4. He commits crimes against three aspects of society:	4. He commits crimes against three aspects of society:	4. He commits crimes against three aspects of society:
A. sacrilege/lèse-majesté: he kills a king, with sacrifice as a pretext	A. sacrilege/lèse-majesté: he interferes with the regal horse-sacrifice	A. sacrilege/lèse-majesté: he robs a temple
B. behavior unbecoming of a warrior: he flees from battle	B. behavior unbecoming of a warrior: he makes sneak attacks	B. behavior unbecoming of a warrior: he makes a sneak attack
C. wantonness: he accepts a bribe out of greed.	C. wantonness: he rapes.	C. wantonness: he commits bigamy.
5. He commits suicide by having a hero kill him for a reward. He then tries to have his essence absorbed by his killer.	5. He is killed by the hero Kṛṣṇa, who is the god Viṣṇu in human form. His essence is absorbed by his killer.	5. He commits suicide by having a hero kill him for a reward. His essence is then transported by Zeus to Olympus and he is reconciled with his antagonist, Hera. He is thus made immortal.

to be "normalized," but he has overweening strength from birth: it took Zeus three nights to impregnate Alkmene, his mother, which is described as an explicit sign of Herakles' excess in strength (Diodorus 4.9.2).

All three heroes have superhuman lineage. Herakles is the son of Zeus. Starkaðr is the progeny of many-handed giants, whence the excess arms. As for Śiśupāla, he can be traced back to the god Śiva, among other reasons because this god, too, has the corresponding excess arms.[5]

All three experience divine intervention at early stages of their lives. Both Starkaðr and Śiśupāla are literally "normalized" in the sense that they are made to look like normal humans by the intervening deities. These deities, beneficent at first, turn out to be antagonists to the respective heroes. Herakles too is helped at first by Hera, who breast-feeds him, but who thereafter turns out to be his antagonist (Diodorus 4.9.7–8). Each hero also has a corresponding benevolent deity: Odin for Starkaðr, Śiva for Śiśupāla, and Zeus for Herakles. Either overtly or latently, these protective heroes are presented as parents of the heroes.

All three heroes are kingmakers, not kings. That is, though they are constantly involved in the affairs of kings, they do not achieve king-ship themselves. Starkaðr is in the service of several kings; Śiśupāla is the subordinate of Jarāsandha; and Herakles serves King Eurystheus throughout his Labors—not to mention his bondage to Omphale, Queen of the Amazons.

Herakles and Starkaðr commit suicide by having another hero kill them. Both pass on to their slayer some form of supernatural gift. Starkaðr offers invulnerability to weapons while Herakles passes on to the hero Philoktetes his miraculous bow, a key to the destruction of Troy. Both Starkaðr and Śiśupāla are cut in two and undergo a process of absorption by the killing hero, directly in the case of Śiśupāla, indirectly in the case of Starkaðr. As a result of their death and trans-formation, Herakles and Śiśupāla both become immortal. In the case of Starkaðr, where the absorption is indirect, the analogue to immor-tality is the invulnerability conferred upon his killer by virtue of having absorbed the hero's essence. All three heroes, then, undergo a process suggesting rebirth. In the case of the Herakles myth, the rebirth is actually dramatized by Hera, who simulates giving him birth when Herakles attains immortality (Diodorus 4.39.2).

In the three columns outlining parallels in the myths about the three heroes, the second entry under "Herakles" is left blank, because

[5] Ibid. 64–66.

Dumézil does not single out a point in the story of Herakles where the hero is "normalized." Walter Pötscher, however, has written two articles that we may use as indirect corroboration of Dumézil's comparison of these three heroes.[6] From Pötscher's work, we may derive a theme involving Herakles' normalization that counts as a Greek cognate with the corresponding themes in the Germanic and Indic traditions. It appears that the Greek form *Hērā* is a root variant of the form *hōrā* 'season, ripeness, timeliness, being seasonal'. The goddess *Hērā* is the divine force that presides over whatever is in season or out of season. The goddess of seasons, then, has the power to make Herakles be born out of season by delaying the delivery of the hero in childbirth (*Iliad* 19.95–133). Herakles' career can be interpreted as a change in state from being out of season to being in season, from abnormality to normalcy, for, once he dies and ascends to Olympus, Hera regularizes him by "giving birth" to him. She then accepts him by having him marry Hebe, her daughter (Diodorus 4.39.3). Thus the career of Herakles is what his name means: *Hera-klēs* can be translated as 'he who has the glory of Hera' (cf. Diodorus 4.10.1). From Pötscher's work, we may infer that even the noun *hērōs* 'hero' contains the same basic root of seasonality—let us call it regulation—for it too contains the root of *hōrā* 'season' and *Hērā* 'goddess of seasons'.

Turning from myth in general to epic in particular, note that the crucial passage involving Herakles' being out of season is directly attested in Greek epic, *Iliad* 19.95–133. One preoccupation of this Herakles passage, the theme of a superior hero in the service of an inferior king, is also central to the *Iliad* itself. We see it in the relationship of Achilles to Agamemnon. As Nestor says, Agamemnon has dishonored the most superior man in his service (9.110–111). Achilles says as much about himself, both to Agamemnon (1.244) and to his mother, Thetis (1.410–411). In the words of the hero, Agamemnon suffered from an *atē* 'aberration' in failing to give him his due honor (1.411). The importance of Achilles' use of this word *atē* becomes clear at a later point of the narrative, where Agamemnon blames the goddess *Atē* personified for his having dishonored Achilles (19.88, 91, 126, 129). In giving this excuse, Agamemnon cites the myth of the

---

[6] Pötscher 1961, 1971.

birth of Herakles, a story that tells how a superior hero came to serve an inferior hero, to his own dishonor (19.95–133).

We have already seen how Hera, by making Herakles be born *out of season,* provides the pressure for his embarking on his heroic career, which culminates in his becoming *in season* after he dies and joins the gods of Olympus in their immortality. I emphasize that Herakles, like Achilles, was in the service of a social superior who was his inferior as a hero. For this theme of the dishonoring of a superior Herakles by an inferior Eurystheus, we may observe the description of Zeus as he contemplates the Labors of Herakles: he bemoans the *atē* 'aberration' (*Iliad* 19.132) every time he sees his son Herakles enduring a Labor at the behest of Eurystheus (132–133).

It remains to be asked whether the Iliadic references to Herakles are references to the general myth or to a specific epic tradition. For an answer, we may turn to Wolfgang Kullmann's work on the epic divine apparatus, or *Götterapparat.*[7] His book surveys the Homeric treatment of several myths involving gods and men, showing in each case how epic selectively shapes and reshapes myth in order to adapt it for its own unified themes. Kullmann refers to the Herakles myth, though he draws no specific conclusions about it. But his book is helpful for its discussion of how epic diction refers to myth in general and to "epic myth" in particular. Two key passages are *Odyssey* 1.337 and Hesiod *Theogony* 99–101, where it is said that the *aoidos* 'singer' gives *kleos* 'fame, glory' to the *erga* 'deeds' of gods and men. As Kullmann argues convincingly, the *klea* 'glories' of gods refers to the general mythical framework while the *klea* of men refers specifically to epic.[8] Since *kleos* is a word that designates not just 'fame' in general but also *poetic* fame in particular,[9] I suggest that the name of Herakles, *Hēra-klēs,* refers to both the *klea* of men and the *klea* of gods—the *klea* of both Hera and his human antagonist. Thus the name of Herakles fits both a broader "saga" treatment and a narrower epic treatment of the myth.

With regard to the epic treatment, a valuable article by Walter Burkert analyzes in detail just such a perspective on Herakles.[10] There

[7] Kullmann 1956.25–35.
[8] Ibid. 10–11.
[9] Nagy 1974.244–261.
[10] Burkert 1972.

is a myth that tells how Homer once composed a now lost epic, *The Capture of Oikhalia,* for Kreophylos, the ancestor of rhapsodes called the Kreophyleioi.[11] Burkert proposes, on the basis of the wording of Homeric references to the capture of Oikhalia, that such references were not Homeric fabrications but traces of an independent epic tradition. Moreover, these references are not incidental, since they constitute themes that are coherent in themselves and that match some main themes of the *Iliad.* These themes, moreover, are not only coherent in the *Iliad:* they are also congruent with the overall Herakles myth. This fact, along with Dumézil's comparanda in the Indic and Germanic traditions, makes it likely that the Herakles myth was epic in nature.

The Greek model of Achilles, as an internal parallel to the model of Herakles, is especially pertinent for comparison with the Iranian model of Rostam. Just as the hero Rostam is king in his own right in his remote native region of Sistān, the hero Achilles is a king in his own right in his remote native region of Phthia. Another parallelism is equally instructive: just as Achilles is primarily a hero and secondarily a king while Agamemnon is primarily a king and secondarily a hero, so also with Rostam and the royal line of the Keyānids in the *Shāhnāma.* This point will be taken still further at a later stage of the discussion.

Whereas the kingship of Rostam and the kingship of the Keyānids are distinct in that one is local and the other is national, the heroic nature of Rostam and the heroic nature of the Keyānids do in fact overlap. We have already observed such an overlap in the case of the juxtaposition between the deeds of Rostam and the deeds of the Zoroastrian prince Esfandiyār. Such patterns of juxtaposition, incidentally, will help us better to understand another problem, the rival themes of Rostam's and Khosrow's consecutive defeats of Afrāsiyāb in the *Shāhnāma:* since Afrāsiyāb is himself primarily the national king of Turān and only secondarily a hero or antihero, it stands to reason that his defeat by Khosrow should be primary and his defeat by Rostam only secondary.

Since I argue that the figure of Rostam is really an insider rather than

[11] Ibid. 76.

an outsider to the poetic traditions about the Keyānids, it is important
to reconsider the main reason for thinking of Rostam as an outsider in
the first place: the contents of the *Shāhnāma* itself intentionally make
Rostam *seem* like an outsider. Let us consider some analogues in other
mythmaking traditions, for example, Dionysus in Greek myth.[12] As
we see him in the *Bacchae* of Euripides, this god is Asiatic, a foreigner
threatening the old Hellenic institutions of Thebes by way of his own
novelty. Time after time, his foreign and "new" features are empha-
sized (for example, *Bacchae* 13–16, 64–68, etc.), and scholars of Greek
religious history were led to believe on the basis of such internal
evidence that the god Dionysus was an outsider to the family of Greek
gods, whose pedigree generally goes back to the second millennium
B.C., and that he was borrowed from Asiatic sources at a relatively
recent time, well into the first millennium B.C. This general opinion
was then decisively overturned by the decipherment of the Linear B
tablets. These Greek documents, dating from the second millennium
B.C., clearly attest the name of Dionysus. Why, then, is the god
traditionally represented as foreign and "new" when he is really native
and "old"? A second look at the internal evidence suggests the answer.
The same narrative tradition that represents Dionysus as a "new"
foreigner simultaneously represents him as an "old" native son, for he
is actually the grandson of Kadmos, the founder of Thebes, and a
cousin of Pentheus, the ruler of the city. The function of Dionysus in
the Dionysus myth is to be "the other" within that myth, and the way
to represent "the other" is to assign him genuinely foreign and new
characteristics. But "the other" is basic to the myth, precisely because
he is anomalous, disruptive: *that is his function*. He is an outsider in
terms of the myth, but he is still the essential part of the myth: he is
truly a "native son." A similar explanation can be offered in the case of
Adonis, who is overtly Phoenician in name but thoroughly Greek in
concept.[13]

So also with Rostam, for, as we take a second look at this anomalous outsider, we see a hero who is genetically part *div* 'demon' and
who is qualified to rule the Turanians, enemies of the Iranians, for

[12] In the discussion that follows, I follow the arguments of Boedeker 1974.4–5 and
Nagy 1990a.296–299.
[13] See Detienne 1972.237–238.

seven years. Moreover, his son Sohrāb is born of a Turanian mother, and Rostam himself, as descendant of mace-wielding Garshāsp, is thereby the descendant of Tur himself, the ancestor of all Turanians (*Garshāspnāma* p. 86, *Tārikh-e Sistān* 2). And yet this same hero Rostam, despite all his quarrels with the Keyānids, is the mainstay of all Iran. As we shall see, Rostam's status as an anomalous aspect of the Keyānid stories turns out to be an inherited aspect of these stories. Let us begin by considering the Turanians, since Rostam's affinities to them serve to establish his own anomaly.

The Turanians, the main enemies of the Iranians in the *Shāhnāma*, are themselves paradoxically Iranians from the standpoint of the *Avesta*. As the studies of Nyberg have shown, the institutions represented as Turanian in the *Avesta* are thoroughly Iranian, but they are distinct both in form and content from the institutions represented as orthodox Iranian. Pictured in the *Avesta* as barbarous and predatory nomads, the Turanians seem to have their idiosyncratic cults, especially of Vayu, the wind-god of the warriors, and of Anāhitā, the river-goddess of fertility.[14]

Nyberg views these Turanian institutions as Northeast Iranian in nature, and he attempts to explain the traditional conflicts between Iranians and Turanians as resulting from the proselytizing of Zoroaster in Turanian regions, which split the Turanians into conflicting groups of orthodox "Iranians" and unorthodox "Turanians."[15] Another explanation has been offered by Wikander. His focus of interest is on the semantics of the Avestan word *mairiia-*, the basic meaning of which is 'unmarried male'.[16] The two named figures in the *Avesta* who are specifically identified as *mairiia-* are Fraŋrasiian = Afrāsiyāb and Arəjat̰.aspa = Arjāsp, two consecutive kings of the Turanians.[17] As it turns out, the word *mairiia-* specifically designates a member of a *Männerbund,* a society of unmarried male warriors that exists outside and beyond the confines of society. Wikander concludes from his

---

[14] Nyberg 1938.249–263.

[15] Ibid. 262–263.

[16] Wikander 1938.

[17] Ibid. 34. Arəjat̰.aspa the *mairiia-*: *Yašt* 9.30. Fraŋrasiian the *mairiia-*: *Yasna* 2.7; 19.56, 82. At *Yašt* 5.50, there is a reference to Fraŋrasiian as the *mairiia-*, and that is enough to name him.

findings that the concept "Turanian" refers to Iranian tribal societies that had preserved the institutions of a *Männerbund,* a separate society outside society. Such a *Männerbund* would have its own separate institutions, even cults. Thus Wikander sees the traditional conflict between Iranian and Turanian as a conflict of societies with and without *Männerbund* cults. And he notes that the conflict between the cults of the *Männerbund* and the cults of regular society in the *Avesta* is older, stronger, and more basic than the conflict between non-Zoroastrian and Zoroastrian traditions.[18] Wikander could even go so far as to say that the conflict with *Männerbund* cults is the main theme, the "Hauptthema," of Indo-Iranian religious history.[19]

One problem, however, with Wikander's explanation of the Turanians is that it presupposes a cross-tribal spectrum of Iranians who do and do not have *Männerbund* institutions.[20] It is hard to accept the notion that an all-pervasive conflict between Iranian and Turanian could stem simply from the retention or rejection of a single institution, unless it was one of central importance to society. In fact the studies of Wikander show that the pattern of the *Männerbund* is incorporated into institutions of the national kingship. In the case of the Parthian dynasty of the Arsacids, their official mythmaking traditions as reflected in the mythical dynasty of the Keyānids are permeated with the pattern of the *Männerbund.*[21] This pattern is present even in the concept of *Kāviyān* 'Keyānid' (= descendant of Kāva, the primordial smith and hero), derived ultimately from *kauui* or *kauuay-,* which is attested in the *Avesta* and which is related to the Indic word *kaví-* 'seer, sage': the Avestan form is used not only as the title of the Keyānids (including the Zoroastrian Vištaspa = Goshtāsp himself) but also as an epithet of the enemies of the orthodoxy that is propounded by the *Gāthās.*[22] It is safe to conclude, then, that the patterns of *Männerbund,* even as early as the *Avesta,* affect not only frontier tribes but the national institutions of kingship itself.

Thus the conflict between Turanians and Iranians is not simply

[18] Wikander 1938.87.
[19] Ibid. 96.
[20] See esp. ibid. 86.
[21] Ibid. 107–108.
[22] Ibid. 102.

between outsiders and insiders, societies that do and do not have the pattern of *Männerbund*. It would be more accurate to say that this conflict is *within* society as a whole, not *between* two discrete types of society. The mythical struggle between Turān and Iran as two separate countries is the model for a real struggle within a single but divided Iran. As King Afrāsiyāb of Turān says, Iran belongs to him too, on the grounds that Tur, the ancestor of the Turanians, is just as much a son of Faridun as Iraj, the ancestor of the Iranians (*Shāhnāma* II 148.324–325).

In fact, as Marijan Molé has argued, the conflict between Iranians and Turanians within a broader framework of Iranian society can be seen as a heritage of the conceptual conflict between the so-called first and second functions within Indo-European society.[23] The terms "first and second functions" are derived from Dumézil's basic theory of trifunctionality. He postulates that Indo-European society is founded on the model of three social functions: (1) sovereigns/ministers of state/priests, (2) warriors, and (3) cultivators/herdsmen, as marked by the wealth that accrues to them.[24] Specifically, Molé shows that the myth of the division of roles among the three sons of Faridun, as narrated in the Pahlavi text of the *Ayādgār ī Žāmāspīg*, corresponds to this tripartite principle:

(1) Ēric = Iraj becomes the exponent of law and religion (= first function)
(2) Tōz = Tur becomes a warrior (= second function)
(3) Salm becomes the exponent of wealth (= third function)[25]

The myth goes on to assign

(1) Iran to Iraj
(2) Turān to Tur
(3) "Rome" and the Occident to Salm

[23] Molé 1952–1953; cf. also Puhvel 1987.121.

[24] For more on Dumézil's theory, see Dumézil 1968. We have already seen an example of this trifunctional pattern in the three "sins" committed by the heroes Starkaðr in the Old Norse, Śiśupāla in the Indic, and Herakles in the Greek traditions: see 4A, 4B, 4C in the table.

[25] Cf. Molé (1952–1953), who also interprets a parallel passage in the *Shāhnāma*, I 256–259; also Dumézil 1968.586–588 and 1971.257–258.

Clearly, the social tripartition in the myth is thus reshaped as an ethnic tripartition, with the Turanians eventually becoming equated with the Turks.[26] But, even in terms of the myth, the tripartition is primarily social and only secondarily ethnic. Furthermore, in light of the evidence adduced by Nyberg and Wikander about the theme of the Turanians as a *Männerbund*, it is possible to identify them as exponents of the "second function" within the broader framework of Iranian society.[27] Gnoli, however, wishes to maintain a distinction between the Tūiriias = Turanians and the Airiias = Aryans, the term for "Iranian" in the *Avesta*: "The Avestan Tūiriias are therefore a tribal group that is distinct from the Airiia group, but closely akin to it."[28] But even Gnoli admits that the Tūiriias = Turanians "are no less Iranian than the Airiias," and "we are dealing with the same historical and geographical horizon."[29] He also accepts Molé's and Dumézil's contention that the myth of the tripartition among the sons of Faridun predates the Arsacid period.[30] Thus the only reason we have for Gnoli to consider the Turanians as distinct from the Aryans of the *Avesta* is that the *Avesta treats* them as distinct from the Aryans. In the paragraphs that follow, I attempt to explain this distinct treatment as a matter of mythmaking.

Parallels in ancient Greek civilization may help clarify the status of the *Männerbund* in Iranian society. In an influential essay "The Black Hunter," Pierre Vidal-Naquet has shown that city-states like Athens and Sparta had institutions corresponding to what Wikander would have called *Männerbund*.[31] For example, the *ephēboi* or ephebes of

[26] Molé 1952–1953. As Gnoli remarks (1980.119), "The epical-legendary transposition of Turān to Turkistan is the evident reflection of a vast process of secondary identifications by the enemies of Sasanian Iran or by Iranian princes who boasted of Sasanian ascendancy: from the Tūiryas [= Turanians] to the Turks, as from the Hyaonas to the Chionites." See also Gnoli's bibliography (pp. 118–119).

[27] Molé 1952–1953. Cf. also Gnoli 1980.115, n160, on the mythical theme of a figure called Tur whose task it was to kill Zoroaster himself by assuming the form of a wolf. In a separate study (Davidson 1979), I have argued that the theme of changing into a wolf is an Indo-European pattern that implies joining a *Männerbund,* becoming an outlaw from regular society, and undergoing one facet of a multifaceted process of initiation. Cf. also Lincoln 1975.

[28] Gnoli 1980.116.

[29] Ibid. Cf. Puhvel 1987.121.

[30] Gnoli 1980.116.

[31] Vidal-Naquet 1968a.

Athens were its unmarried young men, the light-armed component of
the city's military force whose main strategic task was to patrol frontiers and to engage in skirmishes.[32] A young man served as an *ephēbos*
before he could join the ranks of the citizens, that is, the married adult
men, who were members of the phalanx or military ranks proper, the
heavy-armed or "hoplite" component of the city's military force, and
whose strategic task was to fight the battles proper.[33] Similarly with
the Spartan institution of the *krupteia* 'secret band': groups of young
male adolescents would be assigned to a temporary life of isolation,
living in the bush, whose task was to police the frontiers in skirmishes
and sneak attacks, generally out of season (winter) and at nighttime.[34]
As Vidal-Naquet points out, this institution for unmarried adolescents
is the symmetrical inversion of the institution for married adults,
namely the phalanx or army of citizens.[35] Whereas the institutions for
adults represent order, the institutions for adolescents, that is, premature citizens, represent disorder, chaos; still, they are institutions,
subordinated to a society at large.[36] Such institutions for adolescents,
then, are the essence of what we call initiation.[37]

These patterns are analogous to those that Wikander has found
associated with the Avestan word *mairiia-* 'young unmarried male', an
inherited designation of a member of a *Männerbund*. But this word, as
we have seen, is also an inherited designation of the Turanian king
Fraŋrasiian = Afrāsiyāb and his successor king Arəjaṯ.aspa = Arjasp.
This is not to say, of course, that Afrāsiyāb and Arjāsp are unmarried
adolescents. Rather, the opposition of Iranian and Turanian represents
the opposition of order as exemplified by adult society and chaos as
exemplified by *Männerbund* society. Granted, the *ephēboi* of Athens do
not fight the phalanx of the adult citizens as the Turanians fight the
established kingdom of the Iranians, but such a comparison is invalid
in the first place. The opposition of *ephēboi* and citizens is a feature of
society, whereas the opposition of Turanians and Iranians is a myth

[32] Ibid. and Vidal-Naquet 1981 chap. 2 (I cite the page numbers of the English
version, Vidal-Naquet 1986a). See also Vidal-Naquet 1986b, esp. p. 144.

[33] Vidal-Naquet 1986a. 106–122.

[34] Ibid. 112–114, 117.

[35] Vidal-Naquet 1981 chap. 2; see also Vidal-Naquet 1986b, esp. p. 144.

[36] Vidal-Naquet 1981 chap. 2.

[37] On the patterns of inversion in initiation, see Gennep 1909.

that tells about a feature of society. As a myth, the opposition of Turanians and Iranians is represented in the form of war. In this way, every current enemy of the Iranians, primarily the "Turks" and the Chinese, can be equated with or at least allied with the Turanians.[38]

The figures of Rostam and his ancestors hover between the diametrically opposed figures of the Iranians and Turanians. On one hand, the Sistanian heroes Sām and Zāl and Rostam are all mainstays of the national kings of Iran, thus meriting the title *"pahlavān* of Iran" (for example, *Shāhnāma* I 244.1575, II 126.599). On the other hand, they are relatives of Tur (by way of Tur's mother) and exhibit characteristics that clearly stem from the pattern of the *Männerbund:* Rostam and his ancestors traditionally stand apart from the organized ranks of the army and from the authority of the central government, preferring one-on-one combat to formal battle. They even tend to fight their own wars (as in the case of Sām's war against the Gorgsārs). Like the Turanians, as we have seen already, the Sistanian heroes have affinities with the frontier regions of Northeast Iran. Moreover, in the *Avesta,* the Turanian king Fraŋrasiian = Afrāsiyāb shares numerous thematic features with Kərəsāspa = Garshāsp, one of Rostam's earlier ancestors.[39] In view of the traditional characteristics of Fraŋrasiian = Afrāsiyāb as *mairiia-,* that is, as representative of *Männerbund,* we thus have indirect evidence that Rostam himself is *mairiia-.* Moreover, the *Shāhnāma* itself depicts Rostam as engaging in such practices as night attacks (for example, in his very first military exploit: I 269.100–109)—deceptive practices that distinctly reflect the pattern of *Männerbund,* not that of the court and its army (compare also II 208.478–498 and V 74.1125–1157 for further examples of Rostam's resorting to this practice). Maguire has the following to say about Rostam's first such exploit: "Strangely enough, throughout the epic this type of military operation is avoided by the Iranians as unmanly and practiced often by

---

[38] In the Pahlavi poem known as the *Žāmāsp-nāmak* 'Book of Jamāsp', there is an apocalyptic vision of a grim future when it will be impossible to distinguish Ērān 'Iran' from Anērān 'non-Iran' (paragraphs 13, 52, 60 in Benveniste 1932b). In this text, the primary representatives of "non-Iran" turn out to be Tačīks (e.g., paragraph 5), who are allied with the Turks (paragraph 95). See also Gnoli 1980.119, 157 (and n26 above).

[39] See Wikander 1938.38. For the Indo-European characteristics of the themes shared by Rostam and his ancestor Kərəsāspa = Garshāsp, see Dumézil 1971.140–142.

the Turanians, thus becoming an action to be censured."[40] Even in such specifics, we see a convergence of themes that are characteristic of (1) the *Männerbund,* (2) the Turanians, and (3) the Sistanian heroes.

We have seen, then, that the combined themes of Rostam's being simultaneously an "insider" and an "outsider" with relation to the Keyānids is an aspect of an overall Indo-European mythmaking tradition about heroes and kings. Moreover, the theme of Rostam's being an "outsider" with relation to the Keyānids is parallel to the conceptual conflict between Turanians and Iranians in Iranian storytelling traditions, which derives from the conceptual conflict between the so-called second and first functions in Indo-European traditions.

[40] Maguire 1973.96, n15. For instances where it is the Turanians who resort to the deceptive practice of night attacks, see *Shāhnāma* IV 83–87.1155–1213, V 134, 137.860–923, V 329–333.1589–1665.

CHAPTER 6

Rostam, Guardian of Sovereignty

Having examined, with a focus on the conceptual conflict between Turanians and Iranians, the theme of Rostam's being an "outsider" to the kingdom of the Keyānids, we have seen that this hero is really intrinsic to the narrative traditions of the Iranian Book of Kings, even though these traditions keep affirming that he is extrinsic. We shall now see, moreover, that Rostam is integral not only to the narrative traditions about kings but also to the concept of kingship itself. This time, our focus will be on the concept of the royal *farr* 'luminous glory' and Rostam's relation to it. This Persian word *farr*, which corresponds to Pahlavi *xvarrah/farrah* and Avestan *xᵛarənah,* designates the visible emblem of power, sovereignty, and authority.[1] As such, it is associated distinctly with kingship, in particular the kingship of the Keyānids: hence the Avestan expression *kauuaēm xᵛarənah* 'the luminous glory of the *kauuis*' (*Yašt* 19.69, etc.). And yet, paradoxically, Rostam too is pictured as possessing *farr* in the *Shāhnāma,* as we see for example in the scene describing the reaction of his grandfather Sām on the occasion of his first glimpse of Rostam:

برو هر زمان نام یزدان بخواند   ز رستم همی درشگفتی بماند

میان چون قلم سینه و بر فراخ   بدان بازوی و یال وآن پشت وشاخ

دل شیر نر دارد و زور ببر   دو رانش چو ران هیونان ستبر

ندارد کس از پهلوانان همال   بدین خوب روئی واین افرّ و یال

[1] For a survey, see Dumézil 1971.282–289; cf. also Puhvel 1987.106, 120–121, 278–283.

He marveled much at Rostam, calling out the name of God upon him:

"With such a forearm and neck, back, and arms, a waist like a reed, a broad chest and torso!

His two thighs are sturdy like the thighs of camels. He has a lion's heart and a tiger's strength.

With this handsome face and this *farr* and this stature, he has no equal among the *pah-lavāns*."

I 244–245.1587–1590

There have been attempts to explain this seemingly anomalous association of Rostam and *farr* 'luminous glory' in terms of the hero's local kingship in Sistān.[2] This explanation, however, is countered by the narrative traditions of the *Shāhnāma* itself. In one scene, for example, Rostam's mother, at the birth of the hero, immediately perceives that he has the *farr-e shāhanshahi* 'the luminous glory of the King of Kings':

بخندید از ان بچه سرو سهی   بدید اندرو فرّ شاهنشهی

She, who was as tall as a cypress, smiled at the child. She saw in him the *farr-e shāhan-shahi.*

I 239.1516

Clearly, this title must apply to the national kings, and it is a striking anomaly that Rostam, unlike other heroes in the *Shāhnāma,* should be explicitly associated with the *farr-e shāhanshahi.*[3] One way to account for this anomaly is to adduce the case of a figure called Garshāsp, who represents the one instance where the genetic line of the Sistanian heroes crosses with the genetic line of the national kings, in that both lines claim him as an ancestor.[4] Along these lines it could be argued that, if Garshāsp as national king once had *farr,* then it might be an appropriate attribute for his descendant Rostam as well.[5]

[2] Maguire 1973.286.

[3] Maguire herself, ibid. 293, points out this anomaly, which tends to undermine her argument that Rostam's affinities with kingship stem from his local sovereignty over Sistān.

[4] Ibid. 84. For a clear statement on the confusing subject of Garshāsp's genetic affinities with both the Sistanian heroes and the national kings, see Hansen 1954.82.

[5] Maguire 1973.84.

Such an argument falls short, however, since there seems to be no internal evidence that Rostam's claim to the attribute of *farr-e shāhanshahi* is based on his ancestry. Besides, even the national kings cannot hold on to *farr* on the basis of ancestry alone. In the narrative scheme of the *Shāhnāma,* the national kings can and do invalidate their *farr* if they turn to evil. Throughout the narrative, the whole nation of Iran is threatened time and again by disaster whenever the national king lapses into evil ways, and such disasters are typically visualized as the blighting of the king's *farr*. A typical example is the case of the ill-fated celestial ascension attempted by Key Kāus.

بگـردانـدش سـر ز یـزدان پـاک   فـشـانـد بر آن فـرّ زیـبـاش خـاك

He turned away from God, the pure,   and cast dust upon that beautiful *farr* of his.

II 151.376

The earlier traditions of the *Avesta* reveal clearly an analogous pattern: the primordial king Yima (= Persian Jamshid) himself serves as a model for the loss of $x^v ar\partial nah$ (= Persian *farr*) on the part of a king who has lapsed into evil ways (*Yašt* 19.34).

Since the loss of the king's *farr* is conventionally linked with national disasters, it is significant that the absence of Rostam in times of national crises is consistently pictured as a disaster for all Iran. For example, Rostam is summoned in a time of crisis as the hope of the Iranians:

ورا پـیـش ازیـن آگـهـی دادہ ام   بـدیـن مـن سـواری فرسـتـادہ ام
سـوی مـا فرسـتـد بدین رزمـگـاه   مـگـر رسـتـم زال را با سـپـاه

For this I have already sent a horse-man,   and informed him of this,
so that he will send Rostam, son of Zāl,   with an army to us in this battle-field.

IV 143.444—445

In another example, the Turanians seize the opportunity to attack the Iranians precisely when Rostam is absent.

بدرگاه او لشکری نو شوند

زیانی بود سهمگین زین درنگ

فسونها و نیرنگها ساختن

نمانیم تا نزد خسرو شوند

ز زابلستان رستم آید بجنگ

کنون ساختن باید و تاختن

We will not allow them [the Iranians] to go to Khosrow	and form a new army at his [Khosrow's] court.
Rostam will come from Zābolestān for combat.	There would be a heavy loss on account of this delay.
It is necessary to hurry and make preparations now,	devising deceits and stratagems.

IV 146.483–485

And, with Rostam absent, the Iranian troops despair:

که گیرند مارا کنون ناگهان

شود کار ایران کنون تال و مال

دریغ آن در و گاه شاه جهان

تهمتن بزاولستانست و زال

Alas for the court and throne of the Shāh of the world,	for they will seize us now in one fell swoop.
Tahamtan [Rostam] and Zāl are in Zābolestān.	Iran's affairs will end up a shambles.

IV 154.599–600

Moreover, the very process of succession from one king to the next is consistently a matter of crisis that calls for the intervention of the Sistanian heroes. An intensive survey yields several distinct but parallel instances in the *Shāhnāma* where (1) a reigning king dies, (2) the transition to the next king is an occasion for a massive attack on Iran by the Turanians, and (3) the Iranians in their distress turn to a Sistanian hero.[6] In short, Rostam is the guardian of *farr* for the national kings.[7] This epic theme is also politicized and historicized: the *Tārikh-e Sistān* (35–36) reports that, even in Sasanian times, the local rulers of Sistān claimed the title of *pahlavān-e jahān* 'world *pahlavān*' in the service of the national king.

By virtue of being a guardian of the king's *farr* 'luminous glory',

[6] Hansen 1954.132–133.
[7] Such is the conclusion of Zajączkowski 1970.688.

Rostam is a mainstay of Iran more consistently than the national kings themselves. It has been said that "Rostam is consistent, while the image of the king is shifty, opaque, perplexing—it emerges radiant only to submerge again; this, certainly, is one of the most interesting aspects of the *Shāhnāma*."[8] Moreover, the Sistanian heroes not only sustain the *farr* of the national kings: they also confer it. For example, it is Zāl who assembles the *mōbad*s of Iran to ascertain the identity of the new national king, and the *mōbad*s reveal to him that it is Key Qobād who will now have the *gorz* 'mace' and *farr* 'luminous glory' of the Keyānids (II 56.110–111). And it is Rostam himself who must then fetch the new king from Mount Alborz (II 56.112–113). In sum, the national hero Rostam seems to be thematically linked with the *farr-e shāhanshahi*.

The theme of Rostam's possession of the *farr-e shāhanshahi* appears to be attested already in the *Avesta,* and yet, perhaps surprisingly, the actual name and figure of Rostam are not. In other words, even though the figure of Rostam is not directly attested in the *Avesta,* at least the figure of a national hero who guards the *farr* is definitely there. In support of this claim, I summarize the main themes of one particular text, *Yašt* 19 in the *Avesta.*

In primordial times, the first three kings had $x^v ar\partial nah$ (= *farr*) 'luminous glory': Haošiiaŋha (= Hushang), the first created man; Taxmō Urupa (= Ṭahmuraṣ), the warrior; and Yima (= Jamshid), possessor of bountiful flocks (*Yašt* 19.23–33). As the studies of Dumézil have shown, this series of three kings corresponds to the inherited Indo-European conceptual pattern of three social functions: (1) sovereigns/ministers of state/priests, (2) warriors, and (3) cultivators/herdsmen as producers of wealth.[9] Then, after Yima (Jamshid) turned evil and lost $x^v ar\partial nah$ (*farr*), this $x^v ar\partial nah$ was tripartitioned among three successors: Miϑra, Kərəsāspa (= Garshāsp), and Θraētaona (= Faridun) (19.34–40).[10] As Dumézil has also shown, this tripartition, like the earlier succession of three kings, likewise corresponds to the

---

[8] Hansen 1954.147: "Rustam ist der Beharrende, während das Bild des Königs wechselt, sich trübt, verwirrt, wieder Glanz gewinnt, um aufs neue abzusinken. Dies ist gewiss einer der interessantesten Aspekte des *Schahname*."

[9] Dumézil 1968.443–452.

[10] On the nature of tripartitioning, see Dumézil 1971.286–287, n1.

pattern of the three social functions.[11] And it is significant that the *xᵛarənah* = *farr* of the warrior par excellence is assigned to Kərəsāspa, the Avestan equivalent of Garshāsp, the ancestor of Rostam.[12]

But we have not yet reached the point in *Yašt* 19 where the theme of Rostam's own possession of the *farr-e shāhanshahi* seems to emerge. At a time not specified, the Good Spirit (Spənta Mainiiu) and the Evil Spirit (Aŋra Mainiiu) engage in a struggle to possess the *xᵛarənah* (*farr*), and their chief protagonists are Ātar 'fire' and Dahāka = Zahhāk respectively (19.45–52). In the course of the struggle, the *xᵛarənah* (*farr*) is seized by a figure called Apąm Napāt 'progeny of the waters', who saves it by taking it down to the depths of the mythical Lake Vouru.kaša (51).[13] Then the chief god Ahura Mazda (= Ohrmazd) challenges (1) priests, (2) warriors, and (3) herdsmen to attain the inaccessible *xᵛarənah* = *farr* (53–54).[14] The first to make such an attempt is Fraŋrasiian = Afrāsiyāb (55–69). This king of the Turanians, this quintessential *mairiia-* (56),[15] enters the lake three times in order to seize the *xᵛarənah* (*farr*), but fails each time; he thus fails to seize the *xᵛarənah* = *farr* that "belongs to the Aryan [= Iranian] nations, born and unborn, and to the just Zoroaster" (*tat xᵛarəno isō yat asti airiianąm dahiiunąm zātanąm azātanąmča yatča ašaonō zaraϑuštrahe: Yašt* 19.63). The role here of Fraŋrasiian (= Afrāsiyāb) is significant from the standpoint of the *Shāhnāma*, where we have seen that the primary threat to the *farr* of the Keyānid kings is Afrāsiyāb and the

[11] Ibid. 282–289. There is another version of this tripartition of the *xᵛarənah* in the *Dēnkart* (7.1.25–27, 32, 36–37), where the first-function recipient is not Miϑra but the wise Ōšnar, who serves as minister of state for Key Ūs = Key Kāus. In this version the pattern of the three social functions is more transparent: see Dumézil 1971.285–286.

[12] The *Tārikh-e Sistān* (35–36) reports that Rostam actually founded a temple dedicated to Garshāsp, which was still in operation in the first centuries after the Prophet; cf. Molé 1963.452. As the *xᵛarənah* leaves Yima and goes to Miϑra, Kərəsāspa, and Θraētaona, it assumes the form of a bird (*Yašt* 19.35–38). Perhaps it is relevant that, when Rostam loses his warrior-*farr* in the course of combat with Esfandiyār, it is restored to him by the wondrous bird Simorgh (*Shāhnāma* VI 294ff.). In *Dēnkart* 7.1.32, Kərsāsp = Garshasp, who is equated with Sāmān = Sām, receives the *xvarr* = *farr* specifically in his role as warrior: see Molé 1963.463.

[13] For an introduction to the mythological theme of Apąm Napāt 'progeny of the waters', see Puhvel 1987.277–283.

[14] For details on the conceptual pattern of trifunctionalism, see Dumézil 1973.25.

[15] See Chapter 5.

primary defender of the *farr* is Rostam himself. Moreover, even in the matter of chronology, the figures of Afrāsiyāb and Rostam seem to match each other's life-spans while all along exceeding the life-spans of the Keyānids themselves.

In brief, the internal evidence of the *Shāhnāma* suggests that the figure of Rostam matches the figure of Apạm Napāt in *Yašt* 19, to the extent that Rostam, like Apạm Napāt, protects the $x^{\vee}ar\partial nah$ (= *farr*) from Fraṇrasiian = Afrāsiyāb, who seeks to possess it.

Still a major obstacle, of course, is the fact that the name of Rostam is nowhere attested in the *Avesta*. Nevertheless, the point that I am making is that the concept of a national hero who guards the *farr*, if not Rostam himself, is actually attested in *Yašt* 19. The crucial passage comes after the narrative about the attempt of Fraṇrasiian = Afrāsiyāb to possess the $x^{\vee}ar\partial nah$ (= *farr*). In this passage of *Yašt* 19, there are words of praise for Lake Kạsaoiia and the Haētumant River that empties into this lake (66). It is in this river, as it empties into the lake, that the $x^{\vee}ar\partial nah$ abides in the "present," and this $x^{\vee}ar\partial nah$ will continue to be the bane for all "non-Aryan" [non-Iranian] nations (67–69). It is clear from this passage in *Yašt* 19 that the mythical Lake Vouru.kaša, abode of the $x^{\vee}ar\partial nah$ of the Keyānids, is identified with Lake Kạsaoiia.[16] And the remarkable fact is that Lake Kạsaoiia and the Haētumant River are identifiable with Lake Hamun and the Helmand River, which are the chief lake and river in the region of Sistān.[17]

Granted, from the standpoint of other hymns in the *Avesta* such as *Yašt* 9 and *Yašt* 17, the mythical Lake Vouru.kaša is localized elsewhere as Lake Čaēčasta = Chichast in West Iran.[18] But the point is that, already in the *Avesta,* one multiform of Lake Vouru.kaša, the abode of the $x^{\vee}ar\partial nah$ of the Keyānids, is clearly situated in eastern Iran, specifically Sistān, the native place of the hero Rostam himself.

Moreover, it has been argued that, before the Achaemenid conquest, in the period when *Yašt* 19 was composed, the "sacred space" of Zoroastrianism itself was centered in the region of Sistān, the basin of the Haētumant = Helmand River.[19] This "sacred space," known as the *Airiianem vaējo* (= Ariana in Greek), was watered by the river *Vaṇuhi*

---

[16] Christensen 1932.22–23; Duchesne-Guillemin 1972.63; Dumézil 1973.26, n3.
[17] Christensen 1932.22–23.
[18] Ibid. 23.
[19] Duchesne-Guillemin 1972.63, following Gnoli 1965a, 1967.7–39.

Dāitī (for example, *Yašt* 19.2), which has been identified as the Haētu-mant = Helmand.[20] In the *Life of Zoroaster* according to *Vičīrkart i dēnīk* (hereafter abbreviated as *VZ*),[21] this river is called *rōt i Veh Daitīk* 'stream of the Vaŋuhi Dāitī' (*VZ* 16), and it is here that Zoroaster himself witnessed the *xvarrah* = *farr* of Ohrmazd.

There is an important consequence of these findings for our under-standing of Rostam's role in the *Shāhnāma*. In the view of Iranists, from Nöldeke to Boyce, Rostam, as the hero of Sistān, was both extraneous to the legends of the Keyānids and a pre-Zoroastrian sur-vival. We have already seen, on more than one occasion, that Rostam's origin as the hero of Sistān is not after all incompatible with his role as protector of the Keyānids and of their *x*ᵛ*arənah* (= *farr*). We see also that there is nothing markedly non- or pre-Zoroastrian about Rostam either. Rostam, further, is not even incompatible with the traditions about Zoroaster. In this light, it is possible to challenge the opinion that Daqiqi is following a "religious" tradition that is "completely separate" from the tradition about Rostam[22] when he tells how Zāl and Rostam were converted to Zoroastrianism by King Goshtāsp, who had traveled to Sistān for this purpose (*Shāhnāma* VI 133.980–981, 987); earlier on in the narrative, we read that prince Esfandiyār had converted the rest of Iran (VI 122–123.830–836).

But there is perhaps an even more important consequence. We have already seen that the figure of Apąm Napāt in *Yašt* 19 is parallel to that of Rostam in the *Shāhnāma:* both guard the *x*ᵛ*arənah* (= *farr*) against Fraŋrasiian (= Afrāsiyāb), who keeps trying to possess it. The Avestan name *Apąm Napāt* means 'progeny of the waters', and it is cognate with the Indic name with the same meaning, *Apām Napāt* (for exam-ple, *Rig-Veda* 2.35).[23] In this light, we must consider the name *Rostam*. Instead of deriving the Pahlavi form *Rōtastaxm*[24] from an unattested Avestan form like **raoda-staxma* 'having the strength of growth [= *raoda*]',[25] it is possible to reconstruct an Avestan form like **raotas-*

[20] Duchesne-Guillemin 1972.63.
[21] Edited by Molé 1967.122–135.
[22] Maguire 1973.134.
[23] Nagy 1990b.99, 100–102; also Puhvel 1987.277–283.
[24] See Yarshater 1983.456.
[25] See Justi 1895.266, 512. For a discussion of the attempts to associate such an epithet with the hero Kərəsāspa, see Christensen 1932.135–136. Unfortunately, Chris-tensen's discussion is predicated on prosopographical principles, not taking into

taxma, which would mean 'having the strength of the stream [= *raoda-* or *raotah-*]'.[26] The component *-taxma* can be found in the name *Ātur-taxm* 'having the strength of fire'.[27] We have also seen it in the name Taxma Urupa = Ṭahmuraṣ, the second primordial king who represents the second or "warrior" function of society in myths conveyed by Indo-European languages. As for the *Rōtas-* of *Rōtastaxm,* we have already seen the Pahlavi word *rōt* 'stream' as *t* applies to the Helmand River itself, which is where Zoroaster is said to have witnessed the *xvarrah* = *farr* of Ohrmazd (*VZ* 16). Granted, the interpretation of **raotas-taxma-* as 'he who has the strength of the stream' does not correspond precisely to the meaning of *Apąm Napāt* 'child of the waters'. But the notion of 'child' may be conveyed by the relationship of Rostam's name to that of his mother: it has long been recognized that the first elements of *Rōtastaxm* and **Rōtābak* (= Persian *Rudāba*) are the same.[28] Thus the name of Rostam's mother conveys, I suggest, 'brightness of the stream' rather than 'brightness of growth'.

More must be said about Apąm Napāt and the Indic cognate of this figure, Apām Napāt. In Indic mythology, as is clear from the "Hymn to Apām Napāt" in the *Rig-Veda* (2.35), the god Apām Napāt is a multiform of the sun itself, the celestial fire that submerges in the waters that surround the universe at sunset and which is "born" again of these same waters at sunrise: hence the image of celestial fire as 'child of the waters'. In Indic ritual, there is a horse sacrifice in which the spirit of the immolated horse is pictured as setting with the sun, and the horse is then to be reborn from the waters *along with the sun at dawn* (for example, "Hymn to Apām Napāt," *Rig-Veda* 2.35.6).[29] In line with this pattern, the conventional epithet of Indic Apām Napāt is *āśuheman* 'driving swift horses' (*Rig-Veda* 2.35.1, etc.). So also with the

---

account the function of multiformity in mythmaking (on which see, e.g., Lord 1960.100).

[26] The possibility of reconstructing **raotas-taxma* was suggested to me in the course of a conversation with Martin Schwartz of the University of California, Berkeley. The Avestan form *raoda-* 'stream' represents a merger of **raotah* and **raodah-*: see Bartholomae 1904.1492 and 1495 respectively.

[27] See Justi 1895.52, 513.

[28] Ibid. viii; also Christensen 1932.141, n3; Nöldeke 1930.19; and Yarshater 1983.454.

[29] See Nagy 1990b.101.

Iranian Apə̄m Napāt in *Yašt* 19: at the moment he seizes the *x^varənah*
and dives with it into the depths of Lake Vouru.kaša, Apə̄m Napāt
is described as *auruuaṯ.aspa* 'having swift horses'. Elsewhere in the
Avesta, this epithet is reserved for the *huuar-* 'sun' itself (*Yašt* 10.90,
etc.).[30]

Having illustrated the specific Indo-Iranian heritage of themes concerning the Avestan Apə̄m Napāt, I will simply make a passing reference to the general Indo-European heritage of these same themes as
examined at length by Dumézil.[31] The scope of this book precludes
any detailed consideration of the comparative evidence, and I limit
myself here to observing that the Iranian myth of the seizure of *x^var-
ənah* by Apə̄m Napāt in *Yašt* 19 has numerous striking parallels in the
narrative traditions preserved in other Indo-European languages besides the Iranian.[32] In Roman traditions, for example, there is the story
of how the waters of the Lacus Albanus all of a sudden burst forth
violently, creating a river that flowed to the sea;[33] in Old Irish traditions, there is a parallel story of how the well of a figure called Nechtan
likewise burst forth, creating the River Bóand (Boyne), source of all
rivers of the world.[34] In both instances, the eruption of the waters is in
reaction to a violation of the principle of sovereignty as upheld by the
"first function," and this theme is paralleled, in the Iranian traditions,
by the triple eruption of Lake Vouru.kaša in reaction to the triple
attempted seizure of the *x^varənah* = *farr* by the Turanian King Fraŋrasiian = Afrāsiyāb (*Yašt* 19.56, 59, 62). The *x^varənah* = *farr* had been
placed in Lake Vouru.kaša by Apə̄m Napāt, the *Napāt* of whose name
is cognate with the Old Irish *Nechtan* and also with Latin *Neptūnus.* As
in the case of the river that issues from Nechtan's well, the *x^varənah* (=
farr) that escapes from Fraŋrasiian (= Afrāsiyāb) passes into a river, the
Haētumant = Helmand (*Yašt* 19.65–69), which is pictured as the source
of all the other rivers of the world (*Yašt* 19.67).

---

[30] As a name, *Auruuaṯ.aspa* (*Yašt* 5.105) is identical to the Lohrāsp of the *Shāhnāma.*
[31] Dumézil 1973.21–84.
[32] Ibid. 21–89; Puhvel 1987.277–283. On the Irish evidence, see also, besides
Dumézil 1973, Ford 1974.
[33] Dionysius of Halicarnassus *Roman Antiquities* 12.11–17; Plutarch *Camillus* 3–4;
Cicero *De divinatione* 1.100, 2.33; Livy 5.15.17.
[34] The testimony from the Irish *dindshenchas* traditions is collected by Ford 1974.

My purpose here in adducing, all too briefly, the comparative evidence of the Indo-Iranian and Indo-European parallels is to show that the figure of Rostam himself fits the inherited patterns concerning Apạm Napāt. Dumézil's investigation of these patterns led him to postulate a type of solar hero, one who vacillates between being either disruptive or regulated and helpful to society: such heroes are the Norse Hadingus, Irish Cú Chulainn, and Russian Il'ja.[35] I propose that we add to this list the Iranian hero Rostam.

Now that we see a solar aspect of the theme of Apạm Napāt and the $x^{v}arənah$, the corresponding theme of Rostam and the *farr* of the Keyānids leads us to consider the semantics of Rostam's name once again: we have seen that *Rōtastaxm* can be explained as 'having the strength of the stream', and that the name of Rostam's mother can be traced back to *Rōtābak* 'having the brightness of the stream'.[36] To round out the picture, it may be worth adding that Rostam begets *Sohrāb* 'having red brightness',[37] whose mother Tahmina shares the element -*taxm*- 'strength' with *Rōtastaxm* (= Rostam). In this connection, I cite a detail recorded from the oral tradition, that *Tahmina* brought the child *Sohrāb* out of the *daryā;* this word *daryā* bears the inherited meaning of 'river'.[38]

The solar themes associated with Rostam and the *farr* of the Keyānids is also suggested by the tradition of similes in the *Shāhnāma* comparing Rostam to the rising sun. For example, the people of Samangān have this to say as they catch sight of the approaching Rostam:

همی‌گفت هر کس که این رستمست   و یا آفـتـاب سـپـیـده دمست

Everybody said: "Is this Rostam   or is it the sun at dawn?"

II 172.n16

Bahman, before he hurls (in vain) a boulder at Rostam, has a similar reaction upon seeing him:

[35] Dumézil 1973.76.
[36] See Justi 1895.204, who adduces Burhān-i qāti' (in Vullers 1855/1864 II 1238b).
[37] Justi 1895.313.
[38] Reported by Page 1977.140; the folk etymology *sorkh-āb* 'red water' (name of a river in Kabul) may be a result of the story, not the cause of it.

بدل گفت بهمن که این رستمست   ویا آفـتـاب سپـیـده دمـست

Bahman said to himself: "This is   or the sun at dawn!"
either Rostam

VI 237.321

Sohrāb has this to say when he imagines the impact of his and Rostam's talents combined:

نبـایـد بگیـتـی کسی تـاجـور   چو رستم پدر باشد و من پـسـر
ستـاره چــرا بـر فــرازد کــلاه   چو روشن بود روی خورشید و ماه

Since Rostam is the father and I am   no one in the world is worthy of the
the son,   crown.
When the faces of the sun and moon   why should the stars flaunt their di-
are bright,   adems?

II 179.140–141

Rostam describes himself as follows:

به آوردگ بر سر افشان کنم   شب تیره از تیغ رخشان کنم

I light up the dark night with my   On the battlefield I scatter heads.
sword.

II 200.391

Another aspect of the solar themes associated with Rostam can be extracted from a comparison of the relationship between Achilles and his immortal horse Xanthos in the *Iliad*. In the case of Achilles and Xanthos, it has been argued that the hero and the divine horse represent two complementary aspects of an earlier unitary figure[39] and that this figure seems to be a cognate of the Indo-Iranian "child of the waters," as attested in the figures of the Iranian Apąm Napāt and the Indic Apām Napāt.[40] The horse Xanthos, by being immortal (*Iliad* 16.149–154), is implicitly a god; in this respect, he is like the Indic Apām Napāt, whose divine and equine associations have already been

[39] Nagy 1979.209–210.
[40] Nagy 1990b.100.

noted. The horse Xanthos, actually speaking to Achilles in *Iliad* 19, tells him that he, Achilles, is a mortal who therefore has to die, and this pronouncement happens at a point in the narrative where the hero has just been compared to Helios the sun-god (19.398), in a simile that is comparable to the similes that we have just examined in the case of Rostam. Thus Achilles in this context is like the Indic Apām Napāt, who is actually equated with the sun.

Before we actually compare the figures of Achilles and Xanthos to those of Rostam and Rakhsh, I wish to emphasize that the solar theme is pertinent to Achilles' horse Xanthos, who is born on the banks of the Okeanos (*Iliad* 16.151); the Okeanos is the cosmic fresh-water river that surrounds the universe, and the sun sets into and rises out of its waters (8.495 and 7.421–423 respectively). The mother of Xanthos was the equine harpy Podarge, who was impregnated by the wind Zephyros (16.150). It is important to notice that the blasts of Zephyros are emitted by Okeanos itself (*Odyssey* 4.567–568); in this sense, Xanthos is a stylized "child of the waters" analogous to the Indic/ Iranian concept of Apām Napāt/Apạm Napāt. In the case of the Indo-Iranian "child of the waters," however, it is clear that this figure is distinct from the horse(s) that he drives: as we have already seen, the Indic Apām Napāt is *āśuheman* 'driving swift horse(s)', while the Iranian Apạm Napāt shares with the *huuar-* 'sun' the epithet *auruuat̰.aspa* 'having swift horse(s)'. But the patterns of Indo-European solar mythology suggest that the solar figures of driver/rider on one hand and horse on the other can actually overlap. For example, the Greek word *phaéthōn* 'shining' can serve as the epithet of the sun-god Helios (*Iliad* 11.735, etc.), as the name of the hero who drove the chariot of Helios and plummeted to his death (Euripides, *Phaethon*), or the name of a horse that pulls the chariot of the dawn-goddess Eos (*Odyssey* 23.246).[41] Thus it is unimportant for comparative purposes that the Indo-Iranian "child of the waters" is distinct from his horse(s).

As we now begin to consider the case of Rostam and Rakhsh in the *Shāhnāma*, we may note first of all that the name of the hero's horse,

---

[41] See ibid. 249–250. A related point of interest is that Vedic *marya-*, when it serves as an epithet of the sun-god Sūrya, connotes that he is both the sexual partner and the horse of the dawn-goddess Uṣas (*Rig-Veda* 1.115.2, 7.76.3). This difficult Indic word *marya-* is cognate with the Avestan *mairiia-*.

Rakhsh, means 'bright' like *Phaéthōn.* More important, we find that, as
in the case of Achilles and Xanthos, there is an interplay of overlap and
distinctness between the hero Rostam and his horse Rakhsh. My focus
will be on four specific indications. The first is the description of
Rostam's acquisition of Rakhsh. The *Shāhnāma* presents this act of
acquisition as if it were the equivalent of possessing the *farr:* this horse
Rakhsh is the key to the salvation of Iran. As the herder of Rakhsh says
to Rostam when the hero asks the price of the horse,

برو راست کن روی ایران زمی   چنین داد پاسخ که گر رستمی

بدین بر تو خواهی جهان کرد راست   مر اینرا بر و بوم ایران بهاست

Thus he answered, saying: "If you
are Rostam,
The price for this one is the land and
region of Iran.

go, make straight the face of the
land of Iran, [riding] on him.
[Riding] upon him you will
straighten out the world."

II 54.83–84

There is a second indication in the fact that the characterization of
Rakhsh is so closely parallel to Rostam. They even share the same
epithets:

بزهره چو شیران که بیستون   بنیروی پیل و ببالا هیون

In strength he [Rakhsh] was an ele-
phant in stature a camel,

and in courage he was like a lion of
Mount Bisotun.

II 53.n4

These are precisely the attributes that distinguish the hero Rostam
himself.[42] The parallelism of the hero and horse even extends to the
level of action: for example, as Rostam begets Sohrāb, so Rakhsh
begets a foal that Sohrāb will choose for his own (II 255.16–29). A
third indication is that, in the course of Rostam's seven deeds, Rakhsh
communicates with Rostam on a near-human level (II 94–96.345–
370). We may compare the speech of Xanthos to Achilles in *Iliad* 19. A
fourth indication is that Rakhsh, like Xanthos, has special gifts of

[42] See Maguire 1973.104.

perception which the hero does not, such as the ability to see an ant on a black cloth from two miles' distance (*Shāhnāma* II 53.n4), and these gifts enable this wondrous animal to foresee the death of Rostam (VI 330–331.160–165). In this respect, too, we may compare the speech of Xanthos to Achilles in *Iliad* 19, where the immortal horse foresees the impending death of the hero.

For internal evidence of themes that relate Rostam to the Indo-Iranian "child of the water," who rescues the *farr* of kings, we may turn to the narratives that tell how Rostam *finds* or *rescues* national kings, the possessors of *farr*. For example, when Rostam is sent out by his father Zāl to bring back Key Qobād as the new national king, the hero finds Key Qobād seated in the shade on a throne *on the bank of a river* near the foot of Mount Alborz.

برو ریـخـتـه مـشـك ناب و گلاب   یکی تـخـت بـنـهـاده نزدیك آب

A throne was placed near the water;   pure musk and rosewater wafted over it.

II 58.133

There is also a variety of stories about the rescue(s) of Key Kāus by Rostam. In one story, where Key Kāus is captured and imprisoned by the king of Hāmāvarān and then rescued by Rostam, it is made explicit that Key Kāus loses his *farr* by virtue of his imprisonment (Mohl II 18.165); implicitly, then, his *farr* is restored when he is rescued by Rostam (II 145–285). In relating another rescue story, the *Bundahišn* (33) reports that, when Key Kāus attempts his ill-fated celestial ascension and plummets to the earth, he loses his *xvarr* = *farr*.[43] As we have seen, this theme recurs in the *Shāhnāma* (II 151.376). In a story transmitted by the Arabic sources (for example, Thaʿālibī p. 161), Key Kāus is captured and imprisoned by the King of Yemen and then rescued by Rostam. Key Kāus also takes back with him the daughter of the King of Yemen, called Suʿāba, as his new wife. Similarly in the story mentioned earlier, Key Kāus takes back with him the daughter of the King of Hāmāvarān, called Suʿāba, as a new wife. In the version preserved by the Arabic sources, there is an interesting detail that is vital to the

[43] Cf. Christensen 1932.62.

argument here: when Key Kāus is captured and imprisoned by the King of Yemen, thereby implicitly losing his *farr,* he is placed specifically *into a well* (Ṭabarī I p. 63). It is also implicit, then, that Rostam restores the *farr* of Key Kāus by rescuing him from a well, just as he establishes the *farr* of Key Qobād by finding him on the bank of a river.

These aquatic associations of Rostam and the *farr* are not fortuitous. According to the *Dēnkart* (9.22.7–12),[44] when Key Kāus attempted his celestial ascension, he not only lost his *xvarr* = *farr* but also had to hide in the depths of Lake Vouru.kaša. The messenger of the gods, Nēryō-sang, then pursued Key Kāus in order to kill him, but was dissuaded by the promise that Key Kāus would beget Siyāvosh who would beget Key Khosrow, the future killer of Frāsayāp = Afrāsiyāb and thereby the future savior of Iran. It is no coincidence that Afrāsiyāb, fleeing from Key Khosrow, also hides in the depths of Lake Chichast (Ṭabarī I pp. 605ff.),[45] which as we have seen is the West Iranian localization of the mythical Lake Vouru.kaša. With the help of a figure called Hōm,[46] Key Khosrow entices Afrāsiyāb out of the lake and then kills him (Thaʿālibī pp. 226–234, *Shāhnāma* V 368.2241ff.).[47]

These themes bring us back to *Yašt* 19, which relates how the *xᵛarənah* was taken by Apạm Napāt down to the depths of Lake Vouru.kaša, which in this case is identified with the East Iranian Lake Kạsaoiia = Hamun in Sistān, the homeland of Rostam. *Yašt* 19 also relates how the *xᵛarənah* was to be united with Key Qobād, Key Kāus, and the other Keyānids (19.71), especially with Key Khosrow, who will kill Afrāsiyāb (74–77), and with (Key) Goshtāsp, who will kill Arjāsp, the son of Afrāsiyāb (84–87). The *xᵛarənah* will also one day be united with the eschatological Saošiiant 'savior' known as As-tuuaṭ.ərəta (89). I infer that, for these unions between the *xᵛarənah* and the king to happen, the *xᵛarənah* has to be brought up from the depths of Lake Vouru.kaša by Apạm Napāt, just as Apạm Napāt had taken it

---

[44] On which see ibid. 78–79 and the rebuttal by Dumézil 1971.206–208, especially p. 207, n1.

[45] Cf. Christensen 1932.116.

[46] In *Dēnkart* 7.4.29 (ed. Molé 1967), the ritual drink *hōm* is drawn by Zoroaster from the river Dāitī. As we have seen, the Dāitī is identifiable with the river Helmand, which empties into Hamun, the eastern Iranian localization of the mythical Lake Vouru.kaša.

[47] Cf. Christensen 1932.116.

down in the first place. In other words, I propose that Apąm Napāt implicitly confers $x^v ar\partial nah$ upon the kings—which is parallel to the ways in which the *farr* of the Keyānids can be conferred upon them by Rostam and his Sistanian ancestors.

In one case, moreover, it would seem that Apąm Napāt brings up from the watery depths not just the $x^v ar\partial nah$ but the recipient of the $x^v ar\partial nah$ himself. It is explicitly said in *Yašt* 19 that Astuuaṯ.ərəta himself will rise up from the waters of Kąsaoiia/Vouru.kaša (92). I infer from this explicit pronouncement that Astuuaṯ.ərəta emerges already united with the $x^v ar\partial nah$. We have already seen the reverse of this process in the story that tells how Key Kāus went down into the depths of Lake Vouru.kaša after he lost his *xvarr* = *farr*. We have also seen the story that tells how Key Kāus was imprisoned in a well. Now the myth of the $x^v ar\partial nah$ and Lake Vouru.kaša, as Dumézil has shown, has striking parallels in Roman and Irish myths.[48] Significantly, in the corresponding Irish myth, the body of water is not a lake but a well.[49] Thus *lake* and *well* seem to be multiforms in this myth, and the retrieval of Key Kāus from the well by Rostam can be considered a parallel to the implicit retrieval of $x^v ar\partial nah$ from Lake Vouru.kaša by Apąm Napāt. Moreover, since Lake Kąsaoiia/Vouru.kaša is in the homeland of Rostam, it may even be true that this hero had been the Apąm Napāt himself in earlier versions of the myth. Such an identification would account for the parallelism, already discussed, between the meanings of the names Apąm Napāt on the one hand and Rostam/Rudāba on the other.

It remains to ask why Key Kāus descended into Lake Vouru.kaša after he lost the $x^v ar\partial nah$. The answer may be that there is a perpetual store of $x^v ar\partial nah$ at the bottom of the lake, since there is enough of it to accommodate all Iranians, born and unborn (as Afrāsiyāb himself is quoted as saying in *Yašt* 19.57, 60, 63; compare also 19.68).[50] Whoever

---

[48] Dumézil 1973.21–89.

[49] Ibid. 21–38; also Ford 1974.

[50] For the related theme of the $x^v ar\partial nah$ (or, alternatively, the embryonic hero) lodged in a reed that grows in a lake, see Dumézil 1971.218–220. In light of Dumézil's emphasis on the epithet *vərəθrajan*-'obstacle-destroying' in this context, it may be worth noting the application of this epithet to the eschatological savior Saošiiant as he emerges from Lake Kąsaoiia in *Vidēvdāt* 19.5.

loses his *x˘arənah* may hope to recover it at the bottom of the lake and then to emerge again, ready to start anew. Since the life of Key Kāus was spared, we may wonder if this is what happened in his case.[51] By contrast, *Yašt* 19 shows that Afrāsiyāb failed when he made three attempts to seize the *x˘arənah* from the bottom of the lake. Perhaps the story of his final attempt to evade Key Khosrow by hiding in Lake Chichast/Vouru.kaša is a variation on this theme: implicitly, Afrāsiyāb may have been trying one last time to seize the *farr* of the Keyānids.[52]

As for Rostam, guardian of the *farr* of the Keyānids, we may bring this discussion to an end by restating what has already been argued in numerous ways: that his role is not only heroic but also central to the very concept of Keyānid kingship. Although in the text he is presented as an outsider to the kingship in the sense that he is disqualified from becoming a king himself, we see finally that he is in fact an insider to the very traditions that represent him this way. He is, after all, central not only to the Iranian heroic tradition but also to the Book of Kings, both of which are incorporated in the monumental *Shāhnāma* of Ferdowsi.

[51] For the doubtless related theme of Key Kāus and the elixir of life, see Dumézil 1971.190–196.

[52] Curiously, Afrāsiyāb is associated with other aquatic themes as well: according to the *Bundahišn* (20.34), he was responsible for the "construction" of a thousand freshwater wells and of the Helmand River itself; cf. Christensen 1932.86–87.

CHAPTER 7

The Concept of Premature and Immature Fatherhood in the Story of Rostam and Sohrāb

The story of Sohrāb and Rostam explores the very limits of how far Rostam must go, as hero of the *Shāhnāma,* to protect the king, and, by extension, society itself, in his role as guardian of the *farr.* For Rostam to outlive his son Sohrāb is tragic enough, but for him to become Sohrāb's killer tests Rostam's very stature as a hero. Such a testing of the hero's identity, however, is part of a larger pattern. There are stories in other Indo-European narrative traditions that are so strikingly parallel to this particular story that one can only conclude that they all stem from a common heritage. I propose here to compare the story of Rostam and Sohrāb with the Middle Irish tale *Aiged Aenfhir Aífe* 'The Tragic Death of Aífe's Only Son'[1] and the Old High German fragment of the *Lay of Hildebrand.*[2] I shall argue that the parallel story patterns in all three traditions express the idea of a particular kind of extremity or excessiveness, similar to what we have examined in our earlier consideration of Herakles, that characterizes the figure of the central hero in various national epic narratives. Such a figure, as I shall also argue, falls into a pattern of immature behavior as dramatized in rituals and aetiological myths of initiation.

In the process of comparing the three myths taken from the Persian, Middle Irish, and Old High German traditions, I propose first to summarize the essential outlines of each myth, underscoring those parts of the individual narrative that we will compare in detail with re-

---

[1] Editions and variants discussed in Cross 1950.
[2] Text as printed in the edition of Mettke 1976.78–84; cf. Braune 1969.84–85.

lated narratives. I then offer an explanation for why these narrative traditions all require their central heroes to kill their sons, concentrating
on finding the reasons for Rostam's killing of his son, Sohrāb. The case
is strengthened on two fronts: (1) a Greek aetiological myth connected
with a rite of initiation called the Apatouria, and (2) Persian myths of
other antagonistic father-son relationships within the *Shāhnāma* itself,
especially the relationship between Lohrāsp and Goshtāsp, and also
between Goshtāsp and Esfandiyār.

Let us begin with a compressed plot summary of the story of
Rostam and Sohrāb as it is told in the *Shāhnāma* of Ferdowsi.[3] Rostam
goes on a hunting expedition completely alone (with the exception of
his horse Rakhsh) outside of Iran, into the Turanian wildland. After he
has killed an onager, he, as is his custom, roasts it over a fire using a
tree as a spit, eats it all, and then falls asleep. Rakhsh, in the meantime,
is roaming free without his bridle, when some Turkomans [i.e., Tura-
nians], seeing that Rostam is off his guard, use this opportunity to steal
Rakhsh. When Rostam wakes up and finds that Rakhsh has disap-
peared, he is devastated. He goes to the city, Samangān, to find his
horse and is invited by the king to stay with a promise of help. The
king's daughter, Tahmina, comes to him in the middle of the night and
tells him that she is from heroic stock:

ز پـشـت هـژبـر و پلـنگان مـنم(

('I am from the race of lions and leopards')[4] and that absolutely no one
has ever laid eyes on her up to this point

نبیند جزین مرغ و ماهی مرا

('No one sees me, save the fish and fowl').[5] She has kept herself for
Rostam because she has heard so much about his prowess *as a hunter
roaming the borders, completely alone.* Tahmina says,

شنیدم همی داستانت بسی   که از شیر و دیو و نهنگ و پلنگ
نترسی و هستی چنین تیزچنگ   شب تیره تنها بتوران شوی
بگردی بران مرز و هم نغنوی   بتنها یکی گور بریان کنی
هوا را بشمشیر گریان کنی

---

[3] *Shāhnāma* II 167–250.1–1059.
[4] Ibid. II 175.71.
[5] Ibid. II 175.83.

That lion, *div,* crocodile, and leopard	Many stories I have heard over and over about you.
During the dark night, alone, you go to Turān;	you fear not, and you are so sharp clawed.
Alone you roast an onager,	you roam that border, and you never even sleep.
	you make the air weep with your sword.

II 175.74–77

Tahmina's name seems to share the same root as the adjective *tahamtan,* meaning 'brave-bodied' or 'warlike', an epithet used primarily for Rostam.[6] She then proposes to him that, if he were to impregnate her, she would get him back his horse. Rostam accepts her proposition and then, the next day, when they part, *he gives her an armband with the instructions that, should she bear a son, she is to put this armband on the child so that his father could recognize him.* A son is born. He is named Sohrāb and grows in the same extraordinary way as his father, looking a year old when he is only a month old, using weapons when he is only three, and other such characteristics that mark him as a special hero. When he learns who his father is, he leaves Turān, with a Turanian host, for the purpose of invading Iran, overthrowing the Shāh of Iran Key Kāus and putting Rostam on the Iranian throne. He then plans to overthrow Afrāsiyāb, the king of Turān and enemy of Iran, and rule Turān himself. Father and son *will rule the world,* in a manner of speaking, being such a powerful, combined force:

نـشـانـمـش بر گاه کاوس شاه	برستم دهم تخت و گرز و کلاه
ابـا شـاه روی اندر آرم بروی	از ایران بتوران شوم جنگ جوی
سـرنیــزه بگــذارم از آفتـاب	بگیرم سـر تـخت افـراسـیـاب
نـبـایـد بگـیـتـی کسـی تاجور	چو رستم پدر باشد و من پسر

To Rostam I will give the throne, mace, and crown.	I will seat him upon the throne of Key Kāus.

---

[6] In a few instances, the Zoroastrian prince Esfandiyār has *tahamtan* as an epithet as well (*Shāhnāma* V 110.651, V 190.408, V 208.726, V 211.790, V 221.64 variant K, I, VI), which is probably to be connected with the parallelisms in theme between stories about Esfandiyār and Rostam.

From Iran I will go to Turān, seeking battle;

there I will face the *shāh*.

I will seize the throne of Afrāsiyāb;

I will raise my spearhead above the
sun.

Since Rostam is the father and I am
the son,

no one else in the world is worthy
of the crown.

II 179.137–140

Afrāsiyāb is of course delighted to have such a fine young champion
try to conquer Iran for him. He is even more delighted at the prospect
that, once pitted against his father, Sohrāb would overcome him,
thereby leaving Iran completely defenseless, having lost its *pahlavān-e
jahān* 'champion of the world'. *Sohrāb, then, must not know who his father
is.* As Sohrāb invades Iran, he wreaks havoc on the outskirts, fighting
the "amazon" Gordafrid, and laying waste her territory. The Iranian
throne panics and summons Rostam to help in this state of emergency.
Since Rostam does not take any threat from Turān seriously, he does
not immediately obey the *shāh*'s command, but feasts drunkenly for
three days instead. When he finally does come as summoned, the *shāh,*
because of the delay, is furious with him and publicly dishonors him.
With these parting words, Rostam withdraws in anger, leaving Iran to
fend for itself:

منم گفت شیر اوژن و تـاج بخش
چرا دست یازد بمن طوس کیست
نگیـن گرز و مغفر کلاه منست
چو خشم آورم شاه کاوس کیست
زمیـن بنده و رخش گاه منست

He said: "I am the lion-conqueror
and crown bestower!

Who is Shāh Kāus when I am angry?

Indeed who is Ṭōs to lay a hand on
me?

The earth is my slave, and Rakhsh
is my throne,

my mace is my seal-ring, and my
helmet is my crown!"

II 200.388–390

Rostam, however, fearful of being accused of cowardice, allows
himself to be persuaded to fight this Turanian terror. Sohrāb once
again terrorizes the Iranian host, forcing it to scatter and causing
chaos. Rostam and Sohrāb meet for a one-on-one confrontation. They

fight, first with weapons, then in a wrestling match. On the second day, Sohrāb overpowers Rostam in a second wrestling match and is about to finish him off when *Rostam tricks him* by telling him that it is an Iranian tradition that one has to defeat the opponent twice before one can take his head. Sohrāb accepts this lie and cheerfully runs off to hunt down an antelope. Rostam, meanwhile, exhausted, asks *khodā* or 'God' to give him back his former strength, *for he used to have such density that his feet would sink into rocks.* Finally, on the third day, having *tricked* Sohrāb out of his victory, Rostam kills him, only then to learn the sad truth about his identity. Overcome with grief, Rostam asks Key Kāus to restore his son's life, but the *shāh* refuses on grounds that two such outstanding champions would be a threat to the throne:

اگر زنده مانـد چنـان پیلتن
هـلاك آورد بـی گـمـانـی مرا
نـــــازیـم پاداش او جز به بد

شـود پـشـت رسـتم بنیروترا
اگر یك زمـان زو بمن بد رسد

If such an elephant-bodied one remains alive
and without doubt he will bring destruction to myself.
We shall not reward him, but with evil.

Rostam's back will become strengthened
If some time evil befalls me from him

II 242.968–970

   As sad as the outcome may have been, Rostam was only doing what he had to do. He is, after all, the defender of the Iranian throne, and must live up to his epithet of *tājbakhsh* 'crown-bestower'—always a kingmaker, never a king (II 96.383, II 104.533, III 189.2887, and so on). Were Sohrāb to succeed in his quest to put Rostam on the Iranian throne and himself on the Turanian, he would have upset the entire order of things. Rostam, though he is amply qualified, is not meant to sit on the Iranian throne—only to defend it. This is not only his "destiny" but also the thematic requirement of the tradition. Achilles does not displace Agamemnon, Siegfried does not displace Gunther, Herakles does not displace King Eurystheus—even though all these heroes could easily overthrow the sovereigns they are serving. As the aforementioned herdsman who reared the steed Rakhsh tells the hero

at the moment when Rostam first sees Rakhsh and inquires about the
price of such a magnificent beast,

چنـیـن داد پاسخ که گر رستمی   بــرو راست کـن روی ایـران زمی
مر اینرا بر و بوم ایران بهاست   بدین بر تو خواهی جهان کرد راست

| Thus he answered, saying: "If you are Rostam, | go, make straight the face of the land of Iran, [riding] on him. |
| The price for this one is the land and region of Iran. | [Riding] upon him you will straighten out the world." |

II 54.83–84

In defending the throne, Rostam is obliged to protect Key Kāus,
even though the hero was publicly dishonored by the king, and Rostam is constrained not to wrest the throne away from Key Kāus, even
though he could do so with ease. Rostam, as he once explains to the
former *shāh,* Key Qobād, is plainly not the type to rule, because he is
too busy defending the empire:

تهمتن بدو گـفـت کای شـهـریار   تـرا رزم جـسـتـن نیاید بـکـار
من و رخش و کوپال و برگستوان   هـمـانـا نـدارنـد بـا من توان

| Tahamtan [Rostam] said to him "O King, | seeking battle does not become you. |
| With myself and Rakhsh, mace and horse-armor, | surely they have no power against me." |

II 60.189–190

I suggest that Rostam, in this very special role of *pahlavān-e jahān*
'champion of the world', the person who single-handedly keeps chaos
at a distance, fits a narrative pattern known in other cultures as the
story of the Black Hunter. Mention has already been made of Vidal-
Naquet's essay "The Black Hunter," about the initiation of Athenian
ephebes, the city's unmarried young men, whose main task was to
patrol frontiers and to engage in skirmishes.[7] As we have seen, young
Athenians served as light-armed ephebes before they joined the heavy-
armed hoplites of the city's military force; in the analogous Spartan in-

---

[7] See Chapter 5.

stitution of the *krupteia* 'secret band', male adolescents policed Sparta's frontiers in skirmishes.

One of the many aspects of the ritual complex of ancient Athenian initiation was the cutting of the adolescent's hair, performed on the third day of the festival called the Apatouria. According to a myth connected with the ritual of the Apatouria, there is a conflict between the Athenians and Boeotians, and it is agreed that it should be settled by a duel. The Boeotian king, Xanthos 'the fair one', is to fight the Athenian, Melanthos 'the black one'. As they are fighting, Melanthos cried out, "Xanthos, you do not play according to the rules—there is someone at your side!" When Xanthos looks around at his side, Melanthos steals this opportunity to kill his opponent.[8]

The festival of the Apatouria commemorates and is ostensibly named after this *apatē* 'wile, deception', and the hero Melanthos serves as a model for the young ephebes. Vidal-Naquet points out that this story takes place in the frontier region; centers on an *apatē* 'trick' achieved in single combat, which is in direct contrast to the activity of "fair" hoplite fighting on even terms; and associates the hero with the color black. At least two of the details highlighted by Vidal-Naquet can be seen in the story of Rostam and Sohrāb. Their battle, too, takes place in the frontier regions, and they fight in single combat, in the course of which Rostam kills Sohrāb by deceit. In fact, Rostam's trick is similar to that of Melanthos, in that it involves his lying about what is fair in combat.

A parallel story exists in the Middle Irish tale known as the *Aiged Aenfhir Aífe*, 'The Tragic Death of Aífe's Only Son', in which the hero Cú Chulainn kills his son Conlai (or Conlaoch) in single combat. The adolescent, Cú Chulainn, is being instructed in feats of arms in a peripheral region called Letha. In the course of this period of testing, he single-handedly fights with an "amazon" called Aífe. When she is about to get the upper hand, he *tricks* her by shouting out that she has just lost her chariot along with its horses and charioteer. Catching her off guard, he spares her life on the condition that she bear him a son.

---

[8] Hellanicus in Jacoby 1923.323a F 23. For a list of other sources, see Vidal-Naquet 1986a.123–124, n15. On the use of myth in traditional societies as an "explanation" or *aetiology* for ritual, see Nagy 1990a.117–118.

Before he departs for home, *he gives her a thumb ring with the instructions that, when it fits the son who shall be born of their union, he is to be sent to Ireland to seek his father,* but he is not to identify himself to anyone under any circumstances nor refuse anyone a fight. When the child, Conlai, is seven years old, he goes to the borders of Ulster in search of his father, Cú Chulainn. Because Conlai is so skillful and terrifying, Conchobar, the king of Ulster, refuses him entry. Conlai persists. Among all the Ulstermen, only Cú Chulainn challenges the boy. Conlai thrusts Cú Chulainn three times between two stones, and Cú Chulainn's *feet sink into the stone up to the ankle. Cú Chulainn then "played the boy foul" with his special weapon called the gae bolga, that none other had, and disemboweled his son.* Before he dies, Conlai says that if he had but five years among the Ulstermen, he would have slaughtered all the warriors of the world for Ulster, *and the Ulstermen would rule as far as Rome.*

Like Rostam, Cú Chulainn gives his son a band (for the thumb, in this case) so that he may recognize him, and, like Rostam, he kills his son by way of deceit. Also like Rostam, his feet sink into stone. Conlai shares the same sort of overwhelming fighting ability that Sohráb has, which makes all warrior feats seem like child's play. Note especially how Sohráb will hunt or wantonly kill several warriors after he has already exhausted his father in single-handed combat. Conlai also, like Sohráb, wants to make his father ruler of the world. In later versions of the story, Conlai, like Sohráb, even reveals his identity at the time of his death.

In the fragmentary ninth-century Old High German *Lay of Hildebrand,* Hildebrand, when he confronts his son Hadubrand in battle, asks him who his father is. Hadubrand tells him that his father is Hildebrand, who had left him when he was a baby, to serve as Theodoric's champion: *degano dechisto miti Deotrichhe / her war eo folches at ente: imo was eo fehta ti leop: / chud was her . . . chonnem mannum* 'he was the dearest of the warriors with Theodoric; he was always foremost among men; to him the fight was ever too dear; he was known . . . among bold men'.[9] *Hildebrand then takes from his arm a twisted ring and*

---

[9] *Lay of Hildebrand* lines 26–28. Thanks to Stephen A. Mitchell for permission to use his unpublished English translation of the Old High German text.

gives it to Hadubrand, who then accuses Hildebrand of being *ummet spaher, / spenis mih mit dinem wortum, wili mih dinu speru werpan / pist also gialtet man, so du ewin inwit fortos* 'greatly cunning, enticing me with your words, wishing to hurl a spear at me. You have become so old a man, that you ever have cunning on your mind'.[10] Hildebrand then tells Hadubrand that he has spent the last thirty years wandering and that now he must be cut down by his son. They begin to fight, and that is the end of the fragment. We may infer that Hildebrand killed Hadubrand because he survives into other stories in the epic tradition—stories that postdate this one in terms of their own narrative logic.

Another version of this Germanic story, the thirteenth-century Old Norse *Saga of Thidrek of Bern*, has a distinctly happy outcome:

> An aging "Hildibrand" engages his son, "Alibrand," in combat; the father had been instructed how to recognize the son, while the son cannot ascertain the identity of the father during the combat. After the father defeats the son in a fair fight, the son almost succeeds in killing his unknown father *by way of a trick*, only to be thwarted in time and forced to reveal his name, just as the father reveals his. At this point, father and son are happily reunited.[11]

The similarities between the Old High German and the Old Norse versions are striking, but even the differences bring out a common theme: both versions emphasize the element of trickery, though the trickery in the Old Norse version, unlike any other of the stories that we have already seen, is undertaken by the son, not the father.

The Germanic stories and the analogous Irish and Iranian stories are all preoccupied with the topic of divided loyalties, where a warrior's obligations to his lord are played off against a father-son relationship. This relationship in fact transcends the specific topic that continues to be the focus of our attention, that of a hero's being forced actually to kill his son in the line of duty and loyalty to his lord. For the moment, then, let us broaden the scope of inquiry and examine other father-son relationships within the *Shāhnāma* that may be comparable to that of Rostam and Sohrāb.

[10] *Lay of Hildebrand* lines 39–41.
[11] Translation of lines 406–409 in Haymes 1988.248–250.

Rostam himself seems to have come from a line of fathers trying to kill off their sons. After all, his father Zāl was rejected at birth by his own father Sām, and exposed in the desert because he was born with white hair. Zāl was saved by the Simorgh, and once he reached manhood was accepted by his father Sām. Upon finding his son, Sām is only too happy to relinquish his kingdom and ride off to fight the Gorgsārs, leaving Zāl to keep order. It seems that Zāl and Sām have a symbiotic relationship, for one is content to stay home and rule while the other goes out and fights. Sām, like Rostam, plays the role of kingmaker, while Zāl plays the role of ruler *and does not fight*. If both wanted to play the same role, there would be conflict between them, and their kingdom would fall into chaos.[12]

The kind of conflict that would take place between father and son if both were to assume roles that are near-identical in matters of state (that is, if both were to stay on the throne and rule, or if both were to go out and defend the throne and fight) is expressed by the relationship of the Zoroastrian hero-prince Esfandiyār with his father, King Goshtāsp, and also by the relationship of Goshtāsp with his own father, King Lohrāsp. What follows is a brief outline of the stories of Lohrāsp, Goshtāsp, and Esfandiyār, as retold in the *Shāhnāma*.

Lohrāsp, once he has ascended the throne, proclaims that his reign as king will be marked by the rejection of aggressiveness and the promotion of peace. In fact Lohrāsp is so opposed to aggression and war that he prefers the grandsons of Kāus to his own rash son Goshtāsp. This preference, of course, angers Goshtāsp to the point that he demands of his father that he relinquish the throne and pass it down to him. Lohrāsp refuses, because he is opposed to the violence of Goshtāsp. Goshtāsp, enraged at his father for not agreeing with him, leaves Iran and goes into self-imposed exile in Byzantium. When he first comes to Byzantium, he has great difficulty in getting any sort of gainful employment because of his belligerent nature and excessive strength. The only tasks that he is able to undertake successfully in Byzantium are hunting, fighting monstrous beasts, and winning brides for less heroic men (*Shāhnāma* VI 24–45.281–598). Hence

---

[12] This type of relationship in Iranian epic traditions is explored further in Chapter 8.

Goshtāsp has taken on the role of an extremely aggressive and warlike hero. He finally comes back to Iran after several adventures and does take over the throne, leaving a "little corner" for his father to rule. He remains aggressive until his father dies and then loses his aggressiveness to the point that he does not even avenge the death of his brother Zarēr. He leaves that task to his son Esfandiyār and his nephew Nastur. Goshtāsp then promises to give Esfandiyār the throne if he were to rescue his sisters, who are being held captive by the Turanian king, Arjāsp. In the course of this quest, Esfandiyār undergoes a lengthy set of ordeals, known as his famous *Haft Khwān*. He fights fabulous beasts and enemies, testing his prowess as a hunter and fighter. When he returns, however, he demands the throne from his father, but his father once again sends him out on another ordeal, promising him the throne on his return. This time he dispatches him to bring Rostam back in chains, knowing full well that Esfandiyār is fated to be killed if he attempts this endeavor (*Shāhnāma* VI 220.49–58). Esfandiyār is of course killed in his famous combat with Rostam, leaving his father to rule in peace, without a son demanding the throne before his time.

If we examine this chain of events, we see a cycle where the son prematurely demands the throne from his father, and then, once denied, goes off on his own, undergoing several ordeals that test his prowess as a fighter and hunter. What seems to be happening is that the father is not ready to abdicate but instead, since the son is a threat, contrives to have him sent away until the father is ready to have the son back and give him the throne. The son bides his time by taking on the role of hero/kingmaker while the father continues to rule. If either one or the other is not content with this relationship, then one of them has to be removed permanently—either the father will kill the son or the son will kill the father. In the case of Lohrāsp and Goshtāsp, they both, be it ever so grudgingly, manage to work out a relationship, so that they may coexist harmoniously, whereas with Goshtāsp and Esfandiyār, Goshtāsp feels it necessary to have Esfandiyār killed. As for Sām and Zāl, though they stem from a line of heroes and are "kings" only in the most provincial sense, still, since Sām would rather fight Gorgsārs, he is more than happy to leave Zāl minding the principality. No overt conflict arises between Rostam and Zāl so long as Rostam is far too busy maintaining his role as *pahlavān-e jahān* or the 'champion of the world'.

One can see, then, that if Sohrāb's plan were to be carried out, that is, if he and Rostam would rule the world together, having overthrown both Key Kāus and Afrāsiyāb, it would not work. There would be a conflict of interest between father and son, because both heroes would take on the aggressive, fighting role, leaving neither to administer the empire. Unless they could work out a symbiotic relationship, unlikely in terms of the tradition, they are a threat to one another and, consequently, one must cancel out the other.

I propose to go one step further in this scenario. When Rostam engenders Sohrāb, he does so while he is out hunting, completely alone, outside the boundaries of organized society. As we have seen from the outline of the story, the woman Tahmina, with whom Rostam has intercourse, is so virginal that she has up to that point been seen by no one, and yet she is now so bold as to walk into the hero's bedroom and proposition him. She wants him because he has such a fine reputation *as a hunter*. If we look at her Old Irish counterpart, Aífe, the "amazon" whom Cú Chulainn conquers in combat before he ravishes her, we can understand that Tahmina is somewhat of an "amazon" or huntress figure herself—someone so virginal as to be like an Artemis. I stress her particular interest in Rostam as a hunter, as opposed to a warrior, which literally does make her an Artemis-like figure. Recent studies of various Greek Artemis myths have shown that if a hero mixes sex or courtship with the activity of hunting, he is bound to suffer dire consequences, inasmuch as hunting counts as a rite of passage, which is invalidated by premature heterosexual activity.[13]

There is no explicit indication that the Persian hero Rostam, by virtue of engaging in the activity of a hunt, is undergoing a rite of passage. But the points of comparison with the Greek narrative, especially the details about sexual relationships with the Artemis-like figure, Tahmina, do suggest that Rostam's patterns of hunting amount to an epic stylization of an ordeal of maturation. Though in the *Shāhnāma* Rostam lives a very long time, he never becomes a member of adult

[13] Rubin and Sale 1983, 1984.

society in the sense that he does not fight as a member of the organized army; rather, he is separate, fighting alone, much like an ephebe who guards the borders and specializes in sneak attacks.

Rostam fathers Sohrāb only because he wants his horse back, not because he wants to raise an heir. Like Achilles and Cú Chulainn, he is so preoccupied with his current reputation as the absolutely best warrior that, given a choice, he prefers death over a life without unwilting fame and honor.[14] We can see this attitude in the famous story of the battle between Rostam and Esfandiyār. When the wondrous bird Simorgh warns Rostam that whoever kills Esfandiyār is fated to die shortly afterward, Rostam replies that he prefers an early death to dishonor:

و گـر بـاز مـانـم بـجـایی ز جنگ   مرا کـشـتـن آسانتر آید ز ننگ

| of my staying back in any place of battle. | To be killed comes easier to me than the shame |

VI 297.1275

Rostam, like Achilles and Cú Chulainn, makes it inevitable that there will be no hero like him. It is almost as if these heroes, these premature or rather immature fathers, go out of their way to ensure that they are one of a kind in their epic traditions. There was no hero as strong before them, nor will there be one as strong after them—of that we may be certain.

The comparative evidence of cognate narrative traditions, then, suggests that a child conceived in the course of a hunt is doomed from the very start, because he should never have been born in the first place. What better epic device is there than to have the father resolve the problem or undo the mistake by killing the child, thereby undoing his child's life? Both the Persian Sohrāb and the Irish Conlai are a menace to their fathers in that they threaten the community that their fathers are protecting. More than that, they are also nightmarish versions of their fathers' physical powers. When they fight their fa-

---

[14] Achilles: *Iliad* 9.413. Cú Chulainn: p. 26 in the edition of the *Táin Bó Cúalnge* by O'Rahilly (1967), with translation at p. 164.

thers, they can destroy them with astonishing ease. Their fathers have to use craft or cunning in order to survive the battle and hence have to resort to deceiving their sons, taking advantage of youthful and trusting innocence. Neither Rostam nor Cú Chulainn looks very "heroic" after these episodes.

CHAPTER 8

Father-Son Dioscurism as a Model
of Authority in the *Shāhnāma*

While the father-son relationship in the story of heroes like Rostam and Sohrāb is doomed from the start, it serves as a foil for another kind of father-son relationship in stories of kings. Where kings are involved, this relationship translates into an ultimate model of authority. This is not to say that father-son relationships are without tensions in the case of Iranian narrative traditions about kings. Still, whatever tension there is tends toward resolution, not doom. An apt way to describe such tension is to call it "father-son dioscurism."

The term *dioscurism* is taken from the Greek name *Dioskouroi,* which means 'children of Zeus' or 'children of the Sky', and which is applied to the divine twins known as Kastor and Polydeukes in Greek myth and ritual, or Castor and Pollux in Romanized versions of the myth. In an influential book, *The Divine Twins: An Indo-European Myth in Germanic Tradition,* Donald Ward uses this term to describe a broad range of patterns that exist in myths about twins.[1] Specifically, he finds a complementarity in behavior, where one twin tends to be aggressive and dynamic while the other one is passive and static. For example, the Roman Castor was characterized as warlike, rash, and hot-tempered, preoccupied with going afield to fight, while his twin brother Pollux was peaceful and docile, disposed to staying at home and minding domestic affairs.[2] Although Ward's book concentrates on

[1] Ward 1968.
[2] Ibid. 23.

occurrences of this pattern in Indo-European languages, especially the Germanic traditions, he shows that it occurs in a wide variety of other cultures as well. A notable example is the biblical narrative of the twins Esau and Jacob in *Genesis* 25:27, where Esau is a strenuous huntsman, while Jacob is a placid shepherd.[3]

Ward's model of dioscurism can actually be applied to dyads that are not twins. For example, Linda Clader has shown that the Homeric heroes Agamemnon and Menelaos in the *Iliad,* who are brothers but not twins, behave in a dioscuric pattern that is analogous to that of the Indic twins Nakula and Sahadeva in the epic *Mahābhārata.*[4] These Indic heroes, as Stig Wikander has suggested, are an epic hypostasis of the Indic Divine Twins known as the *Aśvinau,* who are characterized as generally the same when they are considered together but who are dioscuric when they are considered apart, so that one will be in the light when the other is in the dark, one will be alive when the other is dead, and so on.[5] In the case of Nakula and Sahadeva, their dioscurism can be seen in more detail: "When they do function together, their diction and themes tend to be identical, but when they are apart the epithets and themes may be more specialized (for example, together Nakula and Sahadeva both have warrior epithets, but Sahadeva alone never does; Sahadeva is wise and brilliant, but Nakula seldom is; Nakula alone always is the most beautiful, but together both brothers are beautiful; Draupadī is the wife of both, but only Nakula rescues her)."[6] There is a strikingly similar pattern in the Homeric portrayal of the brothers Agamemnon and Menelaos: taken together, they look the same, but, taken separately, they are dioscuric in their relationships. For example, both are called Atreidai, sons of Atreus, but the singular epithet Atreides belongs primarily to Agamemnon. Also, Agamemnon is frequently referred to as *anax* 'king', but Menelaos, never; or again, Menelaos is *xanthos* 'blond', Agamemnon, never.[7]

The findings of Dale Sinos concerning the complementary relationship of Achilles and Patroklos in the *Iliad* are also pertinent: when these

[3] Ibid. 14.
[4] Clader 1976.50–53.
[5] Wikander 1957.
[6] Clader 1976.51.
[7] For these and other examples, see ibid. 51–53.

two close friends function as a pair, Achilles is aggressive and Patroklos is passive, *except when Patroklos goes off to fight on his own.*[8] As soon as this "recessive" member of the pair is off on his own, he assumes all the characteristics of his "dominant" counterpart. In this case, Patroklos then dies in place of Achilles while he is described as looking just like Achilles, thus becoming the dominant hero's "ritual substitute," as expressed by the Greek word *therapōn.*[9] In fact, the epic treats Patroklos, both thematically and through the assignment of epithets, as the "alter ego" of Achilles.[10] Even the character of Achilles himself identifies with Patroklos to such an extent that the dominant hero specifies, in arranging for his own funeral, to have his bones placed in the same funeral urn that already contains those of his recessive friend (*Iliad* 23.91–92, *Odyssey* 24.72–76).[11]

I propose, therefore, that the term *dioscuric* may be used for any such patterns of complementarity in dyads, whether or not they involve twins. Granted, the concept of twins is probably the most natural model for patterns of complementarity in myth. It may even be the primary symbol of complementarity, but the emphasis must be on what the symbol is actually for, which is, the dynamics of complementarity in binary comparisons. Even if the primary symbol for complementarity may be the relationship of twin-to-twin, we must expect secondary symbols of binarism as played out in such relationships as brother-to-brother,[12] father-to-son,[13] sister-to-sister,[14] even lover-to-lover,[15] and so on.

My intention here is to concentrate on that aspect of dioscurism where the outward-looking warlike nature of one member of the dioscuric dyad is contrasted with the homeward-looking peaceful

[8] Sinos 1980.

[9] Nagy 1979.292–293.

[10] Ibid. 33.

[11] Ibid. 209.

[12] E.g., Agamemnon and Menelaos, as discussed by Clader 1976.50–53.

[13] Besides the case of Lohrāsp and Goshtāsp, note the case of the Germanic pair Tuisto and Mannus in Tacitus *Germania* 2; both cases are discussed later.

[14] E.g., Helen and Clytemnestra (= Klytaimestra), as discussed by Clader 1976.52, n36.

[15] On the mythologization of the homosexual lovers Harmodios and Aristogeiton as a dioscuric pair, see Taylor 1991. On the mythological theme of Achilles and Patroklos as homosexual lovers, see Sergent 1984.285–296.

nature of the other. I must stress, however, that I will also bring in other points of comparison from the mythical pattern of dioscurism as Ward describes it. For example, Ward shows that many characteristics are commonly shared by both members in a dioscuric relationship. In the Indo-European traditions, perhaps the most striking shared characteristics of the Divine Twins are (1) their propensity to save or heal humans, (2) their association with symbolic themes involving horses, and (3) their association with some sort of female water-animal. These characteristics are remarkably evident in Germanic myths about twin kings,[16] as in the example of the Old English tradition about the young twin brothers Hengest and Horsa, who, according to Bede, were said to be descended from Odin and were reported to have led the Saxons in their invasion of the British Isles, thus saving their people from overpopulation and famine.[17] We also learn from the history of Suffridus Petrus that they are connected with swans, for they have a sister called Svana.[18]

The actual names of Hengest and Horsa connote distinctions as well as parallelisms, for the name of Hengest, who turns out to be the more aggressive brother, means 'stallion' or 'steed' (as in German *Hengst*), while the name of the more passive Horsa means 'horse' (as in English *horse*). Ward points out that, whereas both names mean 'horse', they are distinct in that the first denotes a war-horse and the second, a farm-horse.[19]

In the Finn or Finnsburg episode of *Beowulf* (lines 1063–1159) we learn what Hengest does when he no longer has his twin brother Horsa with him. He, as one of the retainers of Hnaef of the Half-Danes, is fighting the Eotens, who are attacking along with the Frisian king Finn. The reason for this fight was apparently to save Hnaef's sister Hildeburh from mistreatment by her husband Finn.[20] After several days of fighting, Hnaef and many of his men are killed. As a result, Hengest takes over the command of the Half-Danes, being the most valiant warrior (*Beowulf* 1080–1085). It seems that the Half-Danes

[16] See Ward 1968.50–56.
[17] Joseph 1983, esp. 104. See also Ward 1968.54–55.
[18] Joseph 1983.110.
[19] See Ward 1968.56.
[20] See Joseph 1983.107.

could have had the upper hand despite the loss of their king, until Hengest makes what could be deemed an "unheroic" decision. He offers overly generous peace terms to the Eotens instead of immediately avenging the death of his lord Hnaef, as is expected of a retainer in Old English society. Indeed, he has chosen a peace-loving solution.

Hengest then spends the winter with Finn in Friesland contemplating vengeance despite the peace treaty (*Beowulf* 1138–1139). He seems, however, almost reluctant to exact vengeance. Hunlafing, a retainer, has to urge him on by giving him a sword, an act which, in the Old English heroic code, serves as a reminder to a retainer of his duty to his lord after death. Finn finally is killed, *not by Hengest himself,* but rather by two Danes, Guthlaf and Oslaf.

Hengest, then, in this episode, seems ambivalent about his role as a warrior, for he (1) makes peace with his lord's killers, (2) stays on with his lord's killers for the winter, (3) needs to be reminded of his duty to avenge his lord, and (4) lets other men do the actual avenging. Clearly, he has the potential to be passive, if not docile. He seems to embody the characteristics of both a warrior and a nonwarrior or, to put it another way, he is acting like both a war-horse and a farm-horse.

As an example of dioscurism, the myth about Hengest and Horsa is particularly useful because it illustrates both the parallelisms and the distinctions of the dyadic figures. Moreover, it also shows what happens if the more passive half is removed from the narrative: in this case the more active half absorbs the passive characteristics of his counterpart, although his active characteristics may stay dominant.[21] The reason that I stress both these aspects is because I will use them to set up a parallel example of dioscurism: the case of the Iranian kings Lohrāsp and Goshtāsp in the *Shāhnāma.* The distinctness between these two figures has not been pointed out by scholars who have noticed patterns reminiscent of the Divine Twins in this particular narrative.

Following the arguments of Wikander,[22] Ward refers to Lohrāsp and Goshtāsp as "a pair of heroic twins," inasmuch as they are "a

[21] See ibid. 112–113 on Hengest as a "stranded twin," following the analysis by Frame 1978.152, n72, who comments on the dioscurism inherent in the single heroic figure of Nestor in Greek myth.
[22] Wikander 1950.

heroic euhemerization of the Indo-Iranian twins," Nakula and Sahadeva.[23] This description, however, does not take into account the fact that the *Shāhnāma* of Ferdowsi presents Lohrāsp and Goshtāsp not as twins but as father and son in a continuing dynasty. Wikander tries to get around this difficulty by pointing to various twinlike parallelisms shared by this pair of kings. For one thing, both have the element *-āsp* in their names, which can be derived from the Avestan form *aspa,* meaning 'horse', cognate with Indic *aśva,* also meaning 'horse', from which can be derived Indic *Aśvinau,* a name of the Divine Twins.[24] It might be relevant that, as Wikander points out, Lohrāsp and Goshtāsp are the only Iranian kings who have the element *- āsp* in their names.[25] We may compare such an onomastic parallelism with what we have already seen in the case of the Anglo-Saxon *Hengest* and *Horsa.* Even aside from the fact that these names all contain the meaning 'horse', the onomastic parallelism by itself is suggestive of dioscurism. From Ward's survey of the phenomenon, I cite the following examples: the twin saints Ferrutius and Ferrutio, the twin Greek heroes Herakles and Iphikles, the young dukes Sintram and Baltram in Swiss folk legend, and so on.[26]

There are also other traces of twinlike parallelisms in the pair Lohrāsp and Goshtāsp. First, Wikander points out that Lohrāsp and Goshtāsp are unique in being the only successive kings to be assigned the same number of years (120) to their reign in Ferdowsi's narrative scheme.[27] Second, Wikander notes a detail in the *Avesta (Yašt* 5.105), namely, the worshipping of the goddess Anāhitā by Auruuaṯ.aspa, the Avestan name for Lohrāsp. The Avestan name Anāhitā corresponds to the Persian name Nāhid, the name of the wife of Goshtāsp in the *Shāhnāma.*[28] These relationships of Lohrāsp and Goshtāsp, as Wik-

[23] Ward 1968.95–96, n25.
[24] Wikander 1950.318. The designations of these Divine Twins (*Aśvinau*) are "son of Sumakha ['Good Warrior']" and "son of Dyaus ['Sky']"; when treated as a pair, however, they are both known as "sons of Dyaus" (further discussion in Nagy 1990b.255–256).
[25] Wikander 1950.318. Garshāsp may be an exception, but the *Shāhnāma* has him die shortly after he has been crowned (II 48.n21).
[26] See Ward 1968.6.
[27] See Wikander 1950.318.
[28] Ibid.; cf. Puhvel 1987.123.

ander argues, recall the common Indo-European theme of "les Di-oscures au service d'une déesse."[29] Third, Wikander proposes that the connections of Lohrāsp and Goshtāsp with the cult of the sacred fires known in Pahlavi as the Adhur Burzin, founded by Lohrāsp, and the Adhur Mihr Burzin, founded by Goshtāsp, associate them with the inherited symbolism of what Georges Dumézil has called the "third function" in the conceptual framework of Indo-European traditions.[30] In this way, Lohrāsp and Goshtāsp would be parallel to the Indic Divine Twins, the *Aśvinau,* who represent the third function in the conceptual world of Indic religion.[31] As an example of the inherited third-function symbolism attached to Lohrāsp and Goshtāsp, Wikander draws a parallel: in Indic myth, the second-function warrior-god Indra is opposed to the participation of the third-function Divine Twins, the *Aśvinau,* in the *soma* sacrifice just as the warrior Zāl is initially opposed to the coronation of Lohrāsp in the *Shāhnāma.*[32] In general, Wikander connects the hypothesized third-function back-ground of the pair Lohrāsp and Goshtāsp with the narrative difficulties encountered in both the *Avesta* and the *Shāhnāma* in accounting for the transition of kingship from Key Khosrow to Lohrāsp.[33]

Coming back to Ward's characterization of Lohrāsp and Goshtāsp as "a heroic euhemerization of the Indo-Iranian twins," we now see that Wikander's argument in favor of this characterization is based exclusively on the existing parallelisms between these two figures. In making this argument, however, Wikander has not taken into account various patterns of contrast between the two figures—patterns which, as I now hope to show, are also a part of the dioscurism of this pair. In noting that Lohrāsp is but a pale, impersonal, and inactive doublet of Goshtāsp, Wikander assumes that his description fits because Lohrāsp was originally just a "twin" of Goshtāsp, parallel in every way.[34]

My point, by contrast, is that the description fits because Lohrāsp

[29] Wikander 1950.318.
[30] Ibid. 313–319.
[31] Ibid.
[32] Ibid. 321.
[33] Ibid.
[34] See ibid. 318. What Ward calls "twin" I prefer to call "dyadic counterpart."

was the passive member in a simultaneously contrasting and parallel pair, while Goshtāsp was the active member. Moreover, I propose that the symbolism of a simultaneously contrasting and parallel pair, even if we choose to call that symbolism dioscuric, does not require that the relationship between the pair be that of twin brother and twin brother. The same sort of dioscuric symbolism could also be expressed in the relationship of father and son. For example, we may compare the following two relationships in Indic and Germanic myths. In the Indic, Manu 'man' is the ancestor of the human race and has a brother called Yama 'twin', the king of the dead ancestors.[35] In the Germanic, we know of a tradition where Tuisto 'twin' is the ancestor of the human race, who has a son called Mannus 'man' (Tacitus *Germania* 2).[36]

In examining the contrasts between Lohrāsp the father and Goshtāsp the son, we may begin by recalling the dioscuric complementarity that we have observed in the pair Castor and Pollux. To repeat, Castor was warlike and rash while his twin Pollux was docile and disposed to staying at home.[37] Another pertinent example of dioscuric complementarity is a set of myths surrounding the Spartan institution of dual kingship. The two Spartan royal dynasties of the Agiadai and the Eurypontidai, which were forbidden to intermarry (Pausanias 3.12), were reputedly descended from the twins Eurysthenes and Prokles, sons of the Heraclid prince Aristodemos who had been assigned the conquest of Sparta at the time of the Return of the Herakleidai. As Bernard Sergent has shown, the myths that reshape the actual historical events surrounding these two dynasties—myths that I would describe as a constitutional theme of dioscurism—distinguish the kings of the Agiadai as characteristically warlike and outward-looking, with a consequently shorter life expectancy, and those of the Eurypontidai as more placid and homeward-looking, with a longer life expectancy.[38] As Sergent has also shown, the conceptual system leading to

---

[35] Cf. Nagy 1990b.111, n104. Vivasvat is father of Yama in *Rig-Veda* 10.14.5 and 10.17.1. Vivasvat is father of Manu in *Atharva-Veda* 8.10.24. Cf. Macdonell 1897.42, 139.

[36] Cf. Puhvel 1981.300–311, esp. 307–308; also Puhvel 1987.284–290.

[37] See esp. Ward 1968.23.

[38] Sergent 1976.

these characterizations becomes reinforced with the passage of time, so that the pattern is far more pronounced in the narrative of Pausanias (second century A.D.) than in that of Herodotus (fifth century B.C.).[39]

From an examination of the narrative about the reigns of Lohrāsp and Goshtāsp in the *Shāhnāma* of Ferdowsi, we can observe a similar pattern of complementarity. Lohrāsp, once he is king, proclaims that his reign will be marked by the rejection of aggressiveness and the promotion of peace:

ز آز و فــزونی بـیـکسو شویم
بنـادانــئ خــویش خـستو شویم
از این تاج شاهی و تخت بــلــنـد
نجویـیــم جز داد و آرام و پند
مگر بهره مان زین سرای سپنـج
نیاید همی کین و نفرین و رنج
من از پند کیخسرو افزون کنـم
ز دل کــیـنــه و آز بـیــرون کنم

From greed and excess, let us go away;

From this kingly crown and high throne

Lest our portion from this house (transient world)

I will augment the counsel of Key Khosrow.

let us confess our own ignorance.

let us seek nothing except justice, tranquility, and wise counsel.

always come to revenge, curses, and suffering,

I will drive out hatred and greed from my heart.

VI 8–9.9–11

Lohrāsp is so opposed to aggression and war that he prefers the grandsons of Kāus to his own rash son Goshtāsp:

وزیشان نکردیز گشتاسپ یاد
بدیشان بدی جان لهراسپ شاد
و زان کار لهراسپ ناشاد بود
که گشتسپراسر پر از باد بود

In them [the grandsons of Kāus] the soul of Lohrāsp delighted,

for the head of Goshtāsp was full of pride,

and on account of them he did not remember Goshtāsp,

and because of that Lohrāsp was saddened.

VI 9–10.27–28

[39] Ibid. Note too the wording of Ward (1968): "certain Spartan twin kings who were considered to be the earthly representatives of the Dioskouroi" (p. 26, with bibliography at 100, n110); "the Dioskouroi were reputed to have founded the city of Sparta" (p. 27, with bibliography at 100, n127).

This preference, of course, embitters Goshtāsp to the point that he wants his father to relinquish the throne and pass it down to him. Lohrāsp refuses because he is opposed to the violence of Goshtāsp.

بگشتاسپ گفت ای پسرگوش دار

که تندی نه خوب آید از شهریار

He said to Goshtāsp: "O son, listen,

for rashness is unbecoming in a monarch."

VI 10.42

Lohrāsp goes on to imply that Goshtāsp is like too much water irrigating the garden: he will flood the garden and destroy it (or, if we accept a variant reading, Goshtāsp is like a weed in the garden that will grow so rapidly as to overwhelm the garden):

مـرا گفت بـیـدادگـر شهـریـار

یکی جو بود پیش باغ بهـار

که چون آب یابد بنیـرو شـود

همـه باغ ازو پر ز آهو شـود

جـوانی هنوز این بلندی مجوی

سخـن را بسنج و باندازه گوی

To me he [Khosrow] said: "The oppressor monarch

For when it finds water, it grows strong

You are still young, do not be so haughty;

is like a stream [variant: weed] in a spring garden.

and so the whole garden is filled with faults.

weigh your words and speak with moderation."

VI 11.44–46

Another indication of Goshtāsp's belligerence is the claim that it comes closest to the nature of the warrior Rostam:

پرسـتـنــدۀ اخـتـر و افسرت

کنون من یکی بنده‌ام بر درت

گر آیند پیشـم بروز نبـرد

ندارم کسی را ز مـردان بمـرد

که با او نـسـازد کـسـی کارزاد

مگر رسـتـم زال سـام سوار

Now I [Goshtāsp] am a slave in front of you,

I do not consider anyone among men manly

except Rostam, son of Zāl, son of the horseman Sām,

a worshipper of your star and crown.

if they come before me on the day of battle,

since nobody is equal to him in battle.

VI 10.36–38

جـز از پـهـلـوان رسـتم نامدار   بـگـیـتـی نـبـیـنـیـم چـون او سوار

بـیلا و دیـدار و فرهانگ و هوش   چـنو نـامور نیـز نـشـنـیـد گوش

From among the heroes other than
    the famous Rostam
In height, in appearance, in culture
    and intelligence,

we have never seen in the world a
    horseman like him.
never has the ear heard of one as
    celebrated as he.

VI 16.131–132

Angry with his father, Goshtāsp leaves for Byzantium, where he
has trouble finding employment because of his belligerent nature and
excessive strength. He tries to support himself as a scribe, for example,
but the other scribes say about him,

کزین کلك پـولاد گریان شود   هـمان روی قرطاس بـریان شود

یکی بـاره بـایـد بزیـرش بلند   بـبـازو کمان و بزیـن بر کمند

Even a steel pen would weep on
    account of this one [Goshtāsp]
A tall steed should be beneath him,

and the very surface of the paper
    would be scorched as well.
a bow on his forearm, and a lasso on
    his saddle.

VI 17.157–158

He also had difficulty being a smith:

بـگـشـتـاسپ دادندپـتکی گران   بـرو انجـمـن گشـتـه آهنـگـران

بزد پتك و بشکست سندان وگوی   ازو گشت بازار پر گفت و گوی

بترسید بوراب وگفت ای جوان   بزخـم تـو آهن نـدارد تـوان

نه پـتك و نه آتش نه سندان نه دم   چو بشنید گشتاسپ زان شد دژم

They gave Goshtāsp a heavy ham-
    mer—
He struck with the hammer and
    smashed the anvil and ball (of
    iron),
Burāb [a smith] was alarmed and
    said: "O Youth,

all the blacksmiths gathered around
    him.
and the bazaar was filled with talk
    about him.

iron cannot withstand your blows,

nor can the hammer, nor the fire,
nor the anvil, nor the bellows!"

When he heard that, Goshtāsp was
dejected.

VI 19.191–194

As noted earlier, the only tasks he is suited for in Byzantium are hunting, fighting monsters, and winning brides for less heroic men.[40] In
short, Goshtāsp is marked by being extremely aggressive and warlike.

Before his self-imposed exile, when Goshtāsp tells Lohrāsp that he
wants the crown and the throne for himself, he also says that even if he
were *shāh*, he would still treat Lohrāsp as his own *shāh* and superior.

گر ایدونك هستم ز ارزانیـــان   مـــرا نـــام بر تـــاج و تـخت کـیـــان

چنین هم کام پیش تو بنده وار   هـمـــی بـاشم و خـــوانـمــت شهریار

If thus I am one among the worthy,

Then, just as I am (now), I will always be

declare to me the crown and the
Keyānid throne.

slavelike before you, and will call
you monarch.

VI 10.40–41

What he wants, in effect, is a dioscuric arrangement where he is the
active king, and his father is the passive one. It is when Lohrāsp refuses
that Goshtāsp chooses exile in Byzantium. Eventually he is recalled by
his father through the agency of his younger brother Zarēr, and is
granted the throne while Lohrāsp keeps a "little corner" for himself:

سـر تـخت با تـاج کشـور تـراست   چنین گفت کایران سراسر تراست

گه تخت مهی را جز از من کس است   ز گیتی یکی کنج مارا بس است

Thus he [Lohrāsp] said: "Iran is
completely yours;

A corner out of the world is enough
for me;

for you is the throne, with the
crown, and the country.

there is someone else, other than
me, for the great throne."

VI 61.846–847

---

[40] *Shāhnāma* VI 24–45.281–598. I should add that Mirin, one of the less heroic men,
not only describes himself as a nonwarrior (VI 26.305) but is also said to be a good
scribe (VI 27.336–337).

The dioscuric arrangement is now in effect. The political relationship of father and son now accurately reflects their temperamental relationship. In the variant readings of manuscripts I and IV of the Moscow edition, the following lines capture beautifully the very essence of this relationship:

از ایران سوی روم بنهاد روی   بـدل گــاه جــوی و روان راه جـوی

From Iran, he turned toward Rum   In his heart he was throne-seeking;
[Byzantium].   in his soul he was way-seeking.
                                                                        manuscript I, VI 15.120

پدر گــاه جــوی و پسر راه جـوی   از ایران سوی روم بنهاد روی

From Iran, he turned toward Rum.   The father was throne-seeking; the
                                                                    son was way-seeking.
                                                                        manuscript IV, VI 15.120

Later on during Goshtāsp's reign, while Lohrāsp is preserving "a little corner" for himself, the Iranians are once again drawn into battle with their old enemies, the Turanians. Zarēr, the brother of Goshtāsp, to the dismay of the Iranian host, is killed in battle by the Turanian Bidarafsh. Though Goshtāsp is urged to avenge Zarēr's death, he does not do it himself but assigns the task to two other warriors, Nastur son of Zarēr and his own son Esfandiyār.[41] They set out together, and Esfandiyār kills Bidarafsh.

In sum, like Hengest and Horsa, Goshtāsp and Lohrāsp work as a complementary dyad, where Goshtāsp is aggressive and Lohrāsp is peace-loving. The reign of Lohrāsp, as Wikander points out, is distinguished neither by martial exploits nor really by any sort of deeds.[42] In fact, the entire narrative about his reign is taken up by the heroic exploits of Goshtāsp during his period of exile in Byzantium. Nevertheless, when Goshtāsp ascends the throne and Lohrāsp fades into his "little corner," Goshtāsp no longer acts with his customary bravura.

---

[41] Goshtāsp does want to avenge Zarēr's death himself but is quickly dissuaded by his ministers. See especially *Shāhnāma* VI 112–113.681–698.

[42] See Wikander 1950.318.

Although he would have liked to do it himself and is even urged, like Hengest, to take vengeance, he leaves the task of avenging the death of Zarēr to others. Hence, like Hengest without Horsa, Goshtāsp without Lohrāsp too shows his potential to be passive, if not docile. In other words, he acts as *both* war-horse and farm-horse.

Although Lohrāsp and Goshtāsp are father and son, not twin brothers, we may conclude that they fit the pattern of dioscurism in general and that they can be compared to dioscuric figures like Hengest and Horsa in particular. The *Shāhnāma* seems to have dispensed with the common motif of twins, for there are no obvious instances of twins throughout the entire epic. Whether this is true of all Iranian narrative traditions I leave for further study. And yet, as I hope to have shown, the concept of twins is not the sole means for expressing the dyadic relationship of dioscurism, though it does indeed convey the yoking of assertive and passive qualities with the greatest clarity and force. The discovery that dioscurism is to be found in Iranian mythology even if the exact parallel of Kastor and Polydeukes is not, and that it is demonstrably present in the relationship of father and son, *shāh* and heir, both underscores the importance of that relationship, which is so powerful and recurrent in Iranian literature, and suggests that it is the nature of dioscurism, not of twins, that is the point of these stories.

CHAPTER 9

Feasting and Fighting: Ultimate Occasions for Hero and Poet

By now we have seen a wide range of dyadic relationships played out in the *Shāhnāma*. There is the king-hero relationship of Rostam and Esfandiyār on the level of heroic activity, then the father-son relationship of Rostam and Sohrāb on the same level, then the father-son relationship of Lohrāsp and Goshtāsp on not one but two levels of activity, both the kingly and the heroic. So far, we have considered the relationship between Rostam and Esfandiyār on the level of heroic activity alone. But another level of kingly activity is implied in their relationship—an activity which becomes visible when we consider the format for the actual narration of parallel stories about Rostam and Esfandiyār. Moreover, this format brings into play yet another level of activity, the poetic activity that produces the Book of Kings tradition. This format, which reveals the poet as a vehicle of kingly authority, is the heroic narrative theme of *Haft Khwān* 'seven banquet-courses'.

First, let us consider a major theme associated with heroic figures in the *Shāhnāma:* they are conventionally described as warriors particularly given to two activities, *bazm* 'feasting' and *razm* 'fighting'. The activity of feasting is also the context for the telling of stories about the exploits of warriors, their activity of fighting. And this context is the ultimate occasion for the expression of kingly authority on the two levels of heroic prowess and poetic skill.

The thematic parallelism of feasting and fighting in the Persian national epic is matched by a corresponding thematic parallelism in Greek epic traditions: in a fragment from Hesiod, the Aeacids (Aiaki-

dai), the lineage of Achilles himself, are described as πολέμωι κε-
χαρηότας ἠΰτε δαιτί 'delighting in war as well as in the *dais*'.[1] The
word *dais* here means 'feasting, feast, banquet', with the emphasis on
the cutting up and apportioning of meat.[2] The wording of this description reveals in microcosm a central theme concerning Achilles that
pervades the macrocosm of all twenty-four books of the Homeric
Iliad, where the excellence of Achilles as warrior hero is conveyed by
his obsession with his *moira*, or fair portion of honor to be accorded
him by his warrior society.[3] In the *Iliad*, this *moira* is primarily abstract,
a matter of fate; in the fragment of Hesiod, by contrast, with its
emphasis on the hero's feasting, we see a topic analogous to the concrete and more fundamental meaning of *moira*, that is, a cut of meat.

This topic of the warrior's obsession with feasting and fighting, as
exemplified by the Greek epic hero Achilles and his whole patriliny, is
hardly a theme restricted to Greek epic traditions. It is a topic well
attested in the native poetic traditions of other societies as well, both
inside and outside the Indo-European language family. We may leave
aside for the moment questions about whether this poetic theme has an
Indo-European heritage, but the actual points of comparison in what
follows are indeed taken from another Indo-European tradition, the
Persian poetic heritage. In the *Shāhnāma*, heroes are conventionally
described as warriors particularly given to *bazm* 'feasting' and *razm*
'fighting'.

In fact, the thematic parallelism in Persian is reinforced by a formal
one: these two words 'feasting' and 'fighting', *bazm* and *razm*, are
actually made to rhyme with each other in contexts of explicit thematic parallelism. That is, these two words are frequently found in
collocation as rhyming verse closures, and occasionally as rhyming
verse openings.[4] Here are three examples of this rhyming pattern,
highlighting the line placement of these words in both the Persian
script and the transliteration:

[1] Hesiod fragment 206 in Merkelbach and West 1967.

[2] See Nagy 1979.128.

[3] Survey of passages, with commentary, in Nagy 1979.128–141.

[4] As Brent Vine points out to me, there is a parallel pattern of rhyming implicit in
Greek epic traditions: *hipposunáōn* (e.g., *Odyssey* 24.40) vs. *daitrosunáōn* (e.g., *Odyssey*
16.253); *hipposúnē* refers to the military/technical aspects of horsemanship and *daitro-
súnē*, to the culinary/technical aspects of preparing feasts.

چنـیـن گفت با سرفرازان رزم   کـه مـا سر نـهـادیـم یکسر ببزم

chonin goft bā sarfarāzān-e **razm**   ke mā sar nehādim yaksar be**bazm**

| Thus he said to the honored men of **battle**: | "We are given to **feasting** . . ." |

II 77.37

(Spoken by Key Kāus as he harangues his troops into action.)

تـرا نـوز پـورا گ رزم نیـسـت   چـه سازم که هـنـگامۀ بزم نیـست

tora nuz purā gah-e **razm** nist   che sāzam ke hangāme-ye **bazm** nist

| Now, O son, is not yet the time for **battle**. | What can I do, for it is not the time for **feasting**? |

II 50.39

(In this example, Zāl is admonishing his young son Rostam, who is desirous of growing up too fast.)

بـبزم انـدرون شیـد تابنـدهای   بـرزم اندرون شیـر پـایـنـدهای

be**razm** andarun shir-e pāyanda-i   be**bazm** andarun shid-e tābanda-i

| Immersed in **battle** you are an enduring lion, | immersed in **feasting** you are a shining sun. |

I 137.34

(Spoken by the hero Sām, Rostam's grandfather, to King Manuchehr.)

We are now ready to consider the Persian epic narrative theme of *Haft Khwān* 'seven banquet-courses'. The word *haft* means 'seven', cognate with Latin *septem*, Greek *hepta*, while *khwān* means 'spread cloth or board covered by a cloth, with meats on it', and, by extension, 'feast, banquet-course'; but it also carries the meaning of 'adventure' or 'exploit', which is ostensibly being narrated at a feast. The *Haft Khwān* is a collection of seven such adventures, and there are two major examples in the *Shāhnāma*.

The first example of *Haft Khwān* is a set of seven ordeals performed by Rostam, the main hero of the *Shāhnāma*. The second is a corresponding set performed by Esfandiyār, the prince credited with spreading Zoroastrianism throughout Iran proper (*Shāhnāma* VI 980–981, 987). In both cases, as we shall see, the hero's respective *Haft Khwān* is being performed as a sort of rite of passage early in the hero's career.

The way in which the poet introduces the topic for Esfandiyār merits particular attention.

سخن‌گوی دهقان چو بنهاد خوان   یکی داستان راند از هفت‌خوان

ز رویسن‌دژ و کار اسفندیار   ز راه و ز آمـــوزش گــرگـــســار

چنین گفت

sokhan guy-e dehqān cho benhād khwān	yaki dāstān rānad az *haftkhwān*
ze ru'indaž o kār-e Esfandiyār chonin goft . . .	ze rāh o ze āmuzesh-e Gorgsar

The *dehqān*, when he set the spread for feasting, knowing the tradition	recited a story about the *Haft Khwān*,
of the brazen hold, and of Esfandiyār's deeds,	of the journey and of Gorgsār's instructions.
Thus he spoke . . .	

VI 167.25–26

Here we see distinct battle narratives framed by distinct banquet settings, ostensibly enjoyed by the hero and also dramatizing the context of the recitation of the narrative itself. Moreover, the poet here is making this dramatization explicit in his introduction to the *Haft Khwān* of Esfandiyār.

The story of the fight between Rostam and Esfandiyār was probably one of the best-known tales in the *Shāhnāma* of Ferdowsi. Though both heroes are prominent in substantial narrative traditions that stand apart from the narrative tradition about their famous fight with each other, it is almost as if the mention of one hero is incomplete without the other, as in the case of Sigfried and Gunther in the Germanic tradition, or of Cú Chulainn and Ferdia in the Old Irish. I attribute this connectedness of Rostam and Esfandiyār to the parallelisms that exist in the stories about them—parallelisms not due to any borrowing of one story-pattern from another but rather to the parallel but independent inheritance of cognate themes. In making this point, I confine myself to studying the parallelisms between the *Haft Khwān* or 'Seven Courses' of Rostam (II 91–110.280–6340) and the *Haft Khwān* of Esfandiyār (VI 166–192.1–451), two distinct sets of seven ordeals roughly comparable to the Labors of Herakles. Let us begin with Rostam:

Rostam, the champion warrior figure of Iran, is sent out to rescue the *shāh,* Key Kāus, who had been imprisoned by the White Div as a result of his foolish attempt to capture a place outside the boundaries of Iran proper, called Māzandarān. There are two routes to Māzandarān, a long and safe one and a short and treacherous one. Rostam sets out completely alone (except for his horse Rakhsh) and naturally takes the short route. It is on this route that he undergoes his seven ordeals or *Haft Khwān.*

In his first course, Rostam falls asleep and is attacked by a monstrous lion. Before the lion can do any harm to him, however, his horse Rakhsh fights and kills it. When Rostam wakes up and perceives what has happened, he suggests to Rakhsh that it would be better if he would leave the fighting to him.

The second course involves the hero's crossing of an arid desert in which he would have perished had not a ram shown him a watering place.

During the third course Rostam once again falls asleep, only to be attacked by a dragon who is guarding the watering-place that the ram had shown. Rakhsh tries to warn Rostam twice but is firmly rebuked for disturbing his sleep. However, the third time that he is warned, Rostam sees the danger and kills the dragon with a sword, while Rakhsh helps by biting the monster's shoulders and tearing its hide.

In the fourth course Rostam comes upon a lovely banquet that is set up near a spring, out in the wilderness. He spots a lute, picks it up, and sings about himself—how hard his life is *all alone in the wilderness.* Soon a sorceress disguised as a beautiful woman joins him, but the moment he praises her beauty in the name of God, she turns into a repulsive hag and he kills her.

Rostam does not behave well in the fifth course. He lets Rakhsh roam freely in a wheat field, and, when the watchman objects to this trespassing, he wrings off the man's ears. The watchman runs off howling to his lord, whose name is Ulād. Ulād tries to protect his field but Rostam wantonly kills almost all his men and then captures him with the purpose of using him as a guide to Māzandarān.

In the sixth course, Ulād brings Rostam to the entrance of Māzandarān, whereupon the hero proceeds to fight and kill the guard Div, Arzhang, and all his troops. Rostam then finds Key Kāus and plans their escape from the White Div.

The following day, that is, in the seventh course, Rostam, having tied up the unfortunate Ulād, attacks the White Div at midday, and after a difficult fight, manages to kill him. Rostam then gives the kingdom of Māzandarān to Ulād as a compensation for his mistreating him, with the reason that, as a warrior, he has no time for running a kingdom himself. In short, Rostam is a true kingmaker!

Now let us turn to Esfandiyār's *Haft Khwān:*

The prince Esfandiyār is sent by his father, the Shah Goshtāsp, to Turān, a region implacably hostile to Iran, to rescue his enslaved sisters from the Brazen Hold. Like Rostam, he has the choice of taking a long and safe route or a short but treacherous one. Like Rostam, Esfandiyār takes the short route. Unlike Rostam, however, he sets out accompanied by an army, his brother, and a minister. So he is hardly alone, though he leaves his entourage behind when he does his fighting. Esfandiyār is also forewarned about what to expect before he encounters any of his adversaries, by his guide, Gorgsār, to whom the prince promises the kingdom of Turān if his mission is successful.

Then, after being warned, he encounters two wolves, whom he valiantly weakens with arrows and then beheads for his first *Khwān.*

For his second course, Esfandiyār kills two lions, again having previously been warned by Gorgsār.

When Esfandiyār fights his dragon for his third course, not only is he forewarned by Gorgsār, but he has the time before his encounter to construct a chariot with swords protruding from it, somewhat like quills on a porcupine. As the dragon tries to swallow this chariot he is of course seriously wounded, thus enabling Esfandiyār to hack his brains out.

For his fourth course, Esfandiyār encounters a sorceress. Like Rostam, he sings a song before the sorceress comes, but *his* is about how he wishes he had some wine and a lovely woman at his side. Instead of invoking God's name when he sees her and thereby causing her to change her shape, he uses a special chain that Zoroaster had given him to capture her and cause her to change her shape. He then kills her.

Esfandiyār kills the Simorgh, a bird that is special to Rostam, in his fifth course.

The sixth course is the most difficult for Esfandiyār and his men. Gorgsār tells him how they all must travel through a very severe snow storm, only to be forced to cross an impossible desert. His men lose heart and beg Esfandiyār to find some alternate route, but he persuades them to stay on course. They all nearly die in the snow, but, after praying to God, the relief of springlike weather comes their way. There is, however, no scorching heat and arid desert to cross, which causes Esfandiyār to question the truthfulness of Gorgsār's warning speech. When Esfandiyār and his company come to a river, a very unexpected source of fresh water, he asks Gorgsār why he had lied and filled his men's hearts with fear of a drought. Gorgsār tells him that he never wanted them all to succeed in their rescue mission.

After that, they all cross the river, which is the seventh course, and Esfandiyār asks Gorgsār how he would feel after they devastate the Turanians. Gorgsār retorts that he wishes Esfandiyār ill, whereupon Esfandiyār kills him.

Some experts believe that the *Haft Khwān* tradition was original to Rostam, and only later transferred to Esfandiyār.[5] Others believe the converse.[6] Though both *Haft Khwān* narratives seem to be very similar in their respective themes, they have differences that are fundamental in understanding the role that their respective heroes play in the epic. I argue that both are variations on an inherited Indo-European theme. What makes Rostam's and Esfandiyār's experiences different is that they inherit different epic roles: Rostam as warrior, Esfandiyār as sovereign. The Greek differentiation between the Aiakidai and the Atreidai is analogous: whereas Achilles and his lineage are primarily warriors, Agamemnon and his are primarily kings (Hesiod fragment 106). Let us consider some details in the differences between Esfandiyār and Rostam.

Rostam goes through his seven ordeals alone, with the exception of his horse, whereas Esfandiyār has an army, a minister, a brother, and

[5] E.g., Molé 1951.133.
[6] E.g., Nöldeke 1930.72–73.

a guide from the very beginning. Esfandiyār's entourage seems to be there to underscore his "princely rank," for what is a prince without followers, or even better, what prince will act without some form of consultation, that is, Gorgsār, to guide him every step of the way? Hence, though Esfandiyār leaves organized society, that is, Iran proper, to go to Turān, a place that is constantly threatening to disrupt the order of Iran, he keeps a link with this ordered society in the form of the organized army, ministers, and so on, who accompany him. If one regards both heroes' *Haft Khwān* as an instance of the warrior's separation from society, as part of a "rite of passage," then Esfandiyār is "marked" (to use a term of the Prague School of Linguistics) whereas Rostam is "unmarked" in that both are warriors but Esfandiyār is a sovereign as well as a warrior.[7]

This difference between Rostam and Esfandiyār is underscored by how they treat their respective guides, Ulād and Gorgsār. Rostam, the kingmaker, gives Ulād the rule of Māzandarān, thereby living up to his ornamental epithet, *tājbakhsh,* meaning 'crown-bestower'.[8] By contrast, Esfandiyār, the sovereign, kills Gorgsār because he is threatened by him.[9] When they fight their respective dragons, Esfandiyār uses elaborate technology created by several men, whereas Rostam uses a simple sword and a little help from Rakhsh, his horse. This detail again underscores their inherent differences as "marked" and "unmarked" warriors, with respect to dragon slaying.

The two *Haft Khwān* are distinct battle narratives framed by distinct banquet settings, ostensibly enjoyed by the hero but also dramatizing the context of the recitation of the narrative itself. This observation can be taken even further if we look at what the heroes sing about while they are at a banquet before they encounter their respective sorceresses. Here is Rostam's song:

كه آواره و بدنشان رستماست   همه جای جنگست ميدان اوی   همه جنگ با شير و نر اژدهاست

كه از روز شاديـش بهره غم است   بيـابـان و كوهست بسـتـان اوی   كجـا اژدهـا از كفـش نارهاست

---

[7] On the terms "marked" and "unmarked," see Jakobson 1984.47.

[8] On the significance of this epithet as it applies to Rostam, see Chapter 7.

[9] The epithet *tājbakhsh* is also given to Esfandiyār, though only twice in the *Shāhnāma* (V 225.3, V 245.465). It seems to me significant that both these contexts concern the antagonism of Esfandiyār with Rostam himself, the primary *tājbakhsh*.

نــکــردســـت بخشــش ورا کردگار   می و جام و بویا گل و میگسار

وگر با پـــلـــنـــگــان بجنگ اندراست   همیشه بجنگ نهنگ اندراست

Rostam is an outcast and ill-signed,   for from his days of joy his portion is grief.

Every battlefield is his arena,   the bushland and mountains are his flower garden.

There is always some battle with a lion or a male dragon.   Where is the dragon not free from his tread?

The wine, the cup, the scented rose, and the drinking companion   are not what the Omnipotent has apportioned to him.

He is always battling with the crocodile   or else battling with the leopard.

II 98.406–410

Here Rostam sings about himself in the third person, how hard his life is fighting all alone in the wilderness, like an outcast, where the wilderness must serve him as a cultivated garden. He mourns that he will never experience the ordered or cultured garden. He will always be an outsider, that is, a liminal figure.

Esfandiyār, on the other hand, has his own song:

که هرگــز نبیــند می و میگسار   همی گفت بداختر اسـفـنـدیـار

ز چنگ بــلاهــا نیــابـد رهــا   نبیند جز از شیر و نر اژدها

بــدیــدار فــرّخ پـری چهـره یی   نیابد همی زین جهان بهره یی

مـــرا گر دهـد چهرهٔ دلـگسل   بیابم ز یزدان همـی کـام دل

فــروهــشــتــه از مشك تا پای موی   ببالا چو سرو و چو خورشید روی

He [Esfandiyār] said continuously: "Ill-starred Esfandiyār,   he never sees wine or drinking-companions.

He sees nothing but lions and male dragons.   He finds no escape from the claws of calamity.

He never finds any gain from this world   in the beautiful sight of a fairy face.

I will find from God all my heart's desire   if he gives me the face of a heart-breaker,

in stature like a cypress and with a face like the sun   with musk-scented hair hanging to her feet."

VI 178.202–206

Though Esfandiyār, like Rostam, bemoans the fact that his life is a succession of continuous fighting, he also mourns that he does not have some fairy-faced one with whom he can drink wine. What I find noteworthy in comparing these two passages is that they accurately describe the nature of their respective heroes. Rostam is a "loner," an outsider, and always will be out of synchronization with society, whereas Esfandiyār is a prince and thereby potentially embodies the very essence of the body politic. Nevertheless, both heroes complain that they are away from ordered society and the comforts of a civilized life. In other words, while they are feasting in the wilderness with an unpleasant dinner partner, they yearn for a civilized dinner in a well-structured social setting. The audience, however, who is listening to them while they literally feast, is also enjoying its own feast, that is, all seven courses or the *Haft Khwān* that the hero is performing.

The person who sets the spread for the feast, as we saw in the introduction to the *Haft Khwān* of Esfandiyār, is a *dehqān*, that is, a landowner who is acknowledged by his community as an authority on Zoroastrian law. It is also a *dehqān* who conventionally performs or recites the stories of the *Shāhnāma*, for Ferdowsi again and again says throughout the *Shāhnāma* that he heard the story from a *dehqān*. Alternatively, the diction of Ferdowsi in numerous passages substitutes the figure of a *mōbad* in place of *dehqān*. This interchangeability concerning the theme of hearing the story from a *mōbad* or *dehqān* leads to near-synonymity.[10] The meaning of the word *mōbad* is revealing in this regard. In a Zoroastrian document known as the *Selections of Zātspram*, the idealized Iranian Empire of the supreme god Ohrmazd is visualized as one in which each village has a true-speaking witness, every district has a judge who knows the law, and every province has a *mōybad*, that is, *mōbad*, who is the guarantor of truth.[11] It would seem that the "truth" of the *mōbad* is a foundation for the structure of the empire, just as it is the foundation for the structure of the poetry that glorifies the empire. If the *dehqān* or *mōbad* is represented as setting the spread (*khwān*) for the feast, he is thereby also arranging the seven courses or *Haft Khwān* which are not only the courses of the meal but also narratives of the heroes' adventures. When the hero has a banquet

---

[10] See Chapter 2.
[11] For a translation of *Selections of Zātspram* 23.5 see Molé 1963.338.

too, just like the people who are listening to the story of the hero at a banquet of their own, then the hero is participating in and approving the institution that keeps bringing him back to life, as it were, every time the epic story is retold. It is no accident that it is a *dehqān* who is represented as setting the spread for feasting, that is, "arranging the banquet." This detail is significant because the *dehqān* is ordinarily represented as the traditional storyteller of tales such as these. Thus if a *dehqān* sets the banquet spread for the characters in the story, we have the notion of crossover, where characters in the story participate in the banquet of those who are listening to their story.

At the beginning of *Odyssey* 9, there is another example of such an emphasis on the notion of a feast or a banquet as the context, the *social* context, of epic recitation.

> It is indeed a good thing to listen to a poet
> such as this one before us, who is like the gods in speech.
> For I think there is no occasion accomplished that is more pleasing
> than when mirth holds sway among all the community [*dēmos*],
> and the feasters up and down the house are sitting in order and
>   listening to the singer,
> and beside them the tables are loaded
> with bread and meats, and from the mixing bowl the wine-steward
> draws the wine and carries it about and fills the cups.
> This seems to my mind to be the best of occasions.
>
> *Odyssey* 9.3–11

In both the Greek and the Persian epic traditions, feasting and fighting are treated as parallel activities worthy of marking the hero. Feasting is also the historical context for the narration of the hero's exploits, and the theme of the feast is a conventional symbol for a well-ordered society, as we have seen in the passage from the *Odyssey*. But the theme of a hero's exploits is *also* a symbol for a well-ordered society, since the hero, by performing his exploit, is thereby undergoing an ordeal that dramatizes the transition from disorder to order in society. So feasting and fighting are parallel symbols for the hero's social identity and function. The parallelism is so strong that the activity of feasting, which is the context for narrating the activity of fighting, can be equated with the narration of the hero's ordeal. By extension, the hero's ordeal *is* the feast, and the feast *is* the hero's ordeal. The *Haft Khwān* of a hero like Rostam is not just a matter of his seven ordeals. It is a matter of seven courses or feasts that are the idealized contexts for the retellings of his seven ordeals. The expression *Haft Khwān,* as we have seen, literally means "seven courses," that is, "seven feasts." For the Persian hero, as also for his Greek counterpart, feasting *is* fighting, because the medium in this case is really the message. The medium, preoccupied with heroic prowess, is the ultimate occasion for the expression, through poetic skill, of the authority of kings in the Book of Kings.

Conclusion

Though the Iranian poetic traditions that I have been calling "epic of heroes" and "book of kings" may be distinct, each with its own rules and capable of independent evolution, they are brought together in the heroic figure of Rostam. The mythical themes surrounding this figure center on the relationship of hero and king, and these themes are old enough to be of Indo-Iranian and even Indo-European heritage. Thus the hero, Rostam, is the perfect traditional focus for Ferdowsi's *Shāh-nāma,* a monumental poetic undertaking that recombines—one more time and all over again—the epics of heroes and the books of kings. The artistic unity that results from this recombination is indebted to that most ancient of mythical traditions that retold how a hero had rescued the luminous glory of his lord the king.

There are, as I see it, two major applications of my conclusions, the first in the specific area of Iranian studies and the second in the general area of comparative literature.

For Iranists, I believe that the thrust of my findings is that Ferdowsi's narratives about Iranian kings in general and about the hero Rostam in particular are drawn from a fully formed tradition that both preceded the poet Ferdowsi and survived well beyond his lifetime. This is not to take anything away from the monumental productivity and artistic achievement of Ferdowsi as master poet. By virtue of his poetic preeminence, Ferdowsi has left as his legacy the definitive version of the Iranian national epic tradition. What would be from the standpoint of a folklorist simply one version or multiform, one "performance" in the oral tradition, has instead become a model of perfection, a unique textual realization that precludes any other realization, appropriating to itself in the form of textual variants any alternatives still offered by the oral tradition. But the key to the definitiveness, the supremacy, and even the survival of Ferdowsi's *Shāhnāma,* as I wish to stress for the last time, is its adherence to tradition. Tradition is not an obstacle for the poetic genius of Ferdowsi: it is, rather, its animating principle. I hope, then, that my work will encourage Iranists to analyze the *Shāhnāma* as an authentic and authoritative corpus of Iranian oral poetic traditions.

As for comparative literature, I think that the most noteworthy contribution of my study is its identification of the *Shāhnāma* as an inherited conventional poetic form that combines narratives about dynasties with narratives about heroes. It is not enough to call it either a poeticized "book of kings" or a politicized "epic of heroes": these two aspects are both poetic traditions, but the combination of the two is itself a poetic tradition in its own right. That the combination generates conflicting situations about king and hero does not invalidate the traditional nature of the combination. Conflict itself is a tradition deeply ingrained in Iranian poetry. And if it is really true that the Turanians, natural enemies of the Iranians, are nothing but another way of looking at Iranians, then the battles that rage between Turanians and Iranians throughout the *Shāhnāma* rage also in the soul of Iranian poetry.

A Formulaic Analysis of Samples
Taken from the *Shāhnāma* of Ferdowsi

In Milman Parry's working definition, a formula is "a group of words . . . regularly employed under the same metrical conditions to express a given essential idea."[1] Using this definition, modified along the lines outlined in Chapter 3, I propose that the poetic diction of the *Shāhnāma* is built on the principle of formulas.

To present this argument, I present as a test case a randomly selected passage, the theme of which concerns the writing of a letter. Applying the dictum of Parry and Lord that the formula is the expression of a given theme, I compare this passage with other passages involving the same context of letter writing. My purpose is to test whether these passages, involving a regular *system* of themes or thought-patterns, also involve a regular *system* of wording, which would be indicative of formulaic behavior. The randomly selected passage is the following (each hemistich of the couplet, shaped o—o—o—o–, will be shown as a separate line):[2]

1.1	cho ān nāmarā zud pāsokh nevesht
1.2	padid āvarid andaru khub o zesht

---

[1] Parry 1971.272.

[2] In the following paragraphs, I adhere to the policy of showing each hemistich as a separate line. I have transcribed the passages so as to show metrical length. Translations are provided in footnotes. In terms of New Persian *mutaqārib* metrics, the full line or *bayt* is divided into metrically equal *misra*'s.

1.3   nakhost āfarin kard bar kerdegār
1.4   kazu did nik o bad-e ruzegār³

V 141.984–985

Every word in this passage, to which I shall refer henceforth as 1, can be generated on the basis of parallel passages involving the same context of letter writing. But first, it is important to add that even the *sequence* of the four hemistichs in 1 is indicative of formulaic behavior. I have found parallels of sequential arrangement in the following four passages (2–5), each likewise involving four hemistichs:

2.1   marān nāmarā zud pāsokh nevesht
2.2   beyārast qartāsrā chun behesht
2.3   nakhost āfarin kard bar dādgar
2.4   khodāvand-e mardi o dād o honar⁴

VII 94.1603–1604

3.1   marān nāmarā khub pāsokh nevesht
3.2   sokhanhāy-e bā maghz o farrokh nevesht
3.3   nakhost āfarin kard bar kerdegār
3.4   jahāndār dādār parvardegār⁵

VII 9.46–47

4.1   be eyvān shod o nāma pāsokh nevesht
4.2   bebāgh-e bozorgi derakhti bekesht
4.3   nakhost āfarin kard bar kerdegār
4.4   kazu bud rowshan del o bakhtyār⁶

IV 266.887–888

³ 1.1 He quickly had a reply written to that letter,
   1.2 In which he showed himself both gentle and harsh.
   1.3 First he praised God the omnipotent,
   1.4 from whom he saw good and bad fortune.
⁴ 2.1 He quickly had a reply written to that very letter
   2.2 on a leaf that was decorated like paradise.
   2.3 First he praised God the all-just,
   2.4 lord of mankind and justice and knowledge.
⁵ 3.1 She had a good reply written to that very letter.
   3.2 She had words written with substance and happiness.
   3.3 First she praised God the omnipotent,
   3.4 possessor of the world, distributor of justice, the all-powerful.
⁶ 4.1 He went to the palace and had a letter written in reply.

5.1	dabir-e kheradmand benvesht khub
5.2	padid āvarid andaru zesht o khub
5.3	nakhost āfarin kard bar dādgar
5.4	kazu did peydā begiti honar[7]

II 110.636–637

The underlines provided for these four passages show the word-for-word correspondences with the first passage. These correspondences are not just a matter of repetitions: rather, as we shall see, they indicate a *system* of regular word placement. From the further correspondences that we are about to explore, it will become clear that the regularity is not a matter of modeling one set of phrases on another but rather, of generating fixed phraseological patterns from fixed thought-patterns. Such a process is the essence of formulaic behavior as described by Michael Nagler.[8]

In the case of the first hemistich of 1 (1.1), the parallelisms provided by 2.1/3.1/4.1 account for every word except the first.

1.1	cho ān nāmarā zud pāsokh nevesht
2.1	marān nāmarā zud pāsokh nevesht
3.1	marān nāmarā khub pāsokh nevesht
4.1	be eyvān shod o nāma pāsokh nevesht

Even for the first word, we can find other passages with the same word in a parallel context of letter writing:

6.1	cho ān nāma benvesht nazdik-e shāh
6.2	gozin kard guyanda'i zān sepāh[9]

VIII 372.957

	4.2	In the garden of greatness he planted a tree.
	4.3	First he praised God the omnipotent,
	4.4	from whom there is clarity of mind and good fortune.
7	5.1	A wise scribe wrote well [a letter],
	5.2	in which he showed himself both harsh and gentle.
	5.3	First he praised God the all-just,
	5.4	who makes manifest knowledge in the world.
8	Nagler 1974.	
9	6.1	Then he had a letter written to the *shāh*.
	6.2	He chose a singer from among his army.

7.1   cho ān nāmarā u beman bar bekhwānd
7.2   por az āb dide hami sar feshānd[10]

IX 264.164

In the case of the second hemistich of 1 (= 1.2), the parallelisms provided by 5.2 account for every word except the last three:

1.1   cho ān nāmarā zud pāsokh nevesht
1.2   padid āvarid andaru khub o zesht

5.1   dabir-e kheradmand benvesht khub
5.2   padid āvarid andaru zesht o khub

The order of *zesht o khub* at 5.2 allows rhyming with . . . *khub* at 5.1, while the inverse order of *khub o zesht* allows rhyming with . . . *nevesht* at 1.1. But the order of *khub o zesht* after *padid āvarid andaru* at 1.2 is just as regular as the order of *zesht o khub* that we see after the same phrase at 5.2. For example, compare the following passage:

8.1   pas ān nāmarā zud pāsokh nevesht
8.2   padidār kard andaru khub o zesht[11]

The parallelism between 8.2 and 1.2 extends beyond the phraseological match *padid . . . andaru khub o zesht*. It involves also the identical rhyme of final . . . *o zesht/. . . nevesht* at 8.2/1 and at 1.2/1. Even more, it involves the phraseological match . . . *ān nāmarā zud pāsokh* . . . preceding the final rhyming . . . *nevesht* at 8.1 and 1.1. I append the following further parallels to 1.1:

1.1   cho ān nāmarā zud pāsokh nevesht
9.1   marān nāmarā zud pāsokh nevesht[12]

VII 20.250

10.1   marān nāmarā khub pāsokh nebesht[13]

VIII 375.1009

10   7.1   When he read that letter out loud to me,
        7.2   my eyes began to shed tears.
11   8.1   Then he had a reply written to that letter,
        8.2   in which he showed himself to be gentle and harsh.
12   9.1   He quickly had a reply written to that very letter.
13   10.1   He had a good reply written to that very letter.

10.1[b]   marān nāmarā zud pāsokh nevesht[14]

VIII 375.1009 mss. I, IV, VI

10.1[c]   marān nāmarā zud pāsokh nebesht[15]

VIII 375.1009 ms. K

10.1[d]   marān nāmarā khub pāsokh nevesht[16]

VIII 375.1009 ms. L

11.1   marān nāmarā niz pāsokh nevesht[17]

IX 130.2044

11.1[b]   hamān nāmarā zud pāsokh nevesht[18]

IX 130.2044 mss. I, IV

11.1[c]   hamān nāmarā niz pāsokh nevesht[19]

IX 130.2044 mss. I, IV

12.1   hamān nāmarā zud pāsokh nebesht[20]

VIII 418.n20

It is worth noting that the variations between variant lines in different manuscripts correspond to those between variant lines in different passages; compare 10.1[b] and 10.1[d] to 2.1 and 3.1, or 10.1[b] and 10.1[c] to 3.1 and 10.1. In other words, it seems that, at least in the case of these variations in phraseology between one manuscript reading and another, the patterns of regular interchangeability suggest formulaic behavior.

We have by now accounted for every word in the first two hemistichs of 1, and we are ready to move on to the next two. The first of these two, the third hemistich, explicitly narrates the first and foremost theme in the contents of any stylized letter in the *Shāhnāma*, praise of God the omnipotent:

14   10.1[b] He quickly had a reply written to that very letter.
15   10.1[c] He quickly had a reply written to that very letter.
16   10.1[d] He had a good reply written to that very letter.
17   11.1 Again he had a reply written to that very letter.
18   11.1[b] Again he had a reply written to that very letter.
19   11.1[c] Again he had a reply written to that very letter.
20   12.1 He had a reply written to that very letter.

1.3   nakhost āfarin kard bar kerdegār

It should come as no surprise, then, that there are numerous exact parallels to be found. There is also a common variant, which is actually attested even as a manuscript variant for 1:

1.3[b]   nakhost āfarin kard bar dādgar[21]

variant of above, ms. K

Instead of listing the numerous exact parallels to 1.3 (two instances of which we have already seen at 3.3 and 4.3) and to 1.3[b] (two instances of which we have already seen at 2.3 and 5.3), it would be more instructive to consider the third hemistich together with the fourth.

At 1.4 and 1.4[b], the final word has to rhyme with the final . . . *kerdegar* and . . . *dādgar* of 1.3 and 1.3[b] respectively. If we take 1.3 and 1.4 together, we find the following exact parallel:

1.3   nakhost āfarin kard bar kerdegār
1.4   kazu did nik o bad-e ruzegār

13.1   nakhost āfarin kard bar kerdegār
13.2   kazu did nik o bad-e ruzegār[22]

IX 313.34

With the second hemistich of this one passage we have at last succeeded in accounting for every single word of the four hemistichs of 1 in terms of formal and functional parallels in other passages involving the themes of letter writing. Another exact parallel to the couplet 1.3/4 comes from a variant in one of the four original passages that we have considered:

4.3   nakhost āfarin kard bar kerdegār
4.4   kazu bud rowshan del o bakhtyār

IV 266.888

---

[21]   1.3   First he praised God the all-just.
[22]   13.1   First he praised God the omnipotent,
         13.2   who grants him good and bad fortune.

4.4^b   kazu did nik o bad-e ruzegār[23]

IV 266.888 mss. K, I, IV, VI

There is still another exact parallel from another variant:

14.1   nakhost āfarin kard bar dādgar
14.2   kazu did mardi o bakht o honar[24]

IX 129.230

14.1^b   nakhost āfarin kard bar kerdegar
14.2^b   kazu did nik o bad-e ruzegār[25]

Now we turn to the variant of 1.3/4:

1.3^b   nakhost āfarin kard bar dādgar
1.4^b   khodāvand-e piruziy-o zur o farr[26]

V 141.985 ms. K

At first, 1.4^b seems idiosyncratic, but if we take a sample of hemistichs that rhyme *only* with either

nakhost āfarin kard bar dādgar   (1.3^b)

or

nakhost āfarin kard bar kerdegār   (1.3),

we shall see that the wording of 1.4^b belongs to the overall system of phraseology that has characterized all the passages surveyed so far. In what follows, parallelisms among phrases to be found in hemistichs that rhyme with the type 1.3^b (. . . *dādgar*) will be marked with

---

[23] 4.4^b who grants him good and bad fortune.
[24] 14.1 First he praised God the all-just,
      14.2 from whom there is manliness, fortune, and wisdom.
[25] 14.1^b First he praised God the omnipotent,
      14.2^b who grants him good and bad fortune.
[26] 1.3^b First he praised God the all-just,
      1.4b lord of victory, chiefs, and luminous glory [*farr*].

a broken underline, in contrast to parallelisms with the phrases of
1.1/2/3/4, which have all along been marked with an unbroken underline. The first example to be compared comes from a variant in one
of the four original passages that we have considered:

1.4^b khodāvand-e piruziy-o zur o farr
2.4   khodāvand-e mardi o dād o honar

VII 94.1604

2.4^b khodāvand-e piruz o dād o honar[27]

VII 94.1604 ms. L

We note the close parallelism with the following example (to repeat,
the hemistichs that are now being considered rhyme with a preceding
hemistich that is identical in phraseology to 1.3^b):

14.2   kazu did mardi o bakht o honar[28]

IX 129.2030

We have already considered a variant of this hemistich, 14.2^b, which
corresponds exactly to the phraseology of 1.4:

14.2^b kazu did nik o bad-e ruzegār[29]

IX 129.2030 VI

To repeat, the crucial difference in this variant is that it rhymes with
the phraseology that we saw in 1.4, whereas 14.2 rhymes with the
phraseology that we are now examining, parallel to what we saw in
1.4^b. Yet another example of the latter type is the following:

15.2   kazu did niruy o farr o honar[30]

III 59.901

This line has a manuscript variant with a striking formal parallelism to
the phraseology of 1.4^b, our point of departure:

[27]   2.4^b lord of victory, justice, and wisdom.
[28] See note 24.
[29] See note 25.
[30]   15.2   from whom there is strength, luminous glory [farr], and wisdom.

15.2[b]   <u>kazu did piruziy-o</u> ruzegār[31]

III 59.901 ms. VI

In fact, since we have already seen that

<u>khodāvand-e</u>

and

kazu did

are interchangeable (2.4 and 14.2), the only difference between 1.4[b] and 15.2[b] is the final phraseology that effects the rhyme with the preceding

<u>nakhost āfarin kard bar dādgar</u>

and

<u>nakhost āfarin kard bar kerdegār</u>

respectively. We come to the conclusion that the phraseology marked by the broken underlines is actually a part of the system of the phraseology marked by the straight underlines:

1.4[b]	khodāvand-e piruziy-o zur o farr[32]
2.4[b]	khodāvand-e piruz o dād o honar[33]
2.4	khodāvand-e mardi o dād o honar
14.2	kazu did mardi o bakht o honar[34]
5.4	kazu did peydā begiti honar
15.2	kazu did niruy o farr o honar[35]
15.2[b]	kazu did piruziy-o ruzegār[36]
16.2	kazu gasht piruz be ruzegār (III 45.663)[37]

[31] 15.2[b] who grants him victory and fortune.
[32] See note 26.
[33] See note 27.
[34] See note 28.
[35] See note 30.
[36] See note 31.
[37] 16.2 who gives glory to one's fortune.

16.2^b   kazuyast piruz be ruzegār (III 45.663 mss. I, IV)[38]
13.2   kazu did nik o bad-e ruzegār[39]
14.2^b   kazu did nik o bad-e ruzegār
4.4^b   kazu did nik o bad-e ruzegār

What I hope to have illustrated with this exercise in the formulaic analysis of one passage is that every word in this given passage can be generated on the basis of parallel phraseology expressing parallel themes.

This limited experiment in formulaic analysis illustrates the principle of compositional variation as reflected by textual variation. As another illustration, let us consider the ornamental epithet *shir'owzhan* 'lion-slayer' and its variant *ru'intan* 'brazen-bodied'. The two are isometric, in that they are always found in identical metrical positions within the bayt (hemistich) of the *mutaqārib*, the canonical meter of the *Shāhnāma*:

$$\text{o} \;-\; -\; \text{o} \;-\; -\; \text{o} \;-\; -\; \text{o} \;-$$
$$[\quad \underline{a} \quad]$$
$$[\quad \underline{b} \quad]$$
$$[\quad \underline{c} \quad]$$

Let us label these positions $\underline{a}$, $\underline{b}$, $\underline{c}$, as indicated. The number of occurrences of these two epithets in the entire *Shāhnāma* is as follows:

	$\underline{a}$	$\underline{b}$	$\underline{c}$
shir'owzhan	1	16	5
ru'intan	1	2	10

The numbers for the occurrences are based on the figures gleaned from the Paris edition of the *Shāhnāma as checked against the Moscow edition*. In one passage (Moscow ed. VI 51.679), however, at position *c,* manuscript K of the Moscow edition reads *ru'intan* instead of *shir'owzhan*, which we read for this passage in all other manuscripts used by the Moscow edition. From the overall patterns of distribution here, we see that manuscript K in this case is just as "correct" as the other manu-

---

[38]   16.2^b who gives glory to one's fortune.
[39] See note 22.

scripts, and that such textual factors as manuscript predominance cannot settle the matter. The examples could be multiplied hundreds and even thousands of times, and by then we would start to see clearly that there are legitimate formulaic variants attested for vast portions of the *Shāhnāma*. We may postpone any questions about how these considerations may affect our evaluation of the Moscow edition. What is important for now is that even a limited test reveals such patterns of variation in the text of the *Shāhnāma*—the surest available sign that we are dealing with oral poetry.

Bibliography

ʿAbd al Munʿim, ed. 1960. al Dīnawarī, Abū Ḥanīfa Aḥmad b. Dāwūd, *Al akhbār aṭ ṭiwāl*. Cairo.

Albright, C. F. 1976. "The Azerbaijani ʿĀshiq and His Performance of a *Dāstān*." *Iranian Studies* 4:220–247.

Asadi. *See* Horn 1897.

Azarpāy, G. 1980. *Sogdian Painting: The Pictorial Epic in Oriental Art*. Berkeley.

Bahār, M., ed. 1935 [1314]. *Tārikh-e Sistān*. Tehran.

——, ed. 1940 [1318]. *Mujmal at tawārikh awʾl qisās*. Tehran.

——, ed. 1963 [1341]. Balʿami, Abu ʿAlī Muḥammad b. Muḥammad, *Tarikh-e Balʿami*. Tehran.

Barbier de Meynard, C. A. C., and A. J. B. Pavet de Corteille, ed. and trans. 1861–1877. Masʿūdī, ʿAlī b. Ḥusayn, *Murūj aẕ ẕahab*. 9 vols. Repr. 1965. Beirut.

Bartholomae, C. 1904. *Altiranisches Wörterbuch*. Strassburg.

Benson, L. 1966. "The Literary Character of Anglo-Saxon Formulaic Poetry." *Proceedings of the Modern Language Association* 81:334–341.

Benveniste, E. 1930. "Le texte du *Drakht asūrīg* et la versification pehlevie." *Journal Asiatique* 217:193–225.

——. 1932a. "Le Mémorial de Zarēr." *Journal Asiatique* 221:245–293.

——. 1932b. "Une apocalypse pehlevie: Le *Zāmasp Nāmak*." *Revue de l'Histoire des Religions* 196:337–380.

——. 1940. *Textes Sogdiens: Mission Pelliot en Asie Centrale* III. Paris.

Bertels, Y. E., et al., eds. 1960–1971. Ferdowsi: *Shāhnāma* I–IX. Moscow. For details about supplementary volumes, see Yarshater 1988.ix.

Boedeker, D. D. 1974. *Aphrodite's Entry into Greek Epic*. Leiden.

Boyce, M. 1954. "Some Remarks on the Transmission of the Keyānid Heroic Cycle." *Serta Cantabrigiensia* 1954:49–51. Mainz.

———. 1955. "Zariadrēs and Zarēr." *Bulletin of the School of Oriental and African Studies* 17.463–477.

———. 1957. "The Parthian Gōsān and the Iranian Minstrel Tradition." *Journal of the Royal Asiatic Society* 18:10–45.

Braune, W. 1969. *Althochdeutsches Lesebuch.* 15th ed. Tübingen.

Browne, E. G. 1902–1924. *A Literary History of Persia.* 4 vols. Cambridge.

———, trans. 1921. Neẓāmi ʿAruḍi Samarqandi, *The Chahār Maqāla ("The Four Discourses").* 2d ed. London.

Burkert, W. 1972. "Die Leistung eines Kreophylos: Kreophyleer, Homeriden und die archaische Heraklesepik." *Museum Helveticum* 29:74–85.

———. 1979. *Structure and History in Greek Mythology and Ritual.* Berkeley and Los Angeles.

Cantilena, M. 1982. *Ricerche sulla dizione epica. I: Per uno studio della formularità degli Inni Omerici.* Rome.

Chaytor, H. J. 1967. *From Script to Print: An Introduction to Medieval Vernacular Literature.* New York.

Christensen, A. 1932. *Les Keyānides.* Copenhagen.

Clader, L. 1976. *Helen: The Evolution from Divine to Heroic in Greek Epic Tradition.* Leiden.

Clinton, J. W. 1972. *The Divan of Mānūchihrī Dāmghānī.* Minneapolis.

———. 1984. "The Tragedy of Suhrāb." *Logos Islamikos: Studia Islamica in honorem Georgii Michaelis Wickens,* edited by R. M. Savory and D. A. Agius, 63–77. *Papers in Mediaeval Studies* 6. Toronto.

———, trans. 1987. *The Tragedy of Sohráb and Rostám.* Seattle.

Cross, T. Peete. 1950. "A Note on 'Sohrab and Rustum' in Ireland." *Journal of Celtic Studies* 1:176–182.

Dabir-Siyāqi, M., ed. 1959 [1338]. *Zarātoshtnāma.* Tehran.

———. 1972 [1350]. *Kashf al-abvāt-e Shāhnāma-ye Ferdowsi* I/II. Tehran.

Darmesteter, J., ed. 1892. *Le Zend-Avesta.* Paris.

Davidson, O. M. 1979. "Dolon and Rhesus in the *Iliad.*" *Quaderni Urbinati* 1:61–66.

———. 1980. "Indo-European Dimensions of Herakles in *Iliad* 19.95–133." *Arethusa* 13:197–202.

———. 1985. "The Crown-Bestower in the Iranian Book of Kings." *Papers in Honour of Professor Mary Boyce, Acta Iranica* 10:61–148. Leiden.

———. 1987. "Aspects of Dioscurism in Iranian Kingship: The Case of Lohrasp and Goshtasp in the *Shāhnāma* of Ferdowsi." *Edebiyāt* 1:103–115.

———. 1988. "Formulaic Analysis of Samples Taken from the *Shāhnāma* of Ferdowsi." *Oral Tradition* 3:88–105.

———. 1990. "The *Haft Khwān* Tradition as an Intertextual Phenomenon in

Ferdowsi's *Shāhnāma.*" *In Honor of Richard N. Frye: Aspects of Iranian Culture,* edited by C. A. Bromberg, Bernard Goldman, P. O. Skjærvø, A. S. Shahbazi, *Bulletin of the Asia Institute* 4:209–215.

Davis, D. 1992. *Epic and Sedition: The Case of Ferdowsi's Shāhnāmeh.* Fayetteville, Ark.

Detienne, M. 1972. *Les jardins d'Adonis: La mythologie des aromates en Grèce.* Paris.

Dresden, M. J. 1970. "Middle Iranian." *Current Trends in Linguistics* 6, edited by T. A. Sebeok, 26–63. The Hague.

Duchesne-Guillemin, J. 1972. "La religion des Achéménides." *Historia Einzelschriften* 18:59–82.

——. 1979. "La royauté iranienne et le *x^varənah.*" *Iranica,* edited by G. Gnoli and A. Rossi, 375–386. Naples.

Dumézil, G. 1968. *Mythe et épopée* I. *L'idéologie des trois fonctions dans les épopées des peuples indo-européennes.* Paris.

——. 1971. *Mythe et épopée* II. *Types épiques indo-européens: Un héros, un sorcier, un roi.* Paris.

——. 1973. *Mythe et épopée* III. *Histoires romaines.* Paris.

Elwell-Sutton, L. P. 1976. *The Persian Metres.* Cambridge.

Endjavi, S. A. 1975. *Mardom o Shāhnāma.* Tehran.

Finnegan, R. 1977. *Oral Poetry: Its Nature, Significance, and Oral Context.* Cambridge.

Ford, P. K. 1974. "The Well of Nechtan and 'La Gloire Lumineuse'." *Myth in Indo-European Antiquity,* edited by G. I. Larson, 67–74. Berkeley and Los Angeles.

Frame, D. 1978. *The Myth of Return in Early Greek Epic.* New Haven, Conn.

Garshāspnāma. *See* Huart and Massé 1926–1951.

Gennep, A. van. 1909. *Les rites de passage.* Paris. Trans. 1960 by M. B. Vizedom and G. L. Caffee. Chicago.

Gnoli, G. 1965a. "Lo stato di 'maga'." *Annali: Istituto Orientale di Napoli* 15:105–117.

——. 1965b. "La sede orientale del fuoco Farnbag." *Rivista degli Studi Orientali* 2:301–311.

——. 1967. *Ricerche storiche sul Sistan antico.* Rome.

——. 1980. *Zoroaster's Time and Homeland. A Study on the Origins of Mazdeism and Related Problems.* Naples.

Goeje, M. J. de, et al., ed. 1879–1901. aṭ-Ṭabarī, Abū Jaʿfar Muḥammad Ibn Jarīr, *Tārīkh ar rusūl wa'l mulūk.* Repr. 1961. Cairo.

Gottwaldt, I. M. E., ed. 1844–1848. Ḥamza al Iṣfahānī, *Tārīkh sinī mulūk al arẓ w'al anbiyā.* Repr. 1961. Beirut.

Habībī, A., ed. 1968 [1347]. Gardīzī, Abū Saʿīd ʿAbd al Ḥayy b. aẓ Ẓaḥḥāk Muḥammad, *Zayn al akhbār*. Tehran.

Ḥamza. *See* Gottwaldt 1844–1848.

Hanaway, W. L. 1971. "Variety and Continuity in Popular Literature in Iran." *Iran: Continuity and Variety*, edited by P. J. Chelkowski, 59–75. New York.

Hansen, K. H. 1954. *Das iranische Königsbuch: Aufbau und Gestalt des Schahname von Firdosi.* Wiesbaden.

Haymes, E. R., ed. and trans. 1988. *The Saga of Thidrek of Bern.* Garland Library of Medieval Literature, Series B, vol. 56. New York.

Henning, W. B. 1942. "The Disintegration of the Avestic Studies." *Transactions of the Philological Society* 1942:40–56.

——. 1946. "The Sogdian Texts of Paris." *Bulletin of the School of Oriental and African Studies* 11:713–740.

——. 1950. "A Pahlavi Poem." *Bulletin of the School of Oriental and African Studies* 13:641–648.

Hillmann, M. 1990. *Iranian Culture: A Persianist's View.* Lanham, Maryland.

Horn, P., ed. 1897. Asadi, *Lughat-e furs.* Berlin.

Huart, C., and H. Massé, ed. and trans. 1926–1951. Asadi Ṭōsi, *Garshāspnāma.* Paris.

Huot, S. 1987. *From Song to Book: The Poetics of Writing in Old French Lyric and Lyrical Narrative Poetry.* Ithaca, N.Y.

——. 1991. "Chronicle, Lai, and Romance: Orality and Writing in the *Roman de Ferceforest.*" *Vox intexta: Orality and Textuality in the Middle Ages,* edited by A. N. Doane and C. B. Pasternack, 203–223. Madison, Wisc.

Ibn Ḥishām. *See* Wüstenfeld 1858–1860.

Jackson, W. T. H. 1982. *The Hero and the King.* New York.

Jacoby, F., ed. 1923–. *Die Fragmente der griechischen Historiker.* Leiden.

Jakobson, R. 1939. "Signe zéro." *Mélanges de linguistique offerts à Charles Bally,* 143–152. Geneva. Repr. in Jakobson 1971.211–219; also in Jakobson 1984.151–160.

——. 1971. *Selected Writings* 2. The Hague.

——. 1984. *Russian and Slavic Grammar: Studies 1931–1981,* edited by M. Halle and L. R. Waugh. The Hague.

Jeremiás, E. M. 1984. "Diglossia in Persian." *Acta Linguistica Academiae Scientiarum Hungaricae* 34:271–287.

Joseph, B. 1983. "Old English Hengest as an Indo-European Twin Hero." *Mankind Quarterly* 24:104–115.

Justi, F. 1895. *Iranisches Namenbuch.* Marburg.

Kellens, J. 1976. "L'*Avesta* comme source historique: La liste des Keyānides." *Acta Antiqua Academiae Scientiarum Hungaricae* 24:37–49.

Khaleghi-Motlagh, D., ed. 1988. *Ferdowsi: The Shahnameh*. I. New York.

Krasnowolska, A. 1987. "The Heroes of the Iranian Epic Tale." *Folia Orientalia* 24:173–189.

Kullmann, W. 1956. *Das Wirken der Götter in der Ilias: Untersuchungen zur Frage der Entstehung des homerischen "Götterapparats."* Berlin.

Lathuillère, R. 1966. *Giron le courtois: Etude de la tradition manuscrite et analyse critique*. Geneva.

Lazard, G., ed. and trans. 1964. *Les premiers poètes persans (IXe–Xe siècles)* I/II. Tehran and Paris.

———. 1971. "Pahlavi, Parsi, and Dari: Les langues de l'Iran d'après Ibn al-Muqaffaʿ." *Iran and Islam (In Memory of V. Minorsky)*, edited by C. E. Bosworth, 361–391. Edinburgh.

———. 1975. "The Rise of the New Persian Language." *Cambridge History of Iran*. 7 vols. 4:595–657. Cambridge.

Lincoln, B. 1975. "Homeric Lyssa: Wolfish Rage." *Indogermanische Forschungen* 80:98–105.

Lommel, H. 1939. "Kavya Uçanas." *Mélanges de linguistique offerts à Charles Bally*, 209–214. Geneva.

Lord, A. B. 1938. "Homer and Huso II: Narrative Inconsistencies in Homer and Oral Poetry." *Transactions of the American Philological Association* 69:439–445.

———. 1960. *The Singer of Tales*. Cambridge, Mass.

———. 1970. "Tradition and the Oral Poet: Homer, Huso, and Avdo Medjedović." *Problemi Attuali di Scienze e di Cultura* 139. *Atti del Convegno internazionale sul tema: La poesia epica e la sua formazione*. Accademia dei Lincei, Quaderno no. 139, 13–30. Rome.

Macan, T., ed. 1829. *The Shah Namah*. Calcutta.

Macdonell, A. A. 1897. *Vedic Mythology*. Strassburg.

Maguire, M. 1973. "Rustam and Isfandiyar in the *Shahnameh*." Ph.D. dissertation, Princeton University.

———. 1974. "The Haft Khvān of Rustam and Isfandiyār." *Studies in Art and Literature of the Near East in Honor of Richard Ettinghausen*, edited by P. J. Chelkowski, 137–147. New York.

Maranda, E. K., and P. Maranda. 1971. *Structural Models in Folklore and Transformational Essays*. The Hague.

Marr, N. 1944. "Vazn-e sheʿri *Shāhnāma*." *Hazāra-ye Ferdowsi*, 188–197. Tehran.

Martin, R. P. 1989. *The Language of Heroes: Speech and Performance in the* Iliad. Ithaca, N.Y.

Masʿūdī. *See* Barbier de Meynard and Pavet de Corteille. 1861–1877.

Meisami, J. S. 1987. *Medieval Persian Court Poetry.* Princeton.

Menéndez-Pidal, R. 1960. *La Chanson de Roland et la tradition épique des Francs.* 2d ed. Trans. by I. M. Cluzel. Paris.

Merkelbach, R., and M. L. West, eds. 1967. *Fragmenta Hesiodea.* Oxford.

Meskub, S. 1964 [1342]. *Moqaddamā'i bar Rostam o Esfandiyār.* Tehran.

Mettke, H., ed. 1976. *Älteste deutsche Dichtung und Prosa.* Leipzig.

Minavi, M., ed. 1932 [1310]. *The Letter of Tansar.* Tehran.

——. 1972 [1351]. "Ferdowsi Sākhtagi o jonun-e eslāḥ-e ashʿār-e qodamā." *Sevvomin kongray-e taḥqiqāt-e irāni* I, 106–128.

——, ed. 1973 [1352]. *Dāstān-e Rostam o Sohrāb az Shāhnāma.* Tehran.

——. 1976 [1354]. "Dāstānhāy-e hamāsa-ye Irān dar ma'akhazi gheyr az Shāhnāma." *Simorgh* 2:9–25.

Minnis, A. J. 1984. *Medieval Theory of Authorship: Scholastic Literary Attitudes in the Later Middle Ages.* London.

Minorsky, V. 1964. "The Older Preface to the Shāh-nāma." *Iranica, Twenty Articles,* 260–274. Publications of the University of Tehran 755.

Mohl, J., ed. 1838–1878. *Le livre des rois* I–VII. Paris.

Molé, M. 1951. "Garshāsp et les Sagsār." *La Nouvelle Clio* 3:128–138.

——. 1952–1953. "Le partage du monde dans la tradition irannienne/Note complémentaire." *Journal Asiatique* 240:455–463/241–273.

——. 1953. "L'épopée iranienne après Firdosi." *La Nouvelle Clio* 5:377–393.

——. 1960. "Deux notes sur le Rāmāyaṇa. I: L'initiation guerrière de Rāma et celle de Rustam." *Collection Latomus* 45 (*Hommages à Georges Dumézil*), 140–150.

——. 1963. *Le problème zoroastrien.* Paris.

——. 1967. *La légende de Zoroastre.* Paris.

Monroe, J. 1972. "Oral Composition in Pre-Islamic Poetry." *Journal of Arabic Literature* 3:1–53.

Moorman, C. 1971. *Kings and Captains.* Lexington, Ky.

Muellner, L. 1976. *The Meaning of Homeric EYXOMAI through its Formulas.* Innsbruck.

Nafisi, S., and A. Vullers, eds. 1934–1936. *Shahnama.* 10 vols. Tehran.

Nagler, M. 1974. *Spontaneity and Tradition: A Study in the Oral Art of Homer.* Berkeley and Los Angeles.

Nagy, G. 1974. *Comparative Studies in Greek and Indic Meter.* Cambridge, Mass.

——. 1979. *The Best of the Achaeans: Concepts of the Hero in Archaic Greek Poetry.* Baltimore.

——. 1990a. *Pindar's Homer: The Lyric Possession of an Epic Past.* Baltimore.

——. 1990b. *Greek Mythology and Poetics.* Ithaca, N.Y.

Nöldeke, T., ed. 1879. *Geschichte der Perser und Araber: aṭ-Ṭabarī*. Leiden.

———. 1894–1904. "Das iranische Nationalepos." *Grundriss der iranischen Philologie*, edited by C. Bartholomae et al., 2:130–211. = *The Iranian National Epic*. Translated 1930 by L. Bogdanov. Cama Oriental Institute, Publication no. 7. Bombay.

———. 1944. "Ein Beitrag zur Schahname-Forschung." *Hazāra-ye Ferdowsi*, 58–63. Tehran.

Nyberg, H. S. 1938. *Die Religionen des alten Iran*. German trans. by H. H. Schaeder. Leipzig.

Olearius, A. 1656. *Vermehrte Neue Beschreibung der Muscowitischen und Persischen Reyse*. Schleswig. Repr. 1971. Tübingen.

Omidsalar, M. 1987. "The Dragon Fight in the National Persian Epic." *International Review of Psychoanalysis* 14:1–14.

Opland, J. 1971. " 'Scop' and 'Imbongi'—Anglo-Saxon and Bantu Oral Poets." *English Studies in Africa* 14:161–178.

O'Rahilly, C., ed. and trans. 1967. *Táin Bó Cúalnge*. Dublin.

Page, M. E. 1977. "Naqqāli and Ferdowsi: Creativity in the Iranian National Tradition." Ph.D. dissertation, University of Pennsylvania.

———. 1979. "Professional Story Telling in Iran: Transmission and Practice." *Iranian Studies* 12:195–215.

Pagliaro, A. 1940. "Lo zoroastrismo e la formazione dell'epopea iranica." *Annali, Istituto Univers. Orientale di Napoli*, n.s. 1:241–251.

Parry, A., ed. 1971. *The Making of Homeric Verse: The Collected Works of Milman Parry*. Oxford.

Pearsall, D. 1984. "Texts, Textual Criticism, and Fifteenth-Century Manuscript Production." *Fifteenth-Century Studies*, edited by R. F. Yeager, 121–136. Hamden, Conn.

Pickens, R. T., ed. 1978. *The Songs of Jaufre Rudel*. Toronto.

Piemontese, A. 1980. "Nuova luce su Firdawsi: Uno Šāhnāma datato 614H./1217 a Firenze." *Istituto Orientale di Napoli, Annali* 40:1–38, 189–242.

Pötscher, W. 1961. "Hera und Heros." *Rheinisches Museum* 104:302–355.

———. 1971. "Der Name des Herakles." *Emerita* 39:169–184.

Puhvel, J. 1975. "Remus et Frater." *History of Religions* 15:146–157. Repr. in Puhvel 1981:300–311.

———. 1981. *Analecta Indoeuropaea*. Innsbruck.

———. 1987. *Comparative Mythology*. Baltimore.

Qazvini, M. 1944. *Muqaddama-ye qadim-e Shāhnāma*." *Hazāra-ye Ferdowsi*, 123–148. Tehran.

———. 1953 [1332]. *Bist Maqāla*. 2 vols. Edited by ʿAbbas Eqbāl. Tehran.

———, and Moʿin, M., eds. 1953 [1331]. *Chahār Maqāla*. Tehran.

———, and Radavi, M., eds. 1960 [1338]. *Shams-i Qays, Al mujʿam fī maʿāyīr ʿashʿār alʿajam*. Tehran.

Rastegār Fasāʾi, M. 1986. *Azhdahā dar asātir-e irān*. Shiraz.

Reichelt, H., ed. 1928–1931. *Die soghdischen Handschriftenreste des Britischen Museums in Umschrift und mit Übersetzung herausgegeben*. 2 vols. Heidelberg.

Rubin, N. F., and Sale, W. M. 1983. "Meleager and Odysseus: A Structural and Cultural Study of the Greek Hunting-Maturation Myth." *Arethusa* 16:137–171.

———. 1984. "Meleager and the Motifemic Analysis of Myth: A Response." *Arethusa* 17:211–222.

Sachau, E., ed. and trans. 1878–1879. *al Bīrūnī, Abū ar Rayḥan Muḥammad b. Ḥamad, Al āthār al baqīya ʿan al qurūn al khāliya*. London.

Ṣafā, D. 1944 [1333]. *Ḥamāsa sarāʾi dar Irān*. Tehran.

Saïd, E. W. 1978. *Orientalism*. New York.

Sarkārāti, B. 1975 [1354]. "Gorz-e niyā-ye Rostam." *Nashriya-ye dāneshkada-ye adabiyāt o ulum-e ensāni*, 323–338. Tabriz.

———. 1979 [1357]. Bonyān-e asātiri hamāsa-ye melli-ye Irān." *Nashriya-ye dāneshkada-ye adabiyāt o ulum-e ensāni*, 1–61. Tabriz.

Sergent, B. 1976. "La représentation spartiate de la royauté." *Revue de l'Histoire des Religions* 189:3–52.

———. 1984. *L'homosexualité dans la mythologie grecque*. Paris.

Servatiyan, B. 1972 [1350]. *Barrasi-ye Farr dar Shāhnāma-ye Ferdowsi*. Tabriz.

Shahbazi, A. S. 1991. *Ferdowsī: A Critical Biography*. Costa Mesa, Calif.

Shāked, S. 1970. "Specimens of Middle Persian Verse." *W. B. Henning Memorial Volume*, edited by M. Boyce and I. Gerschevitch, 395–405. London.

Sims-Williams, N. 1976. "The Sogdian Fragments of the British Library." *Indo-Iranian Journal* 18:43–82.

Sinos, D. 1980. *Achilles, Patroklos, and the Meaning of Philos*. Innsbruck.

Sistāni, Mālik Shāh Ḥussain. 1966. *Iḥyā al Mulūk*. Tehran.

Smith, J. D. 1979. "Metre and text in Western India." *Bulletin of the School of Oriental and African Studies* 42:347–357.

Southgate, M. S. 1974. "Fate in Firdawsī's 'Rustam va Suhrāb.' " *Studies in Art and Literature of the Near East in Honor of Richard Ettinghausen*, edited by P. J. Chelkowski, 149–159. New York.

Spiegel, F. von. 1887. *Die arische Periode und ihre Zustände*. Leipzig.

Ṭabarī. *See* Goeje et al. 1879–1901.

Taqizāda, S. H. 1944. "Shāhnāma o Ferdowsi." *Hazāra-ye Ferdowsi*, 17–107. Tehran.

Tarikh-e Sistān. *See* Bahar 1935.

Tarn, W. W. 1951. *The Greeks in Bactria and India*. 2d ed. Cambridge.

Tavadia, J. C. 1950. "A Didactic Poem in Zoroastrian Pahlavi." *Indo-Iranian Studies* 1:86–95.

——. 1955. "A Rhymed Ballad in Pahlavi." *Journal of the Royal Asiatic Society* 1955:29–36.

Taylor, M. W. 1991. *The Tyrant Slayers: The Heroic Image in Fifth Century B.C. Athenian Art and Politics.* Salem, N.H.

Thʿālibī. *See* Zotenberg 1990.

Unvala, J. M., ed. 1923. "Drakht i Asurik." *Bulletin of the School of Oriental and African Studies* 2:637–678.

Vidal-Naquet, P. 1968a. "Le chasseur noir et l'origine de l'éphébie athénienne." *Annales: Economies, Sociétés, Civilisations* 946–964. = chapter 2 in Vidal-Naquet 1981.

——. 1968b. "The Black Hunter and the Origin of the Athenian Ephebia." *Proceedings of the Cambridge Philological Society* 194:49–64.

——. 1981. *Le chasseur noir: Formes de pensée et formes de société dans le monde grec.* Paris.

——. 1986a. English version of 1981. *The Black Hunter: Forms of Thought and Forms of Society in the Greek World.* Trans. by A. Szegedy-Maszak. Baltimore.

——. 1986b. "The Black Hunter Revisited." *Proceedings of the Cambridge Philological Society* 212:126–144.

Vullers, A. 1855/1864. *Lexicon Persico-Latinum* I/II. Bonn.

——, ed. 1877–1884. *Shāhnāma.* 3 vols. Leiden.

Ward, D. 1968. *The Divine Twins: An Indo-European Myth in Germanic Tradition.* Berkeley and Los Angeles.

Warner, A. G., and E. Warner, trans. 1905–1925. *The Shahnama of Firdausī* I–X. London.

Wikander, S. 1938. *Der arische Männerbund: Studien zur indo-iranischen Sprach- und Religionsgeschichte.* Lund.

——. 1950. "Sur le fonds commun indo-iranien des épopées de la Perse et de l'Inde." *La Nouvelle Clio* 1/2:310–329.

——. 1957. "Nakula et Sahadeva." *Orientalia Suecana* 6:66–96.

Wolff, F. 1935. *Glossar zu Firdousis Schahname.* Berlin.

Wüstenfeld, F., ed. 1858–1860. *Das Leben Muhammeds nach Muhammed Ibn Ishāk bearbeitet von Abd el-Malik Ibn Hischām.* 2 vols. Göttingen.

Yarshater, E. 1983. "Iranian National History." *Cambridge History of Iran* 7 vols. 3:359–477. Cambridge.

——. 1988. Introduction to Khaleghi-Motlagh 1988. v–xi.

Zajączkowski, A. 1970. "La composition et la formation historique de l'épopée iranienne." *Atti del Convegno Internazionale sul tema: La poesia epica e la sua formazione.* Accademia Nazionale dei Lincei, Quaderno no. 139, 679–695. Rome.

Zotenberg, H., ed. 1900. *ath Thaʿālibī, Ghurar akhbar mulūk al furs wa siyari-him.* Paris.

Zumthor, P. 1972. *Essai de poétique médiévale.* Paris.

———. 1983. *Introduction à la poésie orale.* Paris.

———. 1984. *La lettre et la voix: De la "littérature" médiévale.* Paris.

Zwettler, M. 1978. *The Oral Tradition of Classical Arabic Poetry: Its Character and Implications.* Columbus, Ohio.

Index

MYTH AND POETICS

A series edited by

GREGORY NAGY

Helen of Troy and Her Shameless Phantom
by Norman Austin
Masks of Dionysus
edited by Thomas W. Carpenter and Christopher A. Faraone
Poet and Hero in the Persian Book of Kings
by Olga M. Davidson
The Ravenous Hyenas and the Wounded Sun: Myth and Ritual in Ancient India
by Stephanie W. Jamison
Poetry and Prophecy: The Beginnings of a Literary Tradition
edited by James Kugel
The Traffic in Praise: Pindar and the Poetics of Social Economy
by Leslie Kurke
Epic Singers and Oral Tradition
by Albert Bates Lord
The Language of Heroes: Speech and Performance in the Iliad
by Richard P. Martin
Heroic Sagas and Ballads
by Stephen A. Mitchell
Greek Mythology and Poetics
by Gregory Nagy
Myth and the Polis
edited by Dora C. Pozzi and John M. Wickersham
Knowing Words: Wisdom and Cunning in the Classical Traaitions of China and Greece
by Lisa Raphals
Homer and the Sacred City
by Stephen Scully
The Mute Immortals Speak: Pre-Islamic Poetry and the Poetics of Ritual
by Suzanne Pinckney Stetkevych
Phrasikleia: An Anthropology of Reading in Ancient Greece
by Jesper Svenbro
translated by Janet Lloyd